DOUGLAS WIL

CW01521777

THE EXPLORATION

OF

THE CAUCASUS

Volume 1

Elibron Classics
www.elibron.com

THE EXPLORATION

OF

THE CAUCASUS

BY

DOUGLAS W. FRESHFIELD

LATELY PRESIDENT OF THE ALPINE CLUB

FORMERLY HONORARY SECRETARY OF THE

ROYAL GEOGRAPHICAL SOCIETY

VOLUME I

SECOND EDITION

LONDON

EDWARD ARNOLD

1902

In Memoriam

W. F. D.

1888

Mens nive candidior, nivium depingere sollers
    Effigies vivas, sole juvante, manus :
Rupibus aeriis ingens ubi Caucasus horret,
    Quam procul, heu ! patriá, dulcis amice, jaces.
Nulla suburbano posuit te pompa sepulcro,
    Nec tibi supremum vox pia dixit Ave.
Discretos cineres cingunt candentia mundi
    Mœnia ; custodes sidera sola loci :
Corripuit gremio dignum Natura ministrum ;
    Pro tumulo pictæ stant monimenta nives.

White soul, in lands of purer light
    Who caught the secrets of the snow,
For you no priest performed the rite,
    No hireling led the funeral show ;—
Lost on the far Caucasian height,
    We know not how ; we only know
The guardian stars their vigils keep,
    The mountain walls their ward extend,
Where Nature holds in quiet sleep
    Her own interpreter and friend.

D. W. F.

TO THE MEMORY OF

WILLIAM FREDERICK DONKIN

THESE VOLUMES ARE INSCRIBED

BY THE AUTHORS

PREFACE TO SECOND EDITION

IN these volumes I have endeavoured to bring together much material previously scattered and difficult of access to the public. It has been my object to make my chapters such a series of sketches of the Central Caucasus, its scenery and its people, as may stir pleasurable memories, or anticipations among travellers, and also interest that great body of readers who love mountains and like to hear about their exploration. The arrangement of the book is in the main topographical: that is to say, I have abandoned chronological order and continuity in the narrative of particular journeys in order to bring together the facts concerning each district, or portion of the chain, into single, or consecutive, chapters. The method has its drawbacks; but on the whole these have seemed to me in the present instance to be more than counter-balanced by its advantages. The record of adventure may be less vivid, but the pictures of the country and its people should gain in definiteness, and it ought to be easier to select characteristic facts from among trivial details.

The Appendix records every New Expedition which had come to my knowledge at the date of its compilation. In the body of the work I seem to myself to have given too much space to my own doings. If I have erred in this direction, it has been partly in order to preserve some literary unity, partly because I have travelled in the country more widely and at longer intervals of time than most of my countrymen. In the course of three journeys—in 1868 and again in 1887 and 1889

—it has been my good fortune to traverse the main chain of the Caucasus eleven times by eight different passes, and to cross in and out of Suanetia eight times by seven different routes. I have taken part in the first ascents of three of the great peaks, Elbruz, Kasbek, and Tetnuld, and of several lesser summits, as well as in many other glacier expeditions of greater difficulty than any of these ascents.   My travels have led me, I believe, into almost every considerable glen at the foot of the main chain between Elbruz and Adai Khokh, and I have penetrated the pathless forests of the Skenis Skali and the Kodor.

The object of the present edition is to place my volumes within the reach of readers who object to heavy and costly illustrated works.   I have not thought it expedient to revise or modify the original text.   Nor do I feel called on to enter here into the many and minute questions of topography and orthography raised by Dr. Merzbacher in the two thousand pages in which he has recently recorded his travels in the Caucasus.   To do so would involve much argument, hardly interesting to the general public. I gladly, however, take this opportunity to add the title of his work "Aus den Hochregionen des Kaukasus" to the list of books recommended in my Appendix.

TABLE OF CONTENTS

VOL. I.   *b*

ILLUSTRATIONS IN THE TEXT

VIGNETTES

From Photographs by Signor V. Sella.

MAP

CHAPTER I

THE DISCOVERERS OF THE CAUCASUS

*The power of attaching an interest to the most trifling and painful pursuits is one
of the greatest happinesses of our nature.* HAZLITT.

 N the Old World of the
West—the *orbis veteribus
notus* of our atlases—the
World of the Bible and
the Classics—there were
only two great mountain-
ranges whose crests pierced
into the region of eternal
snow, and sent down streams
of ice—those Miracles of
Nature, as a mediæval
scholar aptly called glaciers—among the forests and the corn-
fields of the valleys. These ranges both rose at the farthest
extremities of the civilised earth. The mountains that shadowed
the homes, formed part of the daily life, and were woven into the
enjoyment, the poetry, and the religion of the races who dwelt
round the Midland Sea, were of a different type. The heights
of Lebanon, the pathless crests of Parnassus, the deep glens and
wide pastures of the Apennines [1] have little in common with the
peaks, passes, and glaciers of the High Alps or of the Frosty

---

[1] The upper portions of the Apennines are in many cases wide pastures. They are, in
Tuscany, locally known as *Alpi*, and Dante in more than one passage, I think, used the word
in this sense. The primary meaning of the widespread term 'Alp' is everywhere 'high mountain pasturage,' and it was from its pastures or middle zone, and not from any primitive root
denoting whiteness, that the range we call 'the Alps' got its name.

Caucasus. There is no region or zone in them which is not adapted for some human use; there are few heights which the shepherd and his flock may not climb in search of summer coolness. The less accessible crags and hollows were, indeed, looked up to for ages with a certain reverence as places on the borderland of the spiritual world, sites whence a god might issue his oracles, where a patriarch or a prophet might commune with the Infinite, or himself vanish into the Unseen.

The horror of great mountains and wild scenery among primitive people and in early ages has been, I think, not a little exaggerated by writers imbued with the literature of the last century, and the artificial taste which it expressed. In most of the religions and legends of the world mountains have held a large place. Their importance in Bible story was fully set out for the entertainment of the curious so long ago as A.D. 1606 by Rebmann, a Swiss pastor, who proved in a volume of rhymed verse, much to his own satisfaction, his thesis of the important part played by High Places in the dealings of God with man.[1]

The Greek, who gazed up from the river-plains and sea-beaches to the crests of Olympus, Taygetus, or Parnassus, associated them with the council-chamber of the gods, the home of Pan, or the haunt of Apollo. Mountains—his own mountains—held a large place on his horizon and in his mind. He peopled their groves and streams with airy spirits of human or semi-human shape; throughout his literature he played affectionately with these creatures of his imagination. Aristophanes could venture to embody and bring on the stage the Clouds. But the snowfield and the glacier had no place in the daily surroundings, and therefore no place in the common beliefs or fancies of the Hebrew or the Hellenic race. The snows had no local deities, unless, indeed, the Lares—the nature-spirits whose name still lingers in Tuscany and the Trentino in association with remote and uncanny corners of the mountains—took them under their protection.

Yet the eternal snows, if unfamiliar, were not altogether

---

[1] See J. R. Rebmann's *Naturae Magnalia. Ein lustig poetisch Gespräch von Bergen und Bergleuten.* Bern, 1606. 2nd edition, 1620.

unknown to the ancients, or outside their mythology. A few Greek merchant-adventurers had pierced the Symplegades, had followed the southern coast of the Euxine past the woods and cherry orchards of Kerasund to its farthest bay, had crossed the dangerous bar and pushed their prows against the swift grey flood of the Phasis.[1] They had brought back reports of a realm rich in natural fertility and mineral wealth, where the cities were embowered in orchards, the vines hung wild from the fruit-trees, and the rivers ran gold—gold which the natives secured by the simple device of leaving sheepskins in the mountain streams to catch the precious sediment they brought down.[2] And over the dark waves of the Euxine, or above the shadowy forests of the foot-hills and shining mists that rise from the marshes of the Phasis, these Greek mariners had seen at midsummer a strange sight, a silver indenture on the horizon, the 'star-neighbouring summits'[3] of the Frosty Caucasus.

The romantic tales of the Caucasus must have touched the Greek imagination much as those brought from the new regions beyond the Atlantic fired the fancy of our Elizabethan ancestors. And the great range soon found its *vates sacer*. Before any being more civilised than a dark Iberian or a long-limbed Gaul had looked up to the Alpine heights, Æschylus had secured for the remote snows of the Caucasus their place in the world's poetry. He had celebrated them as the prison of Prometheus, of the hero in whose gift of fire to his fellows was represented the first step in the progress of the human intellect from the level of the lowest savage to the arts of civilisation ; the hero who, in his captivity, stood as the Protagonist of humanity against the apparently blind injustice of the Universe.

Æschylus had done something more. So little do poets know

---

[1] 'Rapidas limosi Phasidos undas,' writes Ovid, *Met.* vii. 6. Observe the accuracy of the epithets applied to a glacier stream.

[2] This practice, already noted by Strabo, is stated by more recent writers to have been continued in modern times on the Lower Ingur, the river of Suanetia.

[3] The Æschylean epithet may be illustrated by a coin of Dioskurias (the site of which, disputed by antiquarians, was probably somewhat east of Sukhum Kale) figured in Captain Telfer's *Caucasus*, vol. i. p. 124, on which are represented two mountain-tops (the summits of Elbruz ?), surmounted by the stars of the Dioskuri.

to what uses they may come! He had made himself the instigator and guide of the first English mountaineers who visited the Caucasus.

As a child I had spent several summer holidays in the Alps. As an Eton boy I had reached the Sixth Form and the top of Mont Blanc at about the same period. When, in 1868, my Oxford terms were over, and I had a larger opportunity of indulging my love of mountain travel, the sonorous phrases of the *Prometheus Vinctus* were ringing freshly in my ears,[1] and I was possessed by an ambition to carry the methods of Alpine exploration, in which I had already taken some part, into a range which, though half in Europe and comparatively near home, was practically unknown, even to the leaders of our learned Societies. I was fortunate in finding three very congenial and capable companions, and together we were able to a great extent to dispel the obscurity which then overhung the recesses of the Caucasian chain, to reveal to our countrymen some of its many beauties, to take, in short, the first step towards converting the Prison of Prometheus into a new Playground for his descendants.[2]

Before going farther, let me clear away a frequent source of popular misunderstanding. The word Caucasus is commonly used in two distinct senses. It may be a term of political, or of physical, geography. It may cover the whole of the Caucasian Provinces, or it may be restricted to a mountain range that occupies only a comparatively small part of those Provinces. In the larger sense the Caucasus has, of course, been more or less well known in

---

[1] I may suggest to commentators that the story of Io's journey is much simplified if the ancient Korax, the modern Bsyb, is identified with the ὑβριστὴν ποταμὸν οὐ ψευδώνυμον of the poet. P.V. 736. Κόραξ was certainly a word connected with insults at Athens, and the Bsyb is still the most formidable and unfordable stream on the Black Sea coast. I wonder whether scholiasts will allow us to read 'Αβασίας for 'Αραβίας ? P.V. 420. 'Αβασίας τ' ἄρειον ἄνθος Ὑψίκρημνον οἱ πόλισμα Καυκάσου πέλας νέμονται. Procopius (*de B. G.*, Book IV., chap. ix.) describes the city-fortress of the Abasci in terms exactly fitting in with the poet's epithet! The fortress was taken and burnt by the Romans, but its ruins still exist near Sukhum Kale under the name of Anakopi. See Laurence Oliphant's 'Travels in Circassia' in vol. xii. of Blackwood's Series, *Travel, Adventure, and Sport.* But, on the other hand, Arabia and Circassia are reputed to have had ancient connections which were strengthened, not created, by the pilgrimage to Mecca.

[2] See *Travels in the Central Caucasus and Bashan*, by Douglas W. Freshfield. Longmans, 1869.

Europe for many centuries. Classical authors had already described its western seaboard. We read of Poti, in Hadrian's time, as surrounded by brick walls and furnished with war engines and a garrison of 400 men to preserve it from the attacks of the barbarians. When Arrian went there he saw an alleged memorial of the Argonauts—nothing less than Jason's anchor—exposed to view. He was critical enough to discredit the relic because it was of bronze, and he thought Jason's anchor must have been of stone! We can even catch glimpses of the snowy range, 'about the height of the Keltic Alps,' says Arrian, making a very fair guess. And he goes on, 'a certain peak of the Caucasus was pointed out (Strobilus is the peak's name) where, it is fabled, Prometheus was chained by Hephæstus by the orders of Zeus.' Strobilus—Elbruz we now call it—is still there, lifting its great pinecone-shaped mass over the crest of the central chain. Strabo and Pliny both tell us how the mountain tribes came over the passes to Dioskurias (near Sukhum Kale) by the aid of climbing-irons and toboggans. Such irons or crampons are still used, and an ancient one, dug up in one of the cemeteries of Ossetia, was given to me by M. Dolbesheff at Vladikavkaz. Similar foot-gear has been found in the Eastern Alps, together with other objects said to be attributable to a date not later than 400 B.C.[1]

In comparatively modern times, the number of travellers who have visited the Caucasus, and thought their experiences worthy of record, is prodigious. The *Bibliographia Caucasica*, published twenty years ago (1876) at Tiflis, is, though incomplete, a catalogue of 800 pages, and nearly 5000 entries, ranging from the stately folios of Chardin down to the half-crown booklet of the Boulevards and the scattered 'communications'—a sore trial to collectors and cataloguers—of the German or Russian Member of Scientific Societies. In point of date, Venetian travellers and Elizabethan merchants head the list. The Empress Catherine in the last century sent a *savant*, Guldenstaedt by name, to collect information about the mountain tribes and their languages, much of

---

[1] See *Mitt. des Deutschen und Oesterr. Alpenvereins*, 1892, No. 9.

which was published, with a map, in London in 1788.[1] At a more recent date we meet with one or two names famous in literature. To those who appreciate facts served up with a strong flavour of wit and romance, Alexandre Dumas, the elder, offers three very entertaining and picturesque volumes. The famous novelist, Count Tolstoi, has written some charming tales, based on the experiences of his early life and full of local colour. Those who prefer more solid fare may be recommended to consult the list given in the second volume of this work. Yet despite this mass of literature, 'the Caucasus,' in the limited sense in which the term is used in these pages, was, up to the middle of this century, even less known in Western Europe than the Alps were throughout the Middle Ages. Nothing had been certainly or accurately ascertained as to the structure or characteristics of the central range, the extent of its snows, the height of its peaks, the character of its passes, the relations of its groups, or the peculiarities of their scenery.

It is, or ought to be, obvious that a chain cannot be fully or scientifically described until its essential features above as well as below the snow-line have been discovered and examined. In this limited sense the members of the first Alpine Club party, that which I organised in 1868, may fairly be called the discoverers of the Central Caucasus. Before our journey no great peak of the chain had ever been climbed, and no pass over the range between Kasbek and Elbruz had ever been described, except from hearsay, in any book of travel.[2]

The mountaineers who have followed us—and as climbers so

---

[1] *Memoir of a Map of the Countries comprehended between the Black Sea and the Caspian, with an Account of the Caucasian Nations and Vocabularies of their Languages* (anonymous). London : Edwards, 1788.

[2] The excellent reasons that exist for not believing in the alleged ascent of Elbruz in 1829 by a Cossack, named Killar, attached to an expedition led by General Emmanuel and described in Kupffer's *Voyage dans les Environs du Mont Elbrouz*, 1830, will be found stated at length by the Rev. H. B. George (*Alp. J.* vol. ii. p. 168), Mr. F. F. Tuckett (*Alp. J.* vol. iv. p. 167), by myself (*Central Caucasus*, p. 497), and by M. de Déchy (*Bull. Soc. Geog. Hongr.* vol. xiii. No. 3, and *Mitt. des D. und Œ. Alpenvereins*, 1885, p. 57. The 'ascents' of Kasbek of Wagner (1808) and Parrot (1811), recounted quite seriously in 1868 by German newspapers, were of the order of the 'ascensions du Mont Blanc jusqu'au Montenvers,' and their makers never claimed more than to have reached the snow-level.

far surpassed us—have played a part in Caucasian exploration
similar to that played in the Alps by the first generation of the
Alpine Club. But their work, it should be remembered, has been
carried through in the face of difficulties and hardships far
greater than those that were encountered by mountain climbers,
even in Dauphiné, thirty to forty years ago. 'The Caucasus
does not suit me,' grumbled a well-known Alpine guide; 'the
valleys are too long, and the peaks are very high, and one
cannot get to the top till late in the day, and has to come
down in the dark.'

If I insist here on the substantial results of the travels of
English climbers in the Caucasus in promoting a better knowledge of the chain,[1] it is not only as an answer to attacks that
have been made on them by certain persons abroad—self-styled
Scientists—who might have been expected to know better. I
trust that nothing I may have occasion to say in these pages
will be construed as implying any want of respect or sympathy
for genuine scientific research or for those who pursue it in the
mountains. My object is to promote genuine research by empha-
sising the necessary connection between mountaineering and the
physical investigation of great ranges, to show that it is as impossible to explore thoroughly the heights of the Earth, without
the aid of ice-craft, as it would be to explore the depths of
the ocean without the aid of seamanship.

The founder of 'mountaineering,' De Saussure, recognised this
connection and created—those who have studied the story of his
life will know that I do not use too strong a word—the first
school of glacier guides at Chamonix. It has been the occupation
and delight of later men of Science to follow in his footsteps.
Tyndall and John Ball were eminent equally in the Alpine Club
and the Royal Society. Forbes and Agassiz employed the best
guides and were themselves active climbers. It is no doubt unfortunate that the character of English education does so little to

---

[1] The number of the *Royal Scottish Geographical Magazine* for June 1895 contains an
article on Suanetia by M. Dingelstedt, who believes that 'no descriptions of this country in
English exist.' I may refer to it more particularly hereafter.

qualify our countrymen to use the many opportunities for physical observation their energy gives them.   The majority of English climbers are, I admit, not physical observers.   I am fully conscious of my friends', and even of my own, deficiencies in this respect. But whatever our shortcomings, we mountaineers have not darkened counsel with vain words, after the manner of the 'Scientist.'

USHBA

I must define a 'Scientist' as a person who bears to a Man of Science the relation that a poetaster does to a poet.   It has been my frequent misfortune to come across specimens of this class. Geography, lying as it were on the Borderland of Science, is one of their favourite hunting-grounds.   One of these gentlemen once undertook to prove to me that there are no glaciers at all in the Himalaya. In the Caucasus there have been of late years not a few such 'specialists,' and their contributions to Caucasian literature have been considerable. They make the most of their own expeditions—generally failures—above the snow-level. Those who are more successful they describe as 'mere tourists.' They see very little; and what they do see is frequently out of focus. Their ignorance of mountain phenomena and the terms properly applicable to them often renders their narratives misleading. They constantly boast that their facts and descriptions are 'scientific,' forgetting that a statement which is neither accurate nor intelligible cannot be made scientific by any initials attached to the name of its author.

Enough of these pretenders who misuse the name of Science! I have dealt with some of them individually elsewhere. I need not waste my readers' time by pursuing in detail their divagations. The only errors I shall correct here are those into which serious students and writers of authority have been led in past years by the imperfect material at their disposal and the partial character of the exploration of the snowy chain. Let us turn back to some of the statements found in works of authority current at the date of my first journey. The 1860 edition of Keith Johnston's *Dictionary of Geography* contained these very remarkable assertions, the first of which was repeated in 1877 :—

'The mountains of the Caucasus are either flat or cup-shaped; the existence of glaciers is uncertain.'

The doubt as to glaciers was shared by Agassiz. The erroneous information as to the main features of the geological structure of the mountains given by Kupffer in 1830 was still current in 1868, and Sir Roderick Murchison was eager for information on this point. The existence of erratic blocks had been denied by Abich; and his assertion, after he had corrected it himself, was repeated by Tchihatcheff, a Russian traveller of considerable reputation. There was similar uncertainty as to the existence of mountain lakes or tarns,

even in the highest quarters. Mr. Darwin told me that in 1869
Sir Charles Lyell, holding my book in his hand, had greeted him
with the exclamation, 'No lakes in the Caucasus!'

Some distinguished fellow-countrymen of our own had, no
doubt, been among the mountains before us, but they had hardly, if
at all, penetrated the central region, or above the snow-level.   Their
objects had been political; Bell and Longworth and Spencer had,
between 1836 and 1845, while the hill-tribes were still struggling
for independence, wandered to and fro in the western ranges among
the mountains of Circassia and along the Black Sea coast.   Mr.
Laurence Oliphant, at the time of the Crimean War, had visited
and vividly described portions of the same region; Mr. Gifford
Palgrave, while Vice-Consul at Sukhum Kale, had ridden in 1867
to the land of the Karatshai, probably over the Klukhor Pass.
But none of these writers had been in the Central Caucasus at all.
At an earlier date Scottish missionaries were settled outside it
at a place called Karass, near the Caucasian Baths, and one of
them, Dr. Henderson, better known as the author of a work of
Icelandic travel, published in 1826 a book containing what was,
perhaps, the first attempt—I cannot say a successful attempt—to
delineate Kasbek.[1]

This mission was founded in 1802, and dissolved by the Emperor
Nicholas in 1835.   It had a branch near Vladikavkaz.   After more
than twenty years' labours Dr. Henderson was compelled to report
that little progress had been made.   He quaintly adds : 'Were the
temporal concerns of the colony entirely abandoned to the care of
pious men of agricultural habits, and a sufficient number of able and
devoted missionaries sent to labour among the Mohammedans in this
quarter, a very considerable abandonment of the delusions of the
Arabian Prophet might be expected to ensue.'   The missionaries,
however, found means to set up a printing press, and in 1807
published the New Testament in the old Turkish dialect spoken
by the mountaineers, which is less mixed with Persian and Arabic

---

[1] *Biblical Researches and Travels in Russia, including a Tour in the Crimea, and the Passage
of the Caucasus*, by E. Henderson.   London : Nisbet, 1826.   See also *Journal of a Tour
from Astrachan to Karass*, by the Rev. William Glen.   Edinburgh, 1822.

than that in use at Constantinople. Copies of this volume doubtless exist.

Sir D. Mackenzie Wallace, in his classical work on Russia, describes his visit to the site of the colony, and his encounter with a convert, a 'Scotch Circassian,' speaking the Lowland dialect, who informed him that his name was John Abercrombie. The missionaries, if they could not evangelise, seem to have done their best to Scotticise, the Caucasus. They even converted Elbruz into Allburrows!

From their home on the spurs of Beshtau our countrymen could watch the shadows pass over the snows of the great mountain, and dawn and evening paint its double crest, but they could not even approach its base. Up to 1820 the fierce tribes of the Karatshai prevented any attempts to penetrate their fastnesses. Dr. Abich, writing in 1854, states that no traveller had up to that date visited Suanetia. The highroad through the Darial was the only track open to traffic across the main chain.

In the northern valleys of the Central Caucasus, our earliest predecessors, other than Russian officials, were the German ethnologists, Klaproth (1808), and Wagner (1843). They confined themselves mostly to their special pursuit, and when they approached the snowy region their descriptions become so general that competent critics are still in doubt how much of their narratives may be based on hearsay, and how much on actual experience.

Our immediate forerunners in the exploration of the central chain were also two Germans, who were in the employment of the Russian Government, and resided at Tiflis, where I had the good fortune to meet them both in 1868.

The correspondence of Dr. Abich, which has recently (1895), been published, shows the extent of his wanderings in the upper valleys. He had visited most of them, including Suanetia, before 1865, and had measured the lower extremities of several of the glaciers. He saw Koshtantau in 1849 from the heights between Balkar and Bezingi, and heard it called Dumala Bashi. But he kept to himself all but a few facts and figures. Dr. Abich was

at heart more a man of science than a man of letters.   He
writes to his wife in 1863 : ' I would rather float with so many
others down the stream of oblivion than run any risk of loading
the vessel of science with useless ballast, in the place of accurately verified observations.   What is the value of showy maps
and pretty drawings which only serve to stereotype errors which
posterity will be called on laboriously to set right?'   Dr. Abich
carried this resolution into practice.   Writing to his relations
during a visit to London, he informs them that Mr. Murray was
prepared to guarantee him 'several thousand pounds' for the
translation of a work on the Caucasus.   But even this belief
failed to spur him to produce such a volume.   He delayed till
his last years publishing the results of his wanderings, and then
issued only the observations made in the Armenian Highlands.
At his death in 1886 his geological map of the Caucasus remained an unfulfilled project, and the fruits of his travels in the
main chain are to be found only in a few scattered pamphlets.

Dr. Radde, a North German by birth, has, both by his continuous
travels and by his energy in organising the Caucasian Museum at
Tiflis, of which he is still the Curator, done more than any man
living to spread abroad a sound knowledge of the country he has
made his home.   A distinguished botanist and an indefatigable
traveller, he has turned his attention to many branches of research, and recorded his observations in several volumes as well as
in numerous contributions to *Petermann's Mitteilungen.*   A lifetime
devoted to the intelligent observation of obscure regions may be
more valuable to science than a single brilliant exploration, and
the honours Dr. Radde has received in this country and elsewhere have been fully earned.   He has done all that was possible
for a man without ice-craft.   Had he succeeded in breaking the
charm that guards the secrets of the snow-world, had he created
a school of glacier guides among the native hunters, he might
have made himself the De Saussure of the Caucasus.   As it
is, although his work will ever be held in high estimation by
serious students, he will leave behind him a scientific reputation
rather than a popular name.

The communications of these German doctors did not reach Europe until 1868, and then they were confined to Germany. For at that time the Council of our Royal Geographical Society had not yet seen its way to fulfil one of its most obvious functions, and despite the individual efforts of Mr. Clements Markham and the late Mr. H. W. Bates, England was still without any magazine for the diffusion of general geographical information comparable to Petermann's famous *Mitteilungen*.

Where books are wanting the intending explorer may often find a most useful and suggestive friend and companion in a map. It was on a German map—Koch's General Map of the Caucasian Isthmus—that Moore and I planned out our journey in 1868. On that map Dykhtau and Koshtantau were not marked. The ridges between the sources of the Rion and the Ingur were very vaguely delineated. But no better map was to be had in Western Europe. It was not until after we had landed in the Caucasus that we learnt that between 1847 and 1863 the Russian staff, under the direction of General Chodzko, had executed a survey of the Caucasian Provinces and part of Armenia, which resulted in the atlas, known from the scale on which it was published—five versts or three miles to the inch— as the Five-Verst Map. The necessary sheets of this atlas were first shown us by Count Levashoff, then the Governor of Kutais, and afterwards placed in our hands at Tiflis by the courtesy of General Chodzko himself.

The Russian surveyors did their work under the greatest difficulties—difficulties which at times took the shape of a shower of bullets. As far as their means and their instructions carried them, they did it adequately. They laid down with surprising accuracy and completeness the general features of the ground below the snow-level, and outside the hidden recesses of the range. They produced an excellent delineation of the habitable country and the practicable bridle-paths. They indicated precisely the extent of forests and the positions of villages and bridges. They were employed for military and administrative purposes, and not for natural research. To have delayed issuing their map until they had made the survey physically complete would have been, under the circumstances, impossible.[1] Accordingly, they were content to fix trigonometrically, mostly, if not altogether, from the northern side, the heights and positions of a few prominent summits. They discovered, and General Chodzko, through *Petermann's Mitteilungen*, communicated to the western world the existence of the three great peaks which they named Dykhtau, Koshtantau, and Adai Khokh. But they omitted altogether Dougusorun, Ushba, Tiktengen, Tetnuld, Janga, Shkara, Ailama and Burdjula—in short, all the peaks that are not conspicuous from the northern steppe. The frozen fastnesses were in most cases represented by conventional signs; a blue smear here and there served as an indication of glaciers, and above the snow-level a number of brown ridges were laid down without much care, in some cases with no care at all, as to their correspondence with nature. In taking this course the surveyors followed the precedent of the first staff-maps of the Alps, except those of the Swiss Government.

Government surveyors do not, I think, always realise fully their responsibility to Science. It might be better in most cases if country not at all, or imperfectly, surveyed as to topographical detail were left blank, or at least distinguished in some striking manner from the more authentic portions of a map. For not only the public, but also its teachers, naturally accept a government map as equally authoritative in every part. Even a scientific traveller may easily fall into the same mistake.

The literature of the Caucasus furnishes a striking instance of the confusion and darkening of knowledge that may thus be wrought. The defects of the five-verst map have raised up a crop of delusions that are far harder to eradicate than simple ignorance. In

---

[1] There is in the Royal Geographical Society's Library in Savile Row a curious tract issued in 1863 by General Chodzko, giving some account of his twenty-five years' labours. At times his officers worked under the fire of hostile villagers. Nor were they less brave in facing natural difficulties, so far as their means availed them. The General camped for several days on the top of Ararat; he climbed Zilga Khokh, a peak of 12,645 feet on the watershed south of Kasbek, in order to connect his Ciscaucasian and Georgian stations. More than this without ice-craft he could not do. It is curious that none of the great peaks were triangulated from stations south of the chain. This is the reason why the mountains on the watershed, including Tetnuld, Ushba, and Shkara, escaped notice. See also notes by General Chodzko in the years 1859 and 1862, in *Petermann's Mitteilungen.*

1868, the year of my first visit, and again three years later, in 1871, M. Ernest Favre, then a young Genevese geologist, a son of the well-known writer of the same name, travelled in the central range, and on his return published a small volume and a geological map. M. Favre did wonders in the time and with the opportunities at his disposal : his map was an immense addition to our knowledge ; his geological and orographical observations were most valuable. His

KOSHTANTAU, FROM ABOUT 14,600 FEET ON ULLUAUZ BASHI

work remains the chief and most trustworthy source of information on his special subject. But not being a mountaineer himself, and having no ice-craft at his command, the glacier region necessarily remained as much a *mare clausum* to him as the Palæocrystic Sea has proved to the British Navy. Consequently, he had to go for his facts, or ideas regarding it, to the government map. Finding this map accurate below the snow-level, he readily accepted it as a true picture of the region above the snow-level, to which he had not himself penetrated. The next step followed almost as a matter

of course. M. Elisée Reclus, the encyclopædist of geography, to
whom that Science owes as much as to any living writer, naturally
went for his information with regard to the Caucasian glaciers to a
geologist of standing rather than to a 'tourist.' The passage below,
copied almost word for word from M. Favre, occurs in the English
edition of M. Reclus's monumental *Géographie Universelle* :[1]—

> 'Although with a greater mean elevation than those of the Alps, the
> Caucasian peaks are far less covered with snow and ice, not only in conse-
> quence of their more southerly latitude and other climatic conditions, but
> also owing to the narrowness of the upper crests and the absence of cirques,
> where the accumulated snows might serve as reservoirs of glaciers. . . .
> The absence of snow produces a corresponding scarcity of glaciers.'

Now, in this quotation, I am obliged to traverse, one by one, the
premises—except the statement as to latitude, as well as the conclusion. The climatic conditions are favourable to glaciers—that is,
the snowfall in the Central Caucasus is heavier than in the Central
Alps ; the crest is broad and has a number of high spurs, which
enclose extensive and well-filled snowy reservoirs, the source of
many and great glaciers.

M. Reclus gives, as physical maps illustrative of his statements,
extracts from the five-verst survey of Kasbek, Elbruz, and the
chain north of Suanetia. These are unfortunately false to nature,
and have been proved to be so, first by the perambulations of
mountaineers, and more recently by the one-verst survey now in
progress.

In one of the most original and instructive studies of the nature
and effects of existing glaciers, by a writer of deservedly high
authority, Professor Heim of Zürich, we are met by similar inaccuracies.[2] I need only mention the most startling. We find the
author stating that there are 46 square miles of snow and ice in
the whole Caucasus, of which half are on Elbruz. According to
the new government survey, the glaciers on Elbruz alone cover
about 83 square miles, and those of the chain, including Elbruz,

---

[1] Vol. vi. p. 40, of the English translation. All the heights assigned to peaks in the English
edition are computed wrongly. Vol. vi. p. 36.

[2] *Handbuch der Gletscherkunde*, von Dr. A. Heim. Stuttgart, 1885.

from the Jiper Pass, to the Darial Road, not less than 625 square miles.

This unconscious propagation of error shows no sign of coming to an end. In vain, it would seem, have I been engaged for years in setting out, to the best of my ability, in the *Alpine Journal* and the *Proceedings* of the Royal Geographical Society, the physical facts ascertained by my friends and myself, or by the labour of the officers employed under General Shdanov while putting together the material for a new map. In vain has M. Mikhailovsky, in the *Proceedings* of the Moscow Naturalists' Society, recently taken up the same task with great care and industry, if with some lack of local experience.[1] We find a new, and in many respects excellent guide and road-book to the Caucasus, issued in 1894 at Paris, reproducing from Reclus old scraps of the five-verst map, and particularly those parts of which M. de Déchy and I had years before most clearly demonstrated the entire inaccuracy! The author, M. Mourier, is consistent, for he borrows also from Reclus's *Géographie* the passage I have already quoted with regard to the formation of the chain and the extent of its *névés*.

The repetition of errors, although for the purpose of correction, is an ungrateful task. To the minor writers already referred to in general terms, I have purposely paid no attention : acting on the principle *corruptio optimi pessima*, I have dealt only with authors of eminence and deserved authority. Enough probably has been said to convince my readers that an accurate account of the peaks, passes, and glaciers of the Central Caucasus is called for, and that, if I correct some previous authors, I do so with good reason. Amongst my corrections will be several of errors into which I have myself fallen. The evolution of Caucasian orography has necessarily been gradual ; and it is still in progress. My successors will doubtless find many facts to add to those brought forward in these volumes, and not a few mistakes to put right both in my text and map.

---

[1] See *Alpine Journal*, vol. ix. p. 182 ; xi. p. 471 ; xii. p. 320 ; xiii. pp. 353, 499 ; xiv. pp. 1, 314, 436. *Proceedings of the Royal Geographical Society* (N. S.), vol. x. pp. 325, 677 ; xi. p. 351 ; xii. p. 257 ; xiv. p. 100. *Bulletin de la S. I. des Naturalistes de Moscou*, 1894.

Twenty-eight years ago, in 1868, I first went to the Caucasus with two companions, Mr. Comyns Tucker, afterwards a Fellow of University College, Oxford, and the late Mr. Adolphus W. Moore, C.B., of the Political Department of the India Office, a public servant of rare ability and a true-hearted and unfailing friend, whose premature death, in 1887, was felt as a national as well as a

A. W. MOORE, C.B.

private loss by all who had come intimately into contact with him. We took with us a Chamonix guide, François J. Dévouassoud, the first Alpine guide to carry his ice-axe to the snows of a distant range. In the course of our journey Kasbek and Elbruz,[1] the only two peaks of the Caucasian chain that were then known to fame in Western Europe, were climbed for the first time. We visited the more important valleys between them on the south side of the range, obtained some idea of the importance of the Central Group, and brought to light the existence of a number of great peaks. Travel in the mountains was at that time difficult, and some of the most attractive districts were still far from safe. In 1875 Mr. F. Craufurd Grove published his *Frosty Caucasus*, a very lively and interesting account of the first ascent of the western, which has proved to be slightly the higher, of the two cones of Elbruz, and of a tour through the heart of the mountains, made in the previous year by himself, my former companion Mr. Moore, Mr. Horace Walker, and Mr. Frederick Gardiner, with Peter Knubel, a Zermatt guide. The party crossed the main chain by

---

[1] *Travels in the Central Caucasus and Bashan.* Longmans, 1869.

the old pass near the source of the Rion, visited the northern glaciers of the Central Group and the western flanks of Elbruz, and descended to the Black Sea over the Nakhar Pass, and through the forest-wilderness of the Kodor, where they all had the misfortune to catch the fever of the country.

Wars and rumours of war intervened, and it was not for some years that English mountaineers again looked eastwards to the confines of Europe and the summits of the Caucasus.

Meantime M. de Déchy, a Hungarian gentleman, took up the task of exploration. In 1884, 1885, and 1886, he made three extensive journeys in the range. In 1884, accompanied by two Swiss guides, one of them the well-known Alexander Burgener of Saas, he climbed Elbruz and a fine peak near the Mamison Pass. In the course of his wanderings he made the first passage by travellers of several native glacier passes and collected a considerable amount of scientific information with regard to the glaciers and the snow region. He also took a very large number of most valuable photographs of the scenery and people, thus making himself the pioneer in Caucasian photography. I am indebted to him for some of the most interesting illustrations in these volumes.

In 1886 Mr. Clinton Dent and Mr. W. F. Donkin, with Burgener and Basil Andenmatten, made a rapid onslaught on the snows from the northern side, and, following Mr. Grove's suggestion, climbed one of the peaks of the Central Group, named Gestola, 15,932 feet in height.[1]

In 1887 M. de Déchy joined company with me for a short journey. I had with me François Dévouassoud and two of his relatives, Chamonix guides. We crossed together two high passes over the main Suanetian chain, and I climbed several summits, amongst them Tetnuld (15,918 feet), the beautiful peak which lifts its silver horn above the forest glades of Suanetia.[2]

The year 1888 was marked by great mountaineering activity and success, and by a most lamentable catastrophe. The late Mr.

---

[1] *Alpine Journal*, vol. xiii. pp. 220 and 242. Mr. Dent, mistakenly, at first called the peak he climbed Tetnuld.

[2] *Proceedings of the Royal Geographical Society*, New Series, vol. x. pp. 325 and 677.

A. F. Mummery, with H. Zurfluh of Meiringen, scaled the great southern cliff of the second peak in the Caucasus—if, indeed, Dykhtau's slight advantage over Shkara is authentic—and explored the passes at the heads of the Bezingi and Bashilsu Glaciers.

A second party, Mr. Holder, Mr. H. Woolley, and Mr. Cockin, with Ulrich Almer of Grindelwald, climbed Dykhtau by its northern ridge, Katuintau and Salynan Bashi, and almost climbed Mishirgitau, and Mr. Cockin, who remained behind his companions, had the extraordinary good fortune to add to his trophies Shkara, the eastern peak of Janga, and the northern peak of Ushba.

The third party consisted of Mr. Clinton Dent, Mr. W. F. Donkin, and Mr. H. Fox, with K. Streich and J. Fischer of Meiringen. Owing to indisposition, Dent was forced to leave his companions in Suanetia. Donkin and Fox, with their two guides, climbed the eastern peak of Dongusorun, and, after forcing a fine glacier pass over the Urubashi spur, made their way along the northern side of the chain to the foot of Koshtantau. They left their camp and interpreter in the Dumala glen, four hours from Bezingi, with instructions to meet them in a few days at Karaul, in the Balkar district. They were never seen or heard of again. Their fate was wrapped in mystery, and became not unnaturally the subject of wild conjecture in the country. The local officials suspected foul play, and some of the hangers-on of officialism were perhaps too ready to adopt a belief by which they may have had something to gain.

In 1889 Mr. Clinton Dent and I, with the assistance of Mr. Hermann Woolley and Captain Powell of the Indian Army, set out with three Alpine guides and Andreas Fischer, the brother of the lost guide, to ascertain, as far as might be possible, the fate of our friends. The story of our Search Expedition, of Mr. Woolley's ascents of Koshtantau and Ailama with Christian Jossi, and of Captain Powell's and my subsequent ascent of the Laila and journey through the forests of Abkhasia, will be found in subsequent chapters.

In 1890 the Adai Khokh Group was made the principal field of exploration. Mr. Cockin, Mr. Holder, and Mr. Mummery, with Mr. W. J. Petherick, took part in it. Adai Khokh, Burdjula, and Zikhvarga were climbed and photographed.

In 1891 two German climbers, Herr Merzbacher and Herr Purt-scheller, with two Tyrolese guides, made an extensive tour, in the course of which the three summits of the Laila, Tetnuld, Dongusorun, the northern Adyrsu Bashi of the one-verst map (first ascent), the eastern peak of Janga and Gimarai Khokh (first ascent) were climbed, and Kasbek reached for the first time from the head of the Genaldon Valley, by a route meeting the Devdorak route on the great snow-field north of the summit.

In 1893 four Englishmen, Mr. Solly, Mr. Woolley, Mr. New-march, and Mr. Cockin, and in the following year Mr. Solly and Mr. Newmarch, with Mr. Collier, visited Suanetia. Their climbs are duly chronicled in the Appendix to these volumes.

In 1895 Mr. Clinton Dent and Mr. Woolley again visited the Caucasus, in company with Mr. M'Cormick, an artist who had previously been with Sir W. M. Conway in the Karakoram. The ascent of Ziteli, the second summit of the Laboda Group, from the Urukh Valley, was their chief climb. The results of their journey were mainly photographic and artistic. Mr. Cockin and Mr. New-march were once more drawn to Betsho, and pursued their pro-tracted courtship of the southern peak of Ushba without meeting with any reward for their constancy.

I have left to the last the journeys of Signor Vittorio Sella, my fellow-labourer in the preparation of this work. In 1889 he made, with his younger brother Erminio, a long journey in the mountains : and in 1890 he returned to them, taking with him three Italian farm-servants to carry his photographic apparatus. He climbed, besides Elbruz and the Laila, three high summits, Burdjula, Zikhvarga, and Ulluauz Bashi. But his distinguishing success was in the work that gives their chief value to these volumes. He has illustrated the Caucasian snows as no distant glacier chain has ever been illustrated before. With the help of his sturdy Piedmontese followers, he carried his camera and his glass-plates to elevations of over sixteen thousand feet, and brought back with him images, not only of the valleys and their people, but of the summits and their vast mountain panoramas. He anticipated the Russian surveyors in correcting the representation of the Suanetian glaciers on the five-verst map.

This catalogue, ruthlessly abbreviated as it has been, is perhaps long enough to be tiresome. It seemed necessary, however, from my point of view, to indicate, once for all, how much has been done in the last quarter of a century by *mountaineers* to elucidate the topography and characteristics of the snowy region of the Central Caucasus.

During this period the lower grounds, the valleys and horse-passes, have not been neglected by general travellers, several of

SIGNOR SELLA AND HIS MEN

whom have contributed to Caucasian literature. If I do not include them in my list of mountain explorers, it is not from any disposition to underrate the interest of their travels. I give elsewhere a list of the more important of these authors. I need only mention here, among our countrymen, Captain Telfer, R.N., an ardent archæo-logist, and Mr. Phillipps-Wolley, equally eager as a sportsman. M. de Bernoville's handsome volume contains much that is inter-esting with reference to Suanetia and its antiquities. M. Chantre's ethnological studies have, by the liberality of the French Govern-ment, been embodied in a monumental work. Signor Lerco, a

Piedmontese, has given an account of an ascent of Kasbek by the buttress opposite the post-station made by him in 1887. M. Ivanoff has recounted a vain attempt to ascend Elbruz. Two other Russian travellers, Messrs. Iljin and Dinnik, visited the lower ends of several glaciers, and published in *Petermann's Mitteilungen* instructive accounts of their travels.[1] Professor Kovalevsky and

RUSSIAN SURVEYORS AND ENGLISH CLIMBERS

Dr. Radde have studied on the spot the primitive laws and customs of the mountain tribes.

In 1890 the distinguished botanist, M. S. Sommier, with M. E. Levier, visited Suanetia, and traversed the Forest of Darl and the Klukhor Pass. M. Levier has described their adventures and discoveries in a most entertaining volume, full of valuable botanical information.

---

[1] *Petermann's Mitteilungen*, vol. xxx., 1884.

It would be very ungrateful to leave out in this enumeration of the contributors to our accurate knowledge of the Central Caucasus the Russian engineers who have been charged with the mapping of the chain.

About 1880 an entirely new survey of the Caucasian Provinces was undertaken by the Government. I had, in 1889, opportunities of making the personal acquaintance of two of the officials—they belong to a civil and not a military service—entrusted with this task, Messieurs Jukoff and Bogdanoff, and of appreciating on the spot their zeal and patience. Another of the surveyors, M. Kovtoradze, distinguished himself in 1891 by following Mr. Holder's party to the top of Adai Khokh. Elbruz had been reached in 1890 by M. Pastukhoff, of the Survey, and Kasbek was in 1889 climbed by a resident at Tiflis, who had the boldness to describe his expedition as the 'first authentic ascent of the mountain.'

As a whole, the new survey promises to be excellent. Some of the earlier sheets have not as yet been brought up to the general level. The surveyors went from one extreme to the other : they exaggerated at first, almost as much as their predecessors had diminished, the extent of the snows ; they paid no attention to the spurs that subdivide the glacier basins. But in the more recent, and by far the larger portion of their work, this tendency has disappeared. There is little fault to be found with most of the sheets placed in my hands by the courtesy of General Kulberg. Here and there, perhaps, some glacier recess, invisible from any valley, and only accessible by dint of ice-axes, has been vaguely and inadequately depicted. In all such cases I have ventured, in the map issued with these volumes, to make, as far as the scale allows, what seem to me the necessary corrections.

Of the predecessor of this map, a large diagram I prepared with no slight labour ten years ago for the Geographical Society, I wrote at the time as follows :—

'The sketch map shown, though in some parts without pretensions to scientific accuracy, gives a fairly truthful representation of the heart of the Caucasus. It indicates the complex character of the snowy chain, its numerous spurs, how the glacier basins are distributed, how the ridges encircle and divide them.   The mountains east of the Mamison Pass are laid down from the new survey.   Mr. Donkin has, by means of numerous magnetic bearings and photographs, depicted with considerable accuracy the great Bezingi Glacier.   M. de Déchy has provided me with a mass of photographs.   For the rest, I have had materials of my own, in bearings and sketches taken from many lofty standpoints.   Thirty-six sheets of topographical notes are embodied in that map.'

This work has been in some points superseded, but it has served its purpose.   The map which I am here able to produce owes no doubt its general scientific precision almost entirely to the observations taken during the last ten years by the officers charged to re-survey the great chain.   It would be difficult to speak too highly of the zeal and industry of several of these cartographers.   But it may be permissible to believe that the sympathy and appreciation their work has met with on the spot, the suggestions and criticisms that have been exchanged in mountain camps between them and Alpine explorers, have afforded some help and encouragement to our Russian friends in their labours.   Owing to the delay in the formal publication of the new survey, which is on the large scale of one-verst to the inch, these labours have as yet met with but limited recognition, even in Russia.   M. Golovievsky, who was responsible for the Elbruz sheet, the only one yet officially published, has, I understand, received honours from the geographers of St. Petersburg.   When the importance in the orography of the chain of the Central Group, and the difficulties involved in its accurate survey, are appreciated at a distance, there can be but little doubt that the work of other officers will be duly noticed in their own country.

My only serious difference with the surveyors is in the very knotty question of nomenclature.   It is the general experience of travellers that the names given on the new maps are in many instances not those commonly in use among the people of the country. In some they are obviously clumsy.   Dongus-orun-cheget-kara-bashi, 'The head of the black ridge of the place of pigs'—the name applied to one of the summits visible from Urusbieh—is too much of a mouthful for every-day use.   And in one now famous instance we bow most reluctantly to the decision of the new survey. The second and fourth peak of the chain, the two highest summits of the great spur of the Central Group, the Dent Blanche and Weisshorn of the Caucasus, were named **Koshtantau** and **Dykhtau** by the makers of the five-verst map, and for a quarter of a century these names had held their place in geographical literature and tales of mountain adventure. It was on the Dykhtau of the five-verst map that Donkin and Fox met their fate. These names have been reversed in the still unpublished new sheets, on the ground of local usage. All our remonstrances, on the score of convenience or sentiment, against the change have been fruitless. There is no Court of Appeal from the official verdict. Henceforth Dykhtau must be Koshtantau, and *vice versâ*. We English mountaineers submit, but we do so with infinite regret.[1]

---

[1] Those who read Russian will find a mass of information relating to the Caucasus in the ten or more volumes entitled *Materials for the Study of the Caucasus*, issued by M. Janovsky at Tiflis since 1885. The best general description of the Caucasus in English is that contributed to the *Encyclopædia Britannica* (1875) by one of the early members of the Alpine Club, the well-known geographer, Mr. Edward Bunbury.

CHAPTER II

THE CHARACTERISTICS OF THE CAUCASUS

Why are comprehensive works adapted for the general reader and student of nature to be replaced entirely by studied monographs connected with some single science in some single district? PRINCIPAL JAMES D. FORBES.

GENERAL chapters are apt to be dull. Yet some sort of framework must be provided for the pictures of travel and adventure to follow. The obsolete fiction I have undertaken to get rid of has to be replaced by more correct information. I shall do my best to convey it in a compact and convenient form —dealing here broadly with the outlines, and only indicating the local colours. Topographical details, such as are called for by the explorer and the mountaineer, I shall reserve for an Appendix, where they will not only be accessible to him, but also avoidable by the ordinary reader, who has no time and small patience for such matters.

Let us, with a general map before us, glance, as quickly as possible, at the elements of Caucasian orography. The really mountainous part of the chain, from Fish Dagh on the west to Basardjusi on the east, is over 400 miles long, a distance about equal to that between Monte Viso and the Semmering in the Alps. Its skirts stretch out for another 150 and 100 miles respectively to the neighbourhoods of Baku, on the Caspian, and of Novorossisk, the

new Black Sea corn-port of Ciscaucasia.   It runs from W.NW.
to E.SE., between latitudes 45° and 40° N., its centre being
in the same parallel with the Pyrenees.   The snowy range—' the
frosty Caucasus '—which begins north of Pitzunda on the Black
Sea, stretches without interruption to the eastern source of the
Rion, the ancient Phasis.   Between the Klukhor and Nakhar
Passes and the Mamison Pass—that is, for 100 miles, a distance
as great as from the Col de la Seigne to the St. Gotthard—
there is no gap under 10,000 feet; no pass that does not traverse
glaciers.   Continuous no longer, but broken by gorges, one of which
is the famous Darial, the snowy central crest stretches eastward,
culminating in the glacier groups of Kasbek (16,546 feet) and
Shebulos (14,781 feet).   East of the historical pass of the Caucasus
—commonly known as the Darial, but more correctly as the Krestovaya Gora, or Mountain of the Cross—the mountain ridges diverge,
enclosing between them the barren limestone plateaus and yawning
ravines of Daghestan—' the Highlands,' as the name implies.   The
valleys round Tebulos have been described by Dr. Radde in his
work on the Chevsurs.   Its glaciers, as well as those of Bogos,
have been recently explored, climbed, and photographed by a
German mountaineer, Herr Merzbacher.   Judging from his views,
the forms of the peaks are less bold, and the scenery as a whole
is less varied than in the Central Caucasus.   The range that
forms the southern boundary of Daghestan, and shelters the rich
forests and orchards of Kakhetia, is tame in outline though high
in general elevation, and only becomes picturesque and interesting
in the neighbourhood of the broad basaltic cliffs of Basardjusi
(14,635 feet), a mountain which has lately been climbed and
described by Mr. Yeld and Mr. Baker.[1]

This eastern half of the chain, despite its three glacier groups,
Tebulos, Bogos, Basardjusi, lies outside my field of view.   It will
no doubt be fully dealt with in the volume promised by Herr Merzbacher.   We must be content here to concentrate our attention on
the part of the Caucasian chain between Elbruz and Kasbek.   That

---

[1] *Proceedings of the Royal Geographical Society*, vol. xiii. p. 313.   *Alpine Journal*, vol. xvi.
p. 1.   See also Dr. Radde's paper in *Petermann's Mitteilungen*, Ergänzungsheft 85.

portion is 120 miles long—as long as from Mont Blanc to the
Rheinwaldhorn. From Naltshik to Kutais it is 100 miles broad ;
in its narrowest part about 80 miles broad. A hundred miles is
about the breadth of the Alps from Grenoble to Turin, Chambery
to Ivrea, or Lucerne to Arona. Contrary, therefore, to what has
often been stated, the Central Caucasus is slightly, but not very
much, narrower than the Alps.

It is essential to an understanding of the characteristics of the
Caucasus, to an appreciation of Caucasian scenery, even to the
planning of Caucasian tours, that some correct idea should be formed
of the geological structure of the chain—at any rate, in its main
features. If the zone covered by mountains is nearly as broad as
in the case of the Alps, the orographical detail is much simpler.
Nowhere in the central chain are there more than thirty miles in
a transverse section between the outstanding snow-peaks. There
are about fifty miles between the Wetterhorn and Monte Rosa, or
the Silvretta and the Adamello.

I accept the theory, which has gained ground of late years,
that mountain ranges indicate lines of weakness in the Earth's
crust, and that their elevation is caused by its contraction. The
Alps would appear to be the result of successive and very complicated Earth movements. The Caucasus, by its more uniform
structure, may suggest rather a single if prolonged effort, whereby
the central core of gneiss and granite has been raised, and the
successive layers of crystalline schists, slates, limestone, and
cretaceous rocks thrown up against its flanks.

The key to a correct understanding of much Caucasian orography
may be found in the recognition that the geological axis of the chain
and its water-parting are in many places not identical. The granitic
axis emerges from under the waves of the Black Sea, some distance
west of Sukhum Kale. If a line is drawn along its centre in the
accompanying geological map, it will be seen to form a series of
gentle curves, and to coincide, *in the main*, with the watershed as
far as the Mamison Pass. I qualify my statement because, east of
Dongusorun and again above the Skenis Skali sources and the
western source of the Rion, the dividing ridge is for a short space

composed of friable crystalline schists. This fact, which, as far as I know, has not yet been noticed by geologists, has very important practical effects. The chain in these portions is without conspicuous peaks and crests for a few miles, and is traversed by relatively easy and frequented cattle-passes.

The granitic main chain is not accurately described as a single wall. Nor are the same peaks, as a rule, conspicuous from the steppe and the southern lowlands. Dykhtau and Koshtantau are seen from Piatigorsk on the north, standing out on a bold spur which generally conceals Shkara and Janga. The Adai Khokh group, so conspicuous from the heights of the Lower Rion, is hidden from the north-west by the Bogkhobashi range north of the Urukh.

The central chain of the Caucasus, when studied in detail, recalls the features of the Pennine Alps. It consists of a number of short parallel, or curved horse-shoe ridges, crowned with rocky peaks and enclosing basins filled by the *névés* of great glaciers, the Karagom, the Dykhsu, the Bezingi, the Zanner, and the Leksur. I name only a few of the greatest. In its double ridges, with vast frozen reservoirs between them, it resembles the group of Mont Blanc; it has lofty spurs, like those of the Saasgrat and the Weisshorn. On either side of the main chain the same succession is repeated, with one important difference. On the north the schists come first, sometimes rising into peaks and ridges in a state of ruin most dangerous to climbers—a fact indelibly impressed on my memory—but more often worn to rolling downs; then the limestone range—writing-desk mountains that turn their steep fronts to the central snows; lastly, low cretaceous foothills, that sink softly into the steppe. But on the south side the crystalline rocks are succeeded by a broad belt of slates, as to the age of which the evidence is at present conflicting and the opinion of geologists divided.[1]

East of Adai Khokh, by what seems a strange freak of nature, the granitic range is rent over and over again to its base by gorges, the

---

[1] See Professor Bonney's Note to the Geological Map, Vol. ii. Appendix A.

watershed being transferred to the parallel chain of clay slates—
'palæozoic schists' they have, apparently without conclusive reasons,
been termed abroad—which has followed it from the Black Sea,
attaining on its way the height of 13,400 feet in the Laila, and limit-
ing the great parallel basins of the Rion, Ingur, and Skenis Skali.
The how and why of this transfer of the watershed I leave to professional geologists. Its historical importance has been great. The
slates, less steep, less lofty than the granite, are also far less formidable obstacles to traffic. The Krestovaya Gora—or Cross Mountain
Pass—traverses them at less than 8000 feet; the Mamison Pass
slips over the grassy ridge that links them to the granites of
Adai Khokh at a height of 9200 feet. These are the natural
highways from the north to Georgia and Mingrelia respectively.
The former has long been the Georgian military highroad; the
latter was opened for wheels in 1889. They are easy passes—so
easy that it was not on the mountain crest, but where, in the
gorge of Darial, the granitic range is cleft to its base, that
Chosroes and Justinian combined to raise and garrison a frontier
fortress between the old civilisations of the world and the legendary
hordes, the Gog and Magog, of northern barbarism.   Between
them half a dozen gaps, leading from the head-waters of the
Kur to those of the Ardon, a tributary of the Terek, are frequently
traversed by the Ossetes, whose position astride the chain enabled
them at the beginning of the present century to hand over its
keys to Russia.

Kasbek and Elbruz are volcanic excrescences, trachytic cones
planted close beside the main range, and of much more recent
origin.[1]   M. E. Favre attributes their appearance to a period
before the great Ice Age of the Caucasus, on the apparently conclusive evidence of the erratic boulders found on the steppe. Elbruz
has the regular outlines of a typical volcano. Its characteristic
peculiarity is that it culminates in two comparatively small cones of

---

[1] The distance of Elbruz from the watershed is reduced by the new survey from 11¼ miles
to 7 miles. The position of the north-west peak relatively to the south-east is also shifted in the
new map from N. 41° W., to N. 76° W. The heights of the peaks (given in Russian sajens,
equal to 7 feet), are reduced from 18,526 and 18,453 feet to 18,470 and 18,347 feet respectively.

nearly equal height, separated by a gap some 1500 feet in depth, and 17,000 feet above the sea-level. Each of these cones preserves the features of a crater in a horseshoe ridge broken down on one side, and enclosing a shallow snow-filled basin. Observers from a distance, including M. Favre, have erroneously conjectured the deep hollow between the peaks to be a gap in an immense terminal crater, a supposition which the ascents by Mr. Grove and myself have now finally disposed of.[1]

Kasbek has a far less regular outline than its great rival, and the passing traveller who only sees it from the high-road may be excused for not recognising its volcanic origin. From the south its outline, if compared with the figures (on p. 123) in Judd's *Volcanoes*, has something of the aspect of a breached cone. Signor Lerco, a Piedmontese gentleman, who climbed the mountain in 1887,[2] has sent me a photograph taken on the top of the buttress conspicuous from the post-station (about 14,500 feet), which shows the crags that there protrude to be contorted masses of lava.[3] A great *névé* now clothes the northern face of the peak. Were a hut built on the ridge between the Devdorak and Chach glaciers, the mountain would be less dangerous than Mont Blanc, and not more difficult of ascent. It was by this route that we descended in 1868.

Generalities such as these, first gleaned from maps and books and scattered observations, the mountaineer summarises and fixes in his memory in the vivid moments spent on the mountain tops. De Saussure and Tyndall have both asserted the value of such bird's-eye views as a basis for scientific reasoning. I do not pretend to speak with authority on such high matters. Yet possibly an observer may not bring down less knowledge from these Pisgah-heights because he goes up to them without either a theory to support or a reputation to endanger. Of this much I am certain, that even to men not 'physically minded,' panoramas

---

[1] Grove's *Frosty Caucasus*, 1875.

[2] See *Schweizer Alpenzeitung*, Nos. 17-21. Zürich, 1888.

[3] M. E. Favre has reported as follows on a piece of rock brought from the top and submitted to him by my guide, François Dévouassoud : 'It is a grey rock of a semi-vitrified substance, containing white crystals of oligoclase.'

may be most useful in correcting some of the misapprehensions caused by the conventions of imperfect or uncontoured maps. I shall make bold, therefore, to call upon my readers to climb with me to a height of some 15,000 to 18,000 feet above the sea-level, and while resting on one of the highest crests of the Caucasus, to examine at leisure such a prospect as I saw unrolled before my eyes twenty-eight years ago from Kasbek and Elbruz, and on my subsequent journeys from Tetnuld, Ukiu, and the Laila.

DYKHTAU FROM THE WEST

The heaven overhead is of a deep gentian blue; the neighbouring snows are dazzlingly white; as the range recedes the peaks shine golden, until on the horizon the farthest crests and the thin streaks of cloud take a rich amber tint, shading off into faint sunrise pinks. A luminous, opalescent, transparent haze spreads over the lowlands, softening but hardly obscuring their features. About our solitary pinnacle all is still and silent, save for the lapping of the little waves of warm air that rise up to us from the valleys, the far-off and indistinct, but perpetual murmur of falling torrents, and the momentary roar of avalanches as they plunge from the frozen cliffs of *névé* underfoot into the hidden depths of the glaciers. The vast blue landscape, some 500 miles in diameter, outspread beneath, is spanned by a broad belt of snowy heights and hollows, as the sky is arched at night by the Milky Way. These heights do not show as the single wall indicated on maps, but rather as a system of short crests, running generally at an acute angle to the direction of the chain, and more nearly due east and west. We can distinguish generally two (sometimes more) principal ridges roughly parallel. The peaks are encased in frosty armour, full of subtle lines and delicate flutings, where the corniced crests throw their bands of shadow on to the broad breastplate of snow. Below the *Bergschrund*, or fissure that belts the mountain sides, heavy folds of stainless *névé* fall to the lower glaciers. Where the crags are bare they show the boldness and rigidity of outline characteristic of the harder crystalline rocks. In the Central Group, round Shkara, Koshtantau, and Dykhtau, the forces, whatever they were, that gave the chain its being, seem to have been most strenuously exerted ; the crests are higher, the slopes steeper, the trenches more profound. There is a vigour, an extravagance, one might say, in the mountain structure that may recall the Alps of Dauphiné.[1]

The hollows between the heights are filled by enormous firths of ice, whose basins stretch out parallel to the crests, snowfield beyond snowfield, on a scale hardly found in the Alps except at the bases of the Jungfrau and the Finsteraarhorn.[2] From the 'dusky doors' of the glaciers rivers flash, full-grown, into life, and our eyes follow their course in either direction, north or south, as they linger for a time in broad forest basins or grassy trenches at the foot of the snows, and gather their tributaries before battling a way out through deep ravines and a maze of foothills to the distant steppe or the dim surface of the Black Sea. What is the character of the country

---

[1] The Bezingi Glacier is a geological museum of fragments of crystalline rocks fallen from the neighbouring ranges, as curious to the eyes as obnoxious to the soles of those who tramp up this magnificent ice-stream.

[2] The Aletsch Glacier is longer than any glacier in the Caucasus. But the Bezingi and Karagom are little inferior to any other glacier in the Alps.

they flow through ?   Let us examine it more in detail, and first on
the north.   Here at the base of the central core of the chain spread
broad, smooth, grassy downs, the pastures of the Turk and the
Ossete.   Downs I call them, for the name seems best to suit their
rolling outlines, but their ridges attain 9000 to 10,000 feet.   They
are composed of friable crystalline schists, and atmospheric action has
long ago destroyed the peaks that may once have crowned them.

Beyond these schists rises a broken wall of limestone, cleft to
the base by gorges, through which flow the mountain torrents,

SHEPHERD AND FLOCK, NEAR KARAUL

and capped by pale precipitous battlements, which face the central
chain at a height of 11,000 to 12,000 feet.[1]   Beyond, again, lies a
broad furrow, or 'longitudinal fold,' as geologists call it, parallel to
the ridges, and then rises the last elevation, a belt of low calcareous
hills, on which, here and there among the waves of beech-forest,
purple or blue with distance, a white cliff retains its local colour,
and shines like a patch of fresh snow.   Beyond, once more beyond,

---

[1] Those who know Savoy may recognise an arrangement of rocks similar, though on a
larger scale, to that found round Mont Blanc, in the granitoid rock of the Aiguilles, the
schistose downs of Mégève, and the limestone cliffs of the Aiguille de Varens and Pointe
Percée overshadowing the ravine of the Arve.

spreads the Scythian Steppe; not the dead level of Lombardy, but an expanse of long low undulations, which would be reckoned hills in our Home Counties, seamed by long shining ribbons which mark the courses of the tributaries of the Terek. On the horizon rise boldly—resembling in scale and outline the Euganean Hills—the Five Mountains of Piatigorsk. Farther east, the basin of Vladikavkaz is enclosed by a semicircle of low sandstone hills. They deserve closer inspection, for they might be found to be rich in traces of ancient glacial action.

Now let us turn our faces southwards. Here, too, immediately under the snows, we find 'crystalline schists,' smooth grassy heights separated by shallow trenches, which form the lesser undulations of the three basins, the 'Drei Langenhochthäler Imeritiens' of Dr. Radde. These basins, or 'longitudinal folds,' are enclosed on the south by the long high ridge of dark slates, which extends parallel to the crystalline chain from the neighbourhood of Sukhum Kale to the Krestovaya Gora. Behind this slate crest spreads a confused multitude of hills, jurassic and cretaceous in their formation, the geological features of which are outlined in the accompanying map. Their outer edge, distant some thirty to forty miles from the snows, is marked by a limestone belt, lower and less continuous than that on the north, which frames the gorges of the Rion and rises in the Kuamli (6352 feet) and Nakarala (4774 feet), near Kutais, to its best-known elevations. At the foot of the latter lie the coal-mines of Khibuli, recently connected with Kutais by a railway. Over its high uplands spreads one of the noblest beech-forests in the world, varied by a natural undergrowth of azaleas, laurels, box, and rhododendrons. Further west, on either side of the gorge of the Ingur, this ridge rises to a loftier elevation, and carries small glaciers, on heights designated on the five-verst map as Khodjall (9906 feet) and Larakhanis-chabi.

What ideas or suggestions may we derive from such a landscape? To me, great panoramas—Caucasian or Alpine—confirm the modern belief that the agency that first created mountain ranges was crumpling by pressure. That the original irregularity of surface so produced took the form of one enormous smooth-sided bank or mound appears incredible. In the mountain structure we recognise a series of primary parallel ridges and furrows, enormously modified, possibly by subsequent exertions of forces similar to that which raised the chain, certainly by subaerial denudation in its various forms, but still roughly recognisable. How are we to account for the great clefts that split the crystalline rocks of the central chain to their base in the Upper Cherek, the Darial and Alagir gorges? We seem to require the exertion of some strain acting at right angles to the pressure which raised the chain. The shrinkage of the Earth's crust, to which the elevation of mountain regions is now generally attributed by geologists, might naturally cause such a strain. An alternative theory—held by too high authorities for me to venture to discard it—is that these gorges have been sawn asunder by water following its old channels through a slowly rising ridge of later elevation.

In either case internal forces have produced the rough-hewn blocks. But other agencies have been at work to model the noble forms we see around us: heat and cold, rain and torrent have, century after century, split the mountain crests and furrowed their flanks. Ice moving backwards and forwards along the hollows has polished and smoothed their sides, leaving behind it as it retired immense loads of the broken stuff it had carried down from the higher ranges. Water has followed, scouring the mountain slopes, tapping the hollows, or filling them up with alluvial matter.[1] These agents have done an enormous work, but they have been sculptors and polishers and carriers, not quarriers, and their share of work, even as sculptors, has been perhaps exaggerated. Like Michael Angelo in his colossal statue of David, they have had to follow the form of their material.

---

[1] The conservative action of ice could hardly be better shown than by the contrast between the upper sources of the Ingur and the Skenis Skali, which are closely adjacent. The former occupy shallow U-shaped troughs, the latter trenches 1000 to 2000 deeper, and V-shaped. The reason is obvious, at least to those who accept an axiom of Professor Heim which I have elsewhere (*Proceedings of the Royal Geographical Society*, New Series, vol. x. 1888) pressed on the attention of geologists. 'Glaciation,' Heim lays down, 'is equivalent to the relative cessation of valley formation.' At the Ingur sources the glaciers, owing to the configuration of the chain, always more extensive than those of the Skenis Skali, must have for centuries protected the slopes from the atmospheric action to which the hills of the Skenis Skali were exposed.

Weather and water are sharp tools; ice is Nature's substitute for sandpaper, and a fairly efficient one. But to attribute to it a chief share in the details of the present surface conformation of mountain ranges is surely excessive. On the glaciers an observer might, I fancy, obtain some hints as to mountain structure from what he sees in the ice of the behaviour of an imperfectly elastic body under strain, pressure, and exposure. The surface of the ice and its water channels are finally modelled by exposure to air and water action, but the broader elevations and depressions are the results of other agencies.

THE KALDE GLACIER

Let us now for a moment spread out on the crags before us the old five-verst map, and compare its presentment with Nature herself. So far as physical features are concerned, the most remarkable merit of the map lies in the accurate distinction made between the bare and forested districts. Its most patent inaccuracy is the great reduction of the area occupied by snow and ice.

I had occasion in the last chapter to point out how much mischief had been wrought through the acceptance by geographers of the

five-verst map as a complete physical survey.   In no respect have
the defects of this map been more prejudicial to the formation among
those who instruct the public of a correct conception of the Caucasus
than in the matter of its glaciation.   The map-makers treated this
physical feature with curious carelessness, not to say contempt.   It
may have been difficult for them to delineate or define, with any
approach to accuracy, the limits and extent of the glacier region in
the great chain.   But there was no reason why, while practically
ignoring the central snow and ice, they should have planted
imaginary snows of considerable extent on some of the lower parallel
ranges—for example, those south of the Rion sources.

It is only lately that the completion of many sheets of the one-
verst map has enabled those who have had access to them to realise
how unfounded were the statements current in scientific circles, and
how fully justified we mountain explorers were in our contradiction
of them.

It is now possible to furnish authentic figures as to the total
area and length of some of the greatest Caucasian glaciers.   The
following have been computed for me very carefully by Mr. Reeves,
the Assistant Map Curator of the Royal Geographical Society, from
the new sheets, forwarded to me by the courtesy of the late General
Shdanov and his successor.   The measurements of length are taken
along the centre of the ice-stream from the highest point of its
névé down to its tongue.

	AREA.	LENGTH.
Bezingi Glacier . .	30·8 square miles.	10·6 miles.
Karagom Glacier . . .	14·0	10·0
Leksur Glacier. . . .	19·2	7·6
Dykhsu Glacier . . .	25·6	7·3
Zanner Glacier . . .	21·3	6·6
Tuiber Glacier	21·4	6·6
Irik Glacier	8·7	6·6
Shikildi Glacier [1] . .	10·5	6·0

By way of comparison, I supply the measurements of eight

---

[1] In the statement of area I have tested Professor Heim's figures and find they are calculated
on the same principle as Mr. Reeves's.   The smaller rocks islanded in the ice, and forming part
of a glacier basin, are included in the calculation.

Alpine glaciers, extracted from the publications of the Federal
Staff and Professor Heim's work :—

			AREA.	LENGTH.
Aletsch Glacier	.	.	49·8 square miles.	15·5 miles.
Unteraar Glacier	.	.	15·1	10·0
Mer de Glace	.	.	16·0	9·5
Gorner Glacier	.	.	26·6	9·0
Viescher Glacier	.	.	16·0	9·0
Corbassière Glacier	.	.	9·4	7·0
Morteratsch Glacier	.	.	9·3	6·0
Zmutt Glacier	.	.	10·4	6·0

It will be seen that, putting aside the Aletsch Glacier, which
owes its abnormal size to the combination of a large basin and a
long high-level trough—large glaciers do not make deep troughs,
but shallow troughs make large glaciers—the great Caucasian
ice-streams are about equal in dimensions to those of the Pennine
and Bernese Alps.

The foregoing statistics give, however, but an imperfect idea of
the extent and grandeur of the ice-region in the Caucasus. On the
north side there is a fine glacier at the head of every valley between
the source of the Kuban and that of the Ardon. There are often
several separate glaciers of the first class—as we reckon them in
the Alps—in a single valley, as in the Bashilsu or in the Adyrsu.
If I remember rightly, some writer has reckoned all the ice in the
latter valley as a single glacier, and thus been led to class it as
among the most extensive of the Caucasus. This is true in a
sense, but the mode of classification is not one accepted in the
Alps, and may lead to confusion.

Turning to the lesser chains, the glaciers of the Laila are perhaps
as extensive as those of the Grand Paradis. The range north of
the Urukh valley is very rich in glaciers (the total area of snow
and ice is not less than 31 square miles), and the snowfields
about Kasbek and Gimarai Khokh are of vast extent (total area,
53 square miles).

The lower ends or snouts of the Caucasian glaciers are naturally,
in consequence of the latitude, higher than the Swiss. The

Karagom Glacier, 5700 feet, reaches the lowest point on the northern side; on the southern side the Chalaat and Leksur Glaciers united at about five thousand feet not many years ago, and end now two to four hundred feet higher respectively.   The point to which the glaciers descend would appear to be regulated much more by the size of their *névés* and the conformation of their beds than by their exposure : for instance, the Zanner and

THE SOURCE OF THE INGUR

Bezingi Glaciers, on opposite sides of the chain, both terminate between 6800 and 7000 feet.

The suggestion that there are no more than 46 square miles of ice in the Caucasus may now be finally dismissed. It is too soon to say exactly what extent of ground in the whole chain is under ice. Let us avoid the snare of our predecessors, hasty generalisation, founded on imperfect material. Until the range as a whole has been scientifically mapped, no final and accurate estimate can be possible. But for the Central Caucasus alone,

an estimate of from 625 to 650 square miles will not be very
far wrong. This is not a guess, but the result of very careful
calculation with the best available material.[1]

From the glaciers we naturally raise our eyes to the crests
that overshadow them. The ridges of the Central Caucasus are
far steeper than those of the Central Alps. The whole southern
front of the Central Group keeps up the average slope of the
steepest part of the eastern face of Monte Rosa; it is as if the
Macugnaga precipices extended for ten miles. The northern front
is almost as steep, though less lofty. Take the steepest bit of
the Breithorn, double its height, and spread it along from Monte
Rosa to the St. Théodule, and you may form some faint picture
of what the mountaineer sees from the heights above the Bezingi
Glacier. He fancies nature has here done her utmost in the
perpendicular style of mountain architecture. Then he goes up
the neighbouring Mishirgi Glacier—quite left out in the five-verst
map—and sees precipices profounder and still more impressive.

Sheer rocks are often strange rather than beautiful objects.
The frozen combes of the Caucasus owe their singular fascination to the ample folds and exquisite arrangement of the snowy
drapery that clothes their crags.   In a run I made to the
Bernese Oberland, soon after my return from one of my Caucasian
journeys, the first thing that struck me was the comparative
meagreness of the *névés* and glaciers clinging to the loftier
summits.   A great deal of the Caucasus is like the finest portions of the Alps—the Wengern Alp face of the Jungfrau, or the
Pelvoux above the Glacier Noir. Signor Sella's and M. de Déchy's
photographs of the Bezingi and Mishirgi Glaciers illustrate this
splendid feature in their scenery.

The first feature to attract attention, as we descend from the
mountain crests towards the south, is the exquisite verdure of the
highest uncovered slopes.   Every isolated piece of bare soil among
the Caucasian snowfields becomes a summer garden.   The moraines

---

[1] The glaciers of Switzerland cover 710 square miles. No one, so far as I know, has yet
been at the pains to compute accurately the amount of ice in the whole Alps or even on both
sides of the Pennine Chain.   In the Mont Blanc group the ice covers about 100 square miles.

get covered over very quickly with grass and flowers, which makes them 'look pleasanter'—to borrow the phrase of an Irish peasant discovered covering over with moss the stumps of his landlord's trees, which he had illegally cut down. It is also useful to the student of glacial oscillations; for directly the ice begins to advance, its motion is shown by the barrowfuls of unmistakably raw rubbish it shoots over the grassy banks. Near the foot of the Leksur Glacier I noticed a little island of vegetation on some rocks covering the centre of the ice. It is possible, however, that this may have been not an ordinary moraine, but soil brought down by an avalanche.

I have gathered flowering plants at a height of over 13,000 feet on Ukiu. At this height the stalk and leaves are tiny, the blossoms abundant and vivid in hue. Dr. Radde has described how he found flowers at about the same height on Elbruz.[1]   Thereupon a local 'scientist' took occasion to point out the incredible character of his statement. From the critic's point of view, it was an *a priori* impossibility for flowers to blossom above the snow-level. In the Alps I have found *Ranunculus glacialis* in blossom on the final peaks of the Cima di Castello and the Adamello, at over 11,000 feet, and gentians and forget-me-nots, dwarfed to tiny specks of exquisite brightness, on the southern ridge of the Basodino (10,500 feet). Probably flowering plants will be found in the Caucasus at higher elevations than any that have yet been noted. The slopes above the great Leksur Glacier, from 9000 to 10,000 feet, were green in July, and the grass was enlivened with poppies, *Anemone narcissiflora*, gentians, ranunculus, campanulas, myosotis, veronicas, geraniums, framed by the darker foliage and great cream-coloured blossoms of the *Rhododendron caucasicum*.

The general type of the vegetation is more luxuriant than on the Alps. The giant Caucasian snowdrop, which we grow in our gardens, is typical of the Caucasus. The species are larger, the blossoms more abundant, and near the snow perhaps somewhat less brilliant in colouring; whites and yellows—the colours in

---

[1] *Die drei Langenhochthäler Imeritiens.* Tiflis, 1867. My little specimens were unluckily lost out of a pocket-book; one was, I believe, a pyrethrum.

which lowland nature welcomes the spring—are often prevalent.
There are few cryptogamic plants (as far as I have observed),
few of those lovely little stunted lichens and mosses which enamel
the rocks of the high Alps. No edelweiss (*Gnaphalium leonto-
podium*) has yet been met with in the Caucasus proper, but I
understand from Dr. Radde that he has found the Alpine species
in the Armenian ranges near Kars. Of gentians there are many
varieties, but the species are not identical with the Alpine.
Generally the flora has singularly little in common with that of
the Alps. A German botanist states that the Alps and Himalaya
have more species in common than the Alps and Caucasus.
There is no very marked general distinction between the character of the flora on the two sides of the chain—at least in the
uppermost region. The broad Armenian highlands serve far more
efficiently as a botanical barrier than the lofty but comparatively
narrow line of Caucasian snows. But the vegetation of the forest
zone is much more luxuriant on the Asiatic than on the European
side.

Mountaineers are generally too late to see the flora in perfection. After July it is only close to the snow-line, in northward-
fronting dells, or where a late-melting avalanche has artificially
retarded the spring, that blossoms are found at their best. Botanists
at this season must look out for a green speck just freed from an
avalanche, in order to discover the early mountain blooms. In
August 1887, primulas, which abound, were nearly over. A
beautiful golden crocus we found only on the Goribolo. Tall
yellow lilies were common : of wild roses I noticed several varieties ;
a white rose, delicately flushed with pink, was the commonest.
Strawberries, raspberries, and currants abound on the south side,
particularly in the glen of the Skenis Skali. Plums and pears
almost drop into the mouth of the traveller as he rides down
the valley of the Kodor, and this basin, and still more that of the
Skenis Skali, is a very Brobdingnag of the vegetable world.

From the high pastures of the wild-goats, from secret lawns
no scythe has ever touched, no flock ever grazed, where year
after year the snows of winter are succeeded by the snowy

blossoms of the mountain rhododendron, we descend to the forests, the upper limit of which may be put at from 7200 to 8000 feet. The Caucasian woodlands present the vegetation of Central Europe in its greatest perfection and variety, together with an undergrowth of flowers unique in its richness and profusion.

In a recently published volume, M. Levier, a Swiss botanist, has depicted the forests of the Southern Caucasus with the enthusiasm of an artist joined to the precision of a specialist. His descriptions will naturally carry more weight than any words of mine, and I gladly avail myself of his kind permission to transfer to my pages his account of the first excursion he made among the hills of the upper Skenis Skali. The ridge the travellers ascended lies to the south of Cholur (3400 feet), in the Skenis Skali valley, some twenty-four miles below the sources of that river.

'Immediately above the cultivated fields is the zone of the underwood—rhododendrons, sweetbriar, hazels, crab apples, thorns, mountain ashes; this region and the environs of the village are covered with tufts of a groundsel, with blossoms of rosy white. Soon the true forest is reached, a forest of lofty deciduous trees, where willows, hornbeams, aspens and oaks are interlaced with enormous beeches, festooned with the white beards of the *Usnea*. The birch appears, diminishing in size as one ascends until it becomes little more than a bush. Nordmann's pines are met at first as isolated trees, then, gathering in imposing clusters and groves, they form the predominant element in the forest, where the underwood never entirely disappears.'

Some 3000 feet above Cholur, the travellers issued on a glade of a fairy-like aspect. 'It was a garden, but a garden of the gods. In a vast clearing, an amphitheatre of which the walls were rocks and pines, myriads of monkshoods, surpassing the height of a man on horseback, displayed their blue and white flowers. Raised one above the other and artistically grouped as if by the hand of a skilful landscape gardener, they adorned a long hillside. A crowd of other plants of the most diverse kinds disputed the soil with them, pushing between the straight stalks of their rivals, and prolonging their own blossoms as far as possible towards the light. It seemed a struggle as to which should climb above the heads of its neighbours and exhibit the most brilliant colours. The firework of flowers recalled the artificial bouquets of coloured stars thrown up against the sky at some city festival. A dense mass of verdure, composed principally of the great leaves of a groundsel and of the Alpine sorrel, covered another part of the

THE SKENIS SKALI FOREST

glade, penetrating under the pines, and completely hiding the path. The enormous panicles of an ashy-blue campanula rose out of this confusion, and loftier still, the rival of the monkshoods, a scabious, balanced its great yellow flowers some six to eight feet above the ground.

'A little further there was a display of white umbelliferous blossoms, fine grasses, potentillas with blue-green leaves. In the places where the flowers reached only to our knees we picked handfuls of azure columbines with white centres, ranunculus of several species, an *Astrantia* with pink stars, delicately veined in emerald green, a flower which seemed expressly made to decorate ornamental notepaper or a Valentine. There was also a species of our Alpine snake-weed, with loose spikes and petals of such a vivid crimson that even our servant set to work to gather them for us, and was quite chagrined to see that we neglected them.

'On pushing apart the high stems we discovered another layer of flowers less eager for light : forget-me-nots, herb-Paris, orchids, geraniums, etc.   Close to the ground the soil was covered by a carpet of little round leaves supported by thin stalks like those of the maidenhair fern ; these were the leaves of a shade-loving speedwell (*Veronica liliformis*, G. M.), which, like our violet, blooms modestly beneath great green sunshades.

'I was debating how to pack my immense nosegay when my companion called me from above. I clambered in his tracks, and found him dripping with dew and digging frantically among plants higher than his head. It was real pioneer work to clear a path through this antediluvian vegetation, wherein we were like lost Lilliputians. The high rocky walls, still in the shade, were superb. Here reigned saxifrages, rock-valerians, enchanter's night-shade, groundsels, ferns, and succulent mosses as full of water as sponges. In the air also—for we had to look everywhere—were the winged fruits of maples, which formed the underwood, looking like bouquets of flowers, so vividly did their madder colour stand out under the green cupola of pines. After the first exclamations we collected our spoils in silent haste, oblivious of time, forgetful of the road we still had to travel. We had to come down at last and sort our treasures, and press those that could be pressed.

'Our men were in no hurry. They were well content with this short halt, seasoned with a pipe under the pines. The horses grazed at their will, and seemed as pleased as we were to come across such an El Dorado of tender herbs. They trampled the sorrel and made wide openings among the monkshoods, massacring indiscriminately both common and rare species, while we sat astride a rotten trunk rapidly putting our specimens in paper. Pressed by the advancing hour, we ended by leaving a heap of flowers, enough to have sufficed for three weddings, on the ground, and remounted our horses.

'The path became better, and we could at least botanise with our eyes without having constantly to war with the branches. But the flesh is weak. Before we had gone two hundred paces we had once more jumped to the ground, magnetically attracted by new marvels. The first was a giant campanula, as deeply blue as a gentian, a Caucasian exaggeration of our European *latifolia* ; then a gentian with lilac petals stippled with black ;[1] next an Inula, justly named *grandiflora*, recalling the elecampane, a Pyrethrum with white umbels[2] growing higher than a man ; and, lastly, once more the beautiful yellow lily already gathered in Ajaria, a bulb of which we took away. These bulbs, it may be remarked, are beginning to be exported, and fetch a good price ; and we were told that some European collectors had them pulled up by the hundredweight and sent them to England. They will not succeed, however, in destroying the species very soon, for it is widely distributed throughout the Caucasus, and is found up to the highest meadows, of which it is one of the most beautiful adornments.

'"Forward, signori!" Gosta has just shot an edible bird—a thrush, I think—and he grows impatient. Our little band marches on once more, those on foot in single file, the horsemen behind, determined at last to make up for lost time and to resist the enchantments of the *macroflora*. This is the name we henceforth apply to this vegetation of giant plants, which is not mentioned in treatises on geographical botany, and of which we have read only in certain passages in Dr. Radde's works.[3] *Macroflora* is a hybrid neologism, which might not be tolerated on the plains, but under the domes of the great pines, at 6000 feet above the sea, it may perhaps pass muster.

---

[1] *Sweertia punctata*, Baumg.   *Pyrethrum macrophyllum*, W. K.

[3] *Vier Vorträge über dem Kaukasus, Petermann's Mitt.*, Ergänzungsheft 36 ; *Die drei Langenhochthäler Imeritiens*, Tiflis, 1867. E. Levier, *A Travers le Caucase*. Paris, Fischbacher, 1895.   I dwelt on this characteristic of the Caucasian flora in my *Travels in the Caucasus*, published in 1869, and again in my paper published in 1888 in the *Proceedings of the Royal Geographical Society* (November), where I first wrote the words repeated on p. 43 : 'The general type of the vegetation is more luxuriant than on the Alps. The species are larger the blossoms more abundant.'

'As we rode we exchanged opinions and outlined a theory. From the first, one fact had impressed us. A certain number of species, which we had already seen elsewhere, attained much greater dimensions in the glade of monkshoods than at lower levels, where they grew more or less singly. Other species, and those the largest of all, growing in imposing masses, were absent at lower levels, but they ascended with us after 6000 feet. These probably were the fixed and normal species of the *macroflora*, and the others only adventitious ones, which had found the ground occupied by competitors six to ten feet high, so that, except by inordinately lengthening themselves, they would be in danger of finding neither space nor light. The struggle for existence had made them macro-campanulæ, macro-potentillæ, etc., giants for the nonce. This tendency can also be observed at home on a small scale. Slender and drawn-out plants, such as the cow thistle, the scarlet poppy, the phalaris and other weeds which grow among the brushwood of our forests or between the spikes of grain, often reach a height of five to six feet. But in Europe such occasional giants are thin, with stems of no solidity, whereas here it is quite different. For instance, it is possible to pull up a *Campanula lactiflora* six feet high (this species being only from one and a half to two and a quarter feet in the valley), and yet the stem does not bend in the hand when it is taken out of the ground. The leaf-stalks themselves are often remarkably vigorous; thus the great kidney-shaped leaves of a valerian[1] are borne by very long petioles, which are strong enough to allow them to be used as sunshades, like those of the petasites in Europe.

'Such luxuriance of spontaneous vegetation could not exist without one fundamental condition, that of a fertile soil impregnated with stores of natural manure almost inexhaustible, and this is admirably realised in the rich mould of the Caucasian forest. Beneath the living forest lies a dead forest—not one dead forest, rather the dead forests of several thousand years. On passing through the woods we see and sink into the crumbling rotting

---

[1] *Valeriana alliariæfolia*, Vahl.

trunks which fall everywhere, and slowly get buried after having
yielded life to innumerable epiphytes, large and small, ferns, mosses,
lichens and fungi. Something quite analogous to this burying of
dead trees in the forest goes on in the mountain meadows, where
the masses of giant plants, left to themselves and seldom trampled
by herds, droop in the fall of the year and give back to the
ground the elements of their future renewal.

'No matter how rich a soil may be, however, it can never
lengthen the stem of a cornflower, a poppy, or a tulip, beyond a
certain limit. Something more is needed to explain the extraordinary height of these monkshoods, cephalaria, mulgedia, and
groundsels of the Caucasus, among which men on horseback might
play at hide and seek without stooping, as among the cardoons
(*Cynara cardunculus*) of La Plata. These gigantic dimensions date
neither from yesterday nor from a thousand years ago, but are a
legacy, an inheritance, of still earlier times. We are really dealing
with survivals of the giant flora of past ages, of which a certain
number of characteristic species have been preserved, owing to
specially favourable conditions of soil and climate. These ancients
of the Earth—if the expression may be permitted—are the true
indigenes, and determine the character of the accidental intruders
who have come amongst them. It would make a most attractive subject for research to determine exactly the number of
these veterans and their mode of association, to study them
from one end of the chain to the other, and to distinguish
what are the essential and what the accidental elements of the
macroflora.'

The great screen of forests, spread along the outer northern
flank of the chain, has been less frequently described. The steppe,
except in the sunk river-beds or round the villages, is treeless;
but no sooner does the ground begin to rise than wild fruit-
trees appear, soon to be succeeded by dense groves of beeches.
Azalea and rhododendron—the common lilac variety (*ponticum*)—
flourish under their shade. The glades are bright in summer
with millions of golden flowers, probably the *Telekia speciosa*,
which the ordinary traveller may easily mistake, as I did at

first, for wild sunflowers. In old days these woods were debatable ground, and they long served as one of the chief protections of the mountain tribes. The Turkish tribes on the Cherek and Chegem and Baksan held the fastnesses in their rear. North of them, on the edge of the plain, lay the Cossack *stanitzas*. On their skirts hung the bands of robbers, led by *Jighits* or braves. The word survives. I was myself once saluted as a *Jighit* on the crest of the Caucasus by some grateful Turks whom I had relieved of the labour of step-making in soft snow.

A characteristic saying of Schamyl's has been reported :— ' Would that I could anoint the forests of the Caucasus with holy oil and pour libations of honey on its mud and mire, for these are the best protectors of its independence.' But even before Russian times the forests had served as a barrier. The Turks or Tartars who live behind them have little connection with the Kabardans of the outer hills. They were driven into the mountains by the latter. The Turkish highlanders are broad, big men : the chief of Bezingi stands 6 feet 3 inches at least : the Kabardan is of a different build, slighter and darker, keener-looking, but sometimes effeminate. The Urusbieh princes are of mixed blood, and arguments based on their appearance or manners might be misleading.

The forests extend to the upper end of the limestone gorges. Above them the crystalline schists are bare. Every beam the house-builders of Bezingi and Balkar use must be dragged a journey of several hours. The shepherd's fires are fed on the twigs and roots of the *Rhododendron caucasicum*, and in consequence the plant has in places become almost extinct.

To this barrenness of the upper northern glens, however, there are exceptions. The head-waters of the Baksan and the Urukh, the Bashil valley, and some of the side glens of the Ardon, possess fir and pine woods. Nothing is more striking in the Central Caucasus than the suddenness of the change from woodland to barren scenery. The natural causes in soil and climate of such changes are extremely obscure, and human agency and the ravages of herds further complicate the considerations that have to be taken into account. I have noticed that the crystalline schists are generally bare, while the granites and limestones are clothed in forests. The slates of the southern chain are heavily wooded on the south side, but bare in the Ardon basin.

The deficiencies as well as the excellencies of the Caucasus must be noted. It possesses no remarkable waterfalls, no lakes, and few tarns — neither sub-mountainous lakes like Como, Garda, Geneva, Lucerne, nor clusters of tarns like those that dot certain crystalline districts of the Alps.[1] Waterfalls worth a special visit are not very common even in Switzerland. I would not attach to their absence more weight than it may reasonably bear. An inference might be drawn in favour of the Caucasus having been more waterwashed, of the torrents having had force and time to cut themselves a way out of their difficulties. Geologists may possibly find other reasons in the disposition or dip of the strata.

The absence of lakes is a more serious matter, and must be faced by those who believe that the great prehistoric glaciers excavated lake-basins. They will probably meet it in one of two ways: they may either assert that 'the Caucasus never had a glacial epoch,' or that 'its glaciers excavated basins which have been either tapped or silted up by subsequent water action.' The evidence will, no doubt, be made fuller, but already sufficient facts have been collected by Abich and Favre to show that the glaciers of the Caucasus at one time reached to the northern plains. Erratic blocks have been found near and beyond Vladikavkaz. We are entitled, therefore, to dismiss the first supposition. On the other hand, an existing basin may be emptied of liquid in two ways, either by tapping it or by filling it with solid. It is arguable that lake-basins may have existed in the Caucasus and been subsequently obliterated by either process. A recent traveller in the Sierra Nevada of North America, Mr. Muir, has described very clearly the process of lake - destruction by these methods he witnessed going on

---

[1] According to Dr. Richter (*In hach Regionen*: Berlin, 1895) there are no less than 2460 lakes or tarns in the Alps *east* of the Splugen.

under his eyes in ground from which glaciers had recently with-drawn.

I disbelieve, for reasons I have set out fully elsewhere,[1] in the excavation by moving ice of rock-basins. But that glaciers keep them scoured and leave them empty is obvious, I suppose, to every mountain traveller who uses his eyes. I cannot doubt that glaciers preserve basins formed by other agencies, and that when the protection of the ice is removed such basins are slowly drained or obliterated. The absence of water-filled hollows in the Caucasus is, in my belief, not conclusive, one way or the other, as to the glacial origin of mountain lakes. What it may prove is that the period during which the glaciers have not greatly exceeded their present dimensions has been a longer one in the Caucasus than in the Alps.

The movements of Caucasian and Alpine glaciers have of late years shown a general correspondence. In 1868 the Caucasian ice was in retreat. About 1875 the tide seemed to turn; and in 1887-89 many glaciers were slightly advancing.[2]

Great glaciers, heavily snow-draped peaks and ridges, rampant vegetation, all point to the conclusion that the Western Caucasus has a very moist climate. They point also to the fact that it has no long dry season. The part of the Alps which the general aspect of the flora most recalls—I am not speaking of the identity of species—is the Dolomites, or Venetian Alps. It rains or snows heavily in spring or winter in Corsica or the Maritime Alps; but there, above the zone of artificial irrigation, you find compara-tively few flowers, and the reason is obvious—the long summer drought. Statistics bear out this conclusion; returns of meteoro-logical observations from Stavropol, Vladikavkaz, and the Caucasian Baths north of the chain, from Batum, Kutais, Sukhum, Poti, Gori, Tiflis, to the south. Observations from Oni, or Betsho, or

---

[1] *Proceedings of the Royal Geographical Society* (New Series), vol. x. p. 779, 'A Note on the Conservative Action of Glaciers.'

[2] M. de Déchy has, in his various journeys, taken a certain number of observations with the mercurial barometer of the heights of the ends of glaciers and of the line of *névé*, and also set marks and dates opposite the ends of the ice. See his paper in the *Proceedings* of the Geographical Congress at Paris in 1889. M. Jukoff has also published some measurements in the *Proceedings of the Royal Geographical Society*, vol. xiv. p. 112 (1892).

Balkar, in its heart, are still a desideratum. The rainfall map in Reclus will require correction by the light of the recent publications of the Russian Meteorological Office.[1]

The heaviest fall, sometimes over a hundred inches per annum, is where the sea-winds strike the first hills at Batum and Kutais. It is somewhat less at Sukhum, and diminishes also westwards towards Kertch. Generally, the tendency is to relative dryness as you go eastwards across the isthmus. At first sight it may seem a curious exception that the rainfall at Vladikavkaz (32 inches) should be far in excess of that of the Caucasian Baths (18 inches). This, however, is sufficiently explained by the fact that Elbruz, acting as a great condenser, draws to itself and precipitates clouds which pass more easily through the gap of the Mamison.

Generally, the climate of the Western Caucasus is much moister and less warm than that of the Western Pyrenees. The rainfall at Kutais is double that at Pau, and about equal to that at Tolmezzo, at the head of the Adriatic ; the mean annual temperature is slightly less than at Pau. The climate of Tiflis is less dry, but somewhat hotter, than that of Madrid. The plains north of the chain, which are far colder in winter than the mountain valleys, suffer greater extremes of temperature than the Swiss lowlands. Summer comes in with a burst in May, but June or July are often among the wettest months. The humidity of the summer climate is a danger to the mountaineer, and at once a charm and a vexation to the traveller. When the west wind blows in fine weather, clouds and a shower come up every afternoon from the Black Sea. The explorer risks being befogged —no slight risk on the vast snowfields—and the snow on steep slopes is kept in a very hazardous condition.

Readers will expect to be given a figure for the snow-level. Natural philosophers have spoken disrespectfully of late of the sea-level. I have even heard an ex-President of the Geographical Society suggest that it may vary to an extent of 500 feet,[2] and

---

[1] Wild, H., *Die Regen-Verhältnisse des Russischen Reiches,* and Appendix C.
[2] *Lectures on Geography,* by Lieutenant-General Strachey, R.E., C.S.I., P.R.G.S., p. 33.

I am told that this is a moderate estimate. I may be excused, therefore, if I tell the truth about that vague old abstraction, 'the snow-level.' The figure given for it in an extensive range may serve as a useful mean, but in most places must be locally inexact. For 'the Caucasus' it is impossible to lay down any limit which shall be even approximately accurate for the whole chain and both sides of it. The chain extends over five degrees of latitude; more. than that, its rainfall is at least four times greater at the Black Sea end than it is at the Caspian end. Naturally, at one extremity snow lies permanently down to about 9000 feet, at the other ceases at about 12,000 feet. In the central part of the chain nothing like a continuous snow-bed, not due to avalanches, is found under 9500 feet, and on the northern spurs, where there is less fall, and black rock-slopes facing southwards are exposed to a sun which raises the steppe shade-temperature to over 90° F., the snow-limit will rise in places to over 11,000 feet. For the snow-level in the central chain 10,000 feet may be taken as a fair figure. But as I have said before, this limit should be represented by a zigzag line going up and down, according to accidents of exposure, soil, and vicinity to large glaciers. Let us get rid altogether of a statement frequently repeated, that Dr. Radde found the snow-level 8400 feet at the Rion sources. What he wrote was, that in September he found patches of *fresh-fallen* snow at that height. This is how error may be created by inaccurate copyists![1]

I have given elsewhere a catalogue of 'Peaks and Passes.' It may be enough to mention here a few of the most conspicuous.

Before 1870 the Russian surveyors had triangulated only a few of the snowy peaks—those which are most conspicuous from the northern steppe—Elbruz, 18,470 feet; Koshtantau, 16,880; Dykh-tau, 17,054; Adai Khokh, 15,244; Gimarai Khokh, 15,672; and Kasbek, 16,546. Between the Marukh Pass and the Mamison Pass the five-verst map does not give a single height on the watershed. It was left to the new and still unpublished survey to find figures for Dongusorun, 14,605; Ushba, north peak

---

[1] The figures given are those of the new survey, which differ in many cases from those of the five-verst map.

15,400, south peak 15,409 ; Tiktengen, 15,127 ; Gestola, 15,932 ; Tetnuld, 15,918 ; Janga, 16,569 ; Shkara, 17,038 ; and a crowd of other peaks of between 15,000 and 13,000 feet.   In a space some ten miles square in the Central Group there are found to be no less than twenty distinct summits of over 14,000 feet.

To orographers and map-makers the importance of Shkara long remained unrecognised.   This noble mountain is the Monte Rosa of the Caucasus.   Conspicuous from the southern plains and even from the seaboard, it culminates like its Alpine rival in a five-crested ridge.   It has its Gorner Glacier in the Bezingi Glacier, and its Val Anzasca in the glen of the Zena.

I am responsible for the erroneous identification (in 1868) of Shkara with the Koshtantau of the five-verst map, now called Dykhtau.   Twenty-seven years ago, when I drew the view from the Shtuluvsek, we saw two great mountains where only one was marked on the map.   Here was a dilemma.   Shkara from this point of view was far the more imposing, and we called it Koshtantau, while the peak that had been measured under that name on the map we called an ' unknown peak.'   Consequently, students of Caucasian literature must be careful to remember that the Koshtantau, not only of my *Central Caucasus*, but also of Mr. Grove's book and Mr. Dent's early articles, is always Shkara.

In addition to Shkara we have found and climbed, and the surveyors have now measured, three more great peaks on the actual watershed, and one projecting slightly from it on the south towards Suanetia.   These are the broad-faced Janga—an exaggerated Piz Palu ; the saddle-shaped crest of Katuintau ; the cone of Gestola ; and the white pyramid of Tetnuld.   All these mountains are between 15,900 and 17,100 feet in height—higher, that is, than Mont Blanc.   On the other side of the trench—at their northern base—filled by the Bezingi and Dykhsu Glaciers, the Dykhtau-Koshtantau ridge rises in the form of a horseshoe, with at least five peaks of over 15,000 feet.

Next in prominence to the Central Group, on the main chain, are to the west the peak of Tiktengen, the Schreckhorn of the Caucasus, which dominates the head-waters of the Gara-auz; the

summits that cluster about the twin towers of Ushba, the Matterhorn of the Caucasus, which rise less than a mile south of
the watershed to a height of 15,400 feet; and the broad mass
of Dongusorun.   Farther east, the chief glacier group on the
watershed is best known from the name assigned, somewhat
arbitrarily, to its highest point, as the Adai Khokh group.   It
consists of half a dozen or more summits, closely approaching
15,000 feet, which, like the mountains of the Oberland, gather

CROSSING THE CHAIN

round the *névés* of two great glaciers, the Karagom and Zea, both
of which drain to the north side.   East of the Mamison, all
the more important peaks are in the range that continues the
line of the watershed, though it has ceased to fulfil this function.
Tepli, 14,510 feet, is separated from Gimarai Khokh and Kasbek
by a practicable horse-pass, but may be conveniently treated as
belonging to the same group.

The passes over the main chain of the Central Caucasus crossed
by natives are numerous.   West of the Mamison there are none
but glacier passes, while from this point eastward horses can cross

the chain in many places.   I do not propose to delay my readers
with a catalogue.   Some of the glacier-passes—like the St. Théodule
and Col de Collon in the Middle Ages—are recognised routes for
the passage of cattle and even occasionally, and under favourable
circumstances, of beasts of burden ; others are used only by hunters
or refugees.   The more frequented passes, counting from west to
east, are the Jiper, 10,717 feet ; the Dongusorun, 10,493 ; the
Betsho Pass, 11,474 ; the Tuiber, 11,764 ; the Karaul Passes,
11,679 and 11,270 ; and the Gurdzivsek, 10,976.   Between the
Mamison and the Krestovaya Gora the Bakh-fandak Pass, 9569
feet, seems to be that in most general use.   Professor Hahn states
that the Roki Pass, 9814 feet, which lies slightly more to the
east, has been selected and surveyed as the future route of the
long-projected Caucasian Railway.   Both these passes lead from
the basin of the Liakhva into that of the Ardon.

CHAPTER III

CAUCASIAN HISTORY AND TRAVEL

The use of travelling is to regulate imagination by reality, and instead of thinking how things may be to see them as they are. DR. SAMUEL JOHNSON.

THERE are still several questions to which the reader interested in the Caucasus may be glad of an answer before we leave generalities and plunge into the heart of the mountains. To what races do the inhabitants of the high valleys belong, and what is their character? How does a journey beyond the post-roads compare with ordinary Alpine or Eastern travel? What are the most marked features in Caucasian landscapes, and in what points do they most differ from the familiar scenery of the Alps?

This is hardly the place for an essay on the ethnology of the Caucasus. That difficult, obscure, and extremely complicated subject has already supplied material for several portly volumes and a number of special treatises. M. Chantre's handsome work is valuable in itself, and also for the numerous references contained in the preface. The *Guide au Caucase*, published in Paris by M. Mourier in 1894, contains a useful popular summary of present knowledge. In subsequent chapters I shall find room for sketches of the principal tribes encountered by the mountaineer under the snows of the central chain.

The ethnologist as well as the geographer must be called on to dismiss some time-honoured fictions with regard to the Caucasus. The mountain-fastnesses have not, as was until recently believed, furnished a cradle to a great branch of humanity. In this sense the Caucasian of Cuvier is really 'played out'! Even a poet might now hesitate to write of the 'supreme Caucasian mind.' The highlands between the Black Sea and the Caspian have served as a refuge for portions of many races. They form an ethnological museum where the invaders of Europe, as they travelled westwards to be manufactured into nations, have left behind samples of themselves in their raw condition. Russian ethnologists have been, and are, hard at work. But they have still much to learn before they can render us any complete account of the origin and affinities of these living fragments, which, like the erratic boulders on the hills, serve as records of facts that might otherwise have passed into oblivion.

My travels in the Central Caucasus have led me mostly among three distinct races: first the Ossetes, members of the Iranian branch of the Aryan family, who dwell on both sides of the chain south and west of Vladikavkaz; next the Tauli or Mountain Turks, whose territory includes the highlands between Koshtantau and Elbruz; last, the curious people known as Suanetians, a collection of refugees, grafted possibly on a Georgian, or, as some prefer to say, on a Kolkhian stock.[1] Besides these, we may meet with Cherkess, or Circassians, on the Baksan, with Mingrelians in the valley of the Rion, with Karatshai Tartars near the source of the Kuban. Ossetian is a distinct language; Mingrelian and Suan are dialects of Georgian; the Mohammedan tribes speak an old Turkish dialect. Among the bleak uplands of Daghestan, isolated by deep gorges and arid ridges, there exists to this day a medley of races, some of which bear historic names—Huns and Avars. The western wing of the Caucasus has been occupied from time immemorial

---

[1] I do not find that ethnological writers use this term in any very fixed sense. The most intelligible use is that which restricts it to the Abkhasians, who dwell west of the Georgians. See *Journal of the Royal Asiatic Society*, vol. xvii., and Gifford Palgrave's description of the Abkhasians, *Eastern Studies*, 1872.

by the Adighe, or Cherkess, and the Abkhasians—the Circassians of modern history and romance, primitive peoples of uncertain origin, and with no written languages.

In general history the Caucasus has from the earliest ages played an important part as a barrier. North of it, Herodotus tells us, lived peoples who cared nothing for the Great King. It was the extreme limit of the known and the civilised world. Beyond the mountains spread the land of fable, of Gog and Magog, of gold-guarding Griffins, one-eyed Arimaspians, and Amazons — of all the fabulous creatures who pass slowly out of the atlases of the learned into the picture-books of the nursery. When Roman rule was established on the coast of the Euxine, Chosroes and Justinian combined to maintain the frontier post of the Darial against the northern barbarians. Never, until the Russian eagles crossed the chain, did the same empire hold the lowlands on

ELDERS OF CKUSBIEH

both sides of it. The political condition of the basins of the Kur and the Rion remained the same in its main features throughout the Dark and the Middle Ages. The petty tributary states which had grown up under the Romans maintained an obscure and precarious existence between the Persians, the Turks, and latterly the Russians. The Abkhasians came down to deal at the factories on the coast with the Greeks, the Romans, and the Genoese in succession. But in their mountain-fastnesses they preserved a rude independence. Christianity, introduced at a very early date from Byzantium, retained its hold on the majority of the population of the lowlands; but in the mountains it yielded in many places to Mohammedanism, and as years went on, both faiths became little more than a cover to more primitive forms of religion.   There was a revival of Paganism.   The churches and chapels were desecrated and profaned.   The powers of Nature, the spirits of the storm, the forest, and the flood, were separately worshipped.   Sacred yews and groves regained their former reverence; the spirits of ancestors were appeased or solaced with the ancient offerings.

In modern geography Georgia is equivalent to the basin of the Kur.   But the old Georgian Kingdom extended its territory or its suzerainty to the shores of the Black Sea and the sources of the Rion and the Ingur.   The reign of Queen Thamara, in the first years of the thirteenth century, was the time of Georgia's glory and greatest extent.   In the succeeding centuries the country suffered severely from the Persians and the Turks, until in 1802 its last sovereign secured the peace of his kingdom by putting an end to its separate existence and accepting the rule of Russia. His feudatories, the semi-independent princelets of Mingrelia and Imeretia, the Dadians and Dadish Kilians of Suanetia, soon followed his example.

The beginning of the nineteenth century found the Russians firmly established on both sides of the Caucasus, but holding only a narrow line of communication through the mountains. Vladikavkaz was a fortress exposed to the assaults of hostile tribes.   The hills to the east of it were as much forbidden ground to the Russian as the mountains round Peshawur were to the Englishman—up to last summer.   On the western flank the post-road to the north had to be protected from the forays of the independent Circassians by a chain of Cossack stations.   It was not until 1834 that the Russians undertook the subjugation of Circassia and Daghestan.   The Crimean War found them with the task still incomplete.   Attempts to support the tribes were made by the Allies, but owing to the ignorance of Western statesmen of the political and physical conditions of the Caucasus, they were ill-planned and futile.   The operations of the Turkish army, landed near Sukhum Kale, were entirely misdirected, and the opportunity of setting up an independent Transcaucasian State was lost, probably for ever. It must not be taken for granted that this was any great loss to civilisation. The talents of the Caucasians; Georgians, Armenians, and others, may be better employed in the service of a great nation than in setting up independent and insignificant States, while it is extremely doubtful whether these races could have amalgamated under the leadership of any one of them.

The natives of the highlands of Daghestan, under the leadership of the famous Schamyl—who had no more to do with Circassia than William Wallace had with Wales—carried on until 1859 a separate struggle against the invaders with varying and at times considerable success. In 1860 the conquest of the Caucasus was practically complete; but the tribes which had been subdued would not submit to be ruled, fresh disorders broke out, and ended in 1866 in the famous expulsion of the Circassians and Abkhasians, which has left the Western Caucasus a desert. Happily for the mountaineer, the natives of the valleys of the central chain have as yet found no reason to leave their homes. The Mingrelians have not unwillingly submitted to the results of the abolition of serfdom, which in their case meant the close of a system of oppression by petty nobles, comprising most of the worst features of the feudal

SUANETIANS

system of Western Europe. The Suanetians are beginning to find life endurable without the daily excitement of killing or being killed. The pliant Ossetes have recognised that the Russian service offers a means by which they may rise to fortune. The Turkish and Mohammedan mountaineers alone are still uneasy, and might easily be driven by a clumsy administrator to try their fortunes beyond the frontier. At the present time such a calamity does not appear imminent, and we must trust that it will not be brought about by the blunders of any minor official who has failed to grasp the policy of his chiefs and the true position of his country in the Caucasus. In repressing disorder, improving communications, and welding different races into a political unit, Russia is at once carrying on the work of civilisation and strengthening her own position in Western Asia. The depopulation of the Black Sea coast marks an exception to the comparative success which her rulers have achieved in other parts of the isthmus. In my opinion, the great hope for the future of the country lies in the fact that the Caucasians themselves are acquiring a keen desire for progress. Energy, uprightness, and intelligence in the government will meet with ready appreciation and support from many of the native nobles, from the mercantile classes of the towns, and even from the more intelligent among the mountain people, in whom schools and the vicinity of railways are rapidly developing a new sense of the opportunities of life. The main occupation of the Caucasian Government is no longer the subjugation of lawless tribes. The political problem now before it is the development of the natural resources of the country and of the capabilities of its population. The chief native races, the Armenians and Georgians, are intelligent and progressive; they are well fitted to play an important part in the future of the Russian Empire; but they are also the inheritors of national languages and traditions with regard to which they are justly sensitive. Whether these peoples are to prove the Scotch or the Irish of Russia will depend mainly on the wisdom of the Imperial Government during the next half century. Questions of present politics are, however, outside my immediate purpose, and I shall not attempt in these pages to forecast the doubtful future of the Caucasian Provinces.

I must now endeavour to indicate the general character of travel among the mountains : the difficulties to be overcome, the hardships to be encountered, the pleasures to be won. Twenty-five years ago a journey to the Caucasus was a more or less serious undertaking. Now, by means of the Trans-European railways that extend to Odessa, the quick steamer once a week from that port to Batum, and the two railways that, starting from Batum and Novorossisk, run along either flank of the mountains, to Tiflis or Vladikavkaz, the mountaineer finds himself transported, without discomfort, and in less than a week, from London to the foot of the range. When

I was a boy it took nearly as long to reach Zermatt or the Engadine as it now takes to arrive at Urusbieh or Gebi— that is to say, at points where wheels must stop and climbing may begin. Here, however, the parallel ends. In the Caucasus the traveller is still brought close to barbaric times. Up to 1830, or even later, the marauding habits and savage independence of the tribes rendered it as difficult to penetrate at all into the mountains as it is still to wander in the highlands of Kafiristan. We have the evidence of a Scotch missionary that in 1826 no one could approach Elbruz. In 1829 a Russian general led a little army against the

A SUANETIAN HUNTER

mountain. Even twenty-five years ago, when I first visited the country, it was rough and at times risky work to mix with the mountaineers, and Free Suanetia was independent in fact as well as in name. It was the murder of some Russian officials in 1876 which led to the final subjugation of that remote district.

In the time of Augustus the Swiss Alps had already attained the condition of the Caucasus at the date of my first visit.   In the sixteenth century they were provided with accommodation of a sort.[1] A hundred years ago, De Saussure found their recesses an inhabited and civilised region, traversed in many directions by frequented by-ways of commerce, and within easy reach of centres of civilisation.   The district that is the subject of these pages—the Central

IN THE KALDE VALLEY

Caucasus—is in extent nearly equal to Switzerland.   Its topographical boundaries may be taken as the Ciscaucasian and Transcaucasian Railways on the north and south, the Darial road on the east, and the Klukhor Pass, the new road from Sukhum Kale to the Kuban, on the west.   Now, within these boundaries, there is only one carriage-road across the main chain, the

---

[1] See Simler's *De Alpibus Commentarius*, A.D. 1574. 'Sunt autem in omnibus Alpibus per quas frequentius iter fit, hospitia et xenodocheia quaedam pro viatoribus exstructa.'

Mamison Pass (9284 feet), and the Ardon and Rion Valleys, which this road connects, are the only great valleys accessible up to their heads to vehicles. In the mountains there is not, off the Darial road, a single inn, in the European sense of the word. On the Asiatic side bare sheds, in which boards take the place of beds, built by the Government mainly for administrative purposes, and hence known as 'Cancellarias' or court-houses, are in the principal villages open to the traveller armed with official papers. On the north side the local Mohammedan chiefs place a guest-house at the disposal of strangers. As a rule, they are ready to furnish food also to travellers who are recommended, or appear to them to be distinguished persons. Alpine Clubmen, after a month spent in the mountains, do not as a rule fulfil this description at first sight. But hitherto our merit has never failed to assert itself before long in the eyes of the native aristocracy, and even in the more remote villages the fact that Englishmen are 'paying guests' is beginning to be duly appreciated, and to lead to the usual results—that we are warmly welcomed and handsomely overcharged.

The inconveniences of travel are many. Unless a store of provisions ample for all emergencies is taken, the mountaineer may expect to go supperless while he waits for the mutton that is still walking the hills, or the loaves that are being baked in a distant hamlet. Wine is unknown in the northern valleys, and an exceptional luxury in the southern. Transport, especially for the mountaineer, is a still greater difficulty than commissariat. In African travel—indeed, in much Asiatic travel—porters or horses once secured can be retained. Those who wander to and fro across the Caucasian ridges are often stopped by snows impassable for animals. The porters who act in their stead do not as a rule care to go more than a certain distance from their own homes.

There is no competent local authority to which to appeal in case of difficulties. While the old chieftains have lost much of their feudal or patriarchal authority, the new *starshinas* or village mayors, appointed by the Government, are in the more remote districts treated with very scant respect by their communities. The people are inveterate bargainers and have no sense of time. If a traveller lets them discover that he is in a hurry, or is dependent on their aid, they will take every advantage of the situation. Though not bloodthirsty, they are quick-tempered, and it is their custom to wear arms, and their habit to draw their daggers when excited. The action, it is true, is in most cases little more than an oratorical gesture, but there have been exceptions— a Russian Governor of Mingrelia was once poignarded by a Suanetian Prince—and it is obviously expedient to observe the limits of polite discussion. The high-handed manner which is almost *de rigueur* with a Russian postmaster is quite thrown away on the people of the mountains. The Caucasian traveller has further to guard against the greatest enemy of explorers, and that which the Alpine climber is least prepared for—different forms of illness. The imperfectly baked and coarse rye-bread, poor diet and exposure have in many cases, particularly among the Alpine guides taken out, resulted in dysentery. The lowlands towards the Black Sea breed fevers, and in one party—that of 1874—all the mountaineers were attacked—partly, it is true, through their own imprudence in bathing at sunrise in the notoriously malarious waters of the Kodor. Personally, I have never suffered in any way from the climate, nor has my old guide Dévouassoud, and I believe, with a little care and preventive doses of quinine, the chance of falling ill in the one or two days spent within the fever-level by those who approach the mountains from the south, may be reduced to a very remote one. On the north side there is no risk whatever. The atmosphere, however, is generally damper than that of the Alps, and the effects of a chill are not so quickly thrown off.

In the preceding sentences I have made the most of the difficulties to be encountered. Many of them can be obviated ; others are diminishing year by year. The traveller, if he is a person of ordinary discretion, need now be under no apprehension as to his personal security.

Such being the condition of the country, it is obvious that what is needed to make travel easy is the establishment of a system similar to that which for many years has proved so successful in Syria. A dragoman and camp-equipment—lighter, no doubt, than that used in the comparatively open country of Palestine—ought to be procurable at Kutais and Vladikavkaz. Up to the present time, unfortunately, nothing of the kind exists. Tiflis indeed can furnish half-a-dozen 'dragomen,' or travelling servants and interpreters, but these are for the most part fine gentlemen, not at all eager to encounter the hardships and exposure of mountain exploration, even in the very modified form in which they have to be faced by a commissariat officer at the headquarters' camp. They prefer to accompany celebrated travellers on the post-roads of Daghestan, or the highways of Persian and Central Asiatic travel. Slowly, however—very slowly—as year by year more and more foreigners penetrate the mountain region, some supply is springing up to meet the demand. An intelligent Jew, a young Mingrelian, who has been trained in a consular household, a German who has failed in his private speculations; one of these men may generally be picked up at Kutais or Vladikavkaz and will serve, for better, for worse, as the mountaineer's master of the horse, interpreter, and cook. But none of them, as far as I know, is yet enough of a capitalist to provide himself with camp-equipment, and for a traveller to bring out his own camp-equipment is, owing to the very heavy import duties in Russia, a serious matter for those who contemplate, perhaps, only a six weeks' journey.[1] Members of the Alpine Club have invariably received great courtesy and consideration from the Russian Government. They have also, by leaving part of their equipment behind them at Batum, for their successors' use, extended to one another a certain amount of mutual accommodation. But this resource naturally cannot in all cases be reckoned on, and as a rule the Caucasian traveller has to bring with him tents and provisions, and to find, in a sense often to make, his own dragoman. It is essential that this functionary should be proficient in at least four languages: speak, that is, Russian, Georgian, and Turkish, in addition to the Western language in which he communicates with

[1] Caucasian explorers may be reminded that the duties are very largely diminished in the case of all goods that show marks of previous use.

his employers.   A knowledge of Russian alone is inadequate.   It
is possible to get along in the mountains with Russian, but the
traveller misses much useful information from the inhabitants,
few of whom are as yet familiar with it.   This difficulty will doubt-

ALPINE GUIDES IN A KOSH

less tend to diminish with the spread of schools.   Even a good
dragoman, however, cannot obviate the endless troubles and interminable discussions involved in engaging baggage animals.   My
advice to the traveller is either to buy horses at starting, or to hire
for the whole journey.   To do so may entail arranging his route
so as to cross the main chain by horse-passes.   But he will save

himself much loss of time and of the patience which, as Mr. Donkin once pointed out, is the greatest of all requisites in Caucasian travel.

Hitherto I have dwelt, perhaps too strongly, on the drawbacks and difficulties of travel in the Caucasus. What are its rewards? Does the scenery equal or surpass that of the Swiss Alps? Such questions are often put, but I can hardly hope to give any generally acceptable answer to them. According to my experience, appreciation of scenery for its own sake is far less universal nowadays than is generally assumed. Our contemporaries require social distraction. There are among them comparatively few who can be content to live with a landscape. Painters do so now and then, but their interest in nature is partly professional, and apt to extend only as far as they see their way to reproduce effects. To the public, scenery is welcome as a background for sport, or adventure, or society—for shooting, for climbing, or for picnicing. Our appreciations depend more and more upon accidental circumstances. Thirty years ago the Alps were full of wanderers who might properly be called travellers. Now, most of our countrymen neglect any spot that is not provided with good inns and crowded with their acquaintances. At the same time, a cry is raised that Switzerland is overcrowded, that the Alps are exhausted. It is of our own choice if we submit to be herded in hotels, or packed still closer in the outhouses known as Club-huts. The Playground of Europe has still sufficient quiet corners for those who care to find them. The Alps can never be exhausted, except to tourists of the baser sort. Their old lovers never revisit them without discovering some new beauty. But then we are content to do without such comfort as may be found in *tables d'hôte*, bands, dances, daily newspapers, and a weekly British Chaplain. Those who in their search for scenery are not independent of these luxuries will do well to put up with Zermatt or the Engadine, and to avoid the Caucasus. It is not for them that I attempt here to analyse, from the point of view of an old frequenter of the Alps, the peculiar characteristics of the new region it has been my good fortune to investigate.

I may best convey the broad distinction between the first aspect of the two ranges by saying that, as a whole, the landscapes of the Caucasus are less picturesque, but more romantic. The scenery appeals more to the imagination; even when ugly it is rarely commonplace. It is as Shelley's poetry to Scott's. The scale is larger; mankind is less conspicuous. The view of the great range from the railway, half-way between the Caucasian Baths and Vladikavkaz, dwarfs that of the Alps from the Lombard plain. The rare incidents of the foreground—the grassy barrow of some forgotten Scythian prince, the turbaned headstone of some Tartar chieftain, or the low white cottages, glittering church-spire, and sunflower fields of one of the Cossack villages that line the old military march, will not indeed compensate some cultivated travellers for the absence of frequent villas and campaniles. Many Frenchmen—even Frenchmen of genius—have found the Roman Campagna insupportable. And the old-fashioned and highly respectable sentiment that whatever is waste is horrid (which made Cobbett disparage the heather on Hind Head) is more common among our contemporaries than they sometimes care to avow.

Travellers surely need not be ashamed of their preferences, so long as they are honest. There is scenery, like music, for every mood and mind. Caucasian scenery, I repeat, belongs to the romantic school. It produces impressions rather by broad effects than by crowded details. Compared with the mountains, the forests and flowers of Suanetia, the alps and pinewoods and chalet-dotted[1] meadows of Grindelwald look stiff and tame; even the great Italian valleys yield in sublimity. To those who have seen the sky-cleaving pyramids of Koshtantau and Dykhtau catch the sunset, even the Finsteraarhorn and Schreckhorn may seem small. Elbruz, if the most unequal of mountains, has moments of unequalled majesty. Very seldom in the Alps—I may cite as exceptions Grindelwald and the head of the Val di Genova—is the beauty of forests brought close to the splendour of snow and ice. The interval is generally that

---

[1] I use the word 'alp' here in its proper first sense, a common pasturage. Chalet is seldom circumflexed, except by British authors. It designates properly not a farmhouse inhabited all the year round, but a dwelling on the 'alp' used in summer. The reasons why French writers avoid the circumflex are, I imagine, that there is no written form *chaslet* in old French literature, and that they follow local pronunciation.

grim debatable ground of rock and rubbish which Mr. Ruskin imagines to be an interposition of Providence, but which sometimes seems the reverse to the weary mountaineer. In the Caucasus there are few of these dull barrennesses : the hillsides are clothed, not by monotonous pine-woods, but in a rich medley of European forest-trees ; they are brightened by an undergrowth of laburnums,

THE SOURCES OF THE SKENIS SKALI

azaleas, laurels, and rhododendrons, and broken by glades full of flowers that grow six feet high. The traveller who rides in fair weather over the Latpari Pass, and then crosses the grassy spurs of Tetnuld to Mujal and Betsho, will confess that the Alps must yield, that neither the Oberland nor Monte Rosa can show such a combination of sylvan scenery and sunlit snows. No doubt the scale of the scenery makes it difficult to treat in art. But we must not allow our friends the painters to set up a technical and egotistical standard. We admire in Nature not what is more or less imitable by the brush, but what is most delightful to the eye and most stirring to the imagination.

In the Caucasus the artist will find opportunities, less common in Switzerland, at any rate during the months the Alps are most visited. The atmospheric effects are singularly beautiful and varied. The sky is luminous and soft; the distances are at once distinct and deep in tone; there is none of the harshness of outline of Switzerland. On the northern steppe the light is the glow of the East; the atmospheric colours often recall those of the Roman Campagna, to which there is some general resemblance on an enormously magnified scale in the landscape. Up in the mountains of Suanetia the effect, when the west wind blows, may remind Englishmen of what is called fine weather at our own Lakes. Scarves of mist play in and out of the great towers of Ushba; the tangled maze of low, long wooded ridges and deep glens, of flashing streams and white-towered villages, is now half-veiled in a passing shower, now lit up by brilliant arrows of sunshine. In clear north-wind weather the sky is of a less hard blue than in the Alps; and sometimes in the morning, under a cloudless vault, the mountains gleam through a thin, perfectly transparent golden haze, a Coan drapery which melts as the day goes on.

In my judgment, then, the supremacy of Caucasian scenery lies in the heart of the chain: it consists in the forms of the peaks, their lavish glaciation, and the richness of the flowers and forests that clothe many of the upper valleys. Its inferiority, compared to Alpine scenery, will be found in the outskirts of the mountains. The strength has to be sought; the weaknesses, on the contrary, are obvious at first sight.

The Caucasus has no lakes. It offers nothing to compare to the highly decorated loveliness of Como, the stately charm of Garda and Maggiore, or the pastoral romance of Lucerne and Thun. The landscapes on the flanks of the Alps are full of cheerful trivial human incident; those of the Caucasus are less adorned and varied. How much of the pleasure we derive from the green and red heights that break down in alternate capes and bays on the 'waveless plain of Lombardy' is due to the cities and villages, the castles and campaniles, that crown their brows? How many of the lower valleys of the Northern Alps owe half their attractiveness to the brown huts and quaint steeples that dot their slopes? Again, how large a part is played by literary and historical associations for some, personal associations for all, in the pleasure we derive from distant prospects! What a different sensation it is to look up at a line of nameless snows, and to hail the Jungfrau or Monte Rosa; how much greater is the difference when we know the meaning of every line and scar on the distant peak, when each recalls to us some incident in a hard-won victory? I never felt this more forcibly than when, on my third visit to the Caucasus, I looked up from the Black Sea to a splendid spire, and recognised the peak I had twenty years before compared to the Grivola and the peak I had two years before planted my ice-axe on—Tetnuld—as one and the same.

The Caucasus not only wants lakes; it has very few mountain tarns, and a waterfall worth going out of the way to look at has still to be found. On the north side there is a zone, between the glaciers and the forests of the limestone belt, which is curiously hideous, and it is this district that is traversed by the ordinary horse-tracks.

For these reasons, I fancy that new-comers to the Caucasus are likely to take some time before they fully recognise its fascination. They will miss at first adjuncts to scenery, actual and mental, to which they are accustomed. Yet those who persevere will have their reward. They will learn for themselves within what limits there is truth in the contention put forward by very eminent writers, that traces of man's presence are ingredients essential to our pleasure in scenery. They will find that, if human agency often makes, or adds to, the Picturesque in landscape—and particularly to what is picturesque in the technical sense of the word, reproducible in a picture—there are aspects of nature which need no help from man. The Italian Valley, the Genoese Corniche, depend to a great extent on our additions for their effect. The frosty fastnesses of the Caucasus belong to a separate class of scenery, and excite a different order of emotions. The mountaineer feels transported to the verge of a higher sphere. Great mountains may be only 'the highest parts of the dust of the world,' but they bring us nearer to what lies Beyond.

The man to whom, as Byron wrote, 'High mountains are a feeling,' will be happy in the Caucasus. But how will it be with the 'grimpeur moyen sensuel'? In the minds of the multitude who travel or climb for the sake of health and variety, the quest of beauty or the satisfaction of a 'vague emotion' hold no great place. They are intent on adventure, exercise, change, novelty. Scenery is not enough for them; scientific problems are beyond their ken. For this class, most of all, Switzerland has become inadequate. For, as far as novel adventure and exploration are concerned, it must be admitted that the Alps are almost exhausted. They can hardly be to another generation what they have been to their discoverers, to the men who forty years ago joined to fill up a gap in the maps of Central Europe, to explore the wilds of Tyrol and Dauphiné, to survey the chain of Mont Blanc and the Graian Alps, the then untrodden snowfields of the Ortler, the Adamello, and the Grand Paradis. Mountaineers gifted with acute minds have lately found themselves reduced to studying personal rather than topographical details; ascents have been catalogued under a dozen different headings, from the first of all to the first by ladies without guides. Alpine literature has grown at once highly technical and intolerably minute and voluminous. Ardent climbers, urged on by a thirst for novel adventure, have been led to climb mountains by paths prepared by Providence for the descent of avalanches, or in the search for sensation have broken with the established rules of their craft. The romance of novelty, the excitement of the unknown and the uncertain, have been not unfrequently sought for in ways that are only too likely to bring a noble pursuit into discredit, to turn a game of skill into one of chance in which the stake is what no man has a right to venture deliberately for mere pleasure—life itself. Climbers, both guides and amateurs, have lost their sense of danger. The many succeed, but of a sudden the one—the one least expected, perhaps —fails, and we deplore another Alpine accident. The impulse of youth and energy that, in play as well as in earnest, forgets or does not realise danger has, so long as it is unconscious, a healthy and a fine side. It is often heroism run to waste. But when it begins to boast and glory in its excesses and its imprudences, the time has surely come to seek a cure for a perverted tendency that may be fast hardening into a diseased habit.

To deny the reality of danger on the high mountains is to shut one's eyes in the face of facts and annually recurring warnings. The

SHKARA FROM USHKUL

generation that formed the Alpine Club fully recognised the risks of its favourite pursuit, and devoted its best energy to devising and elaborating a craft or system by which these dangers might be avoided or minimised. It acted on a principle similar to that of the seamen who formed and promulgated an art of navigation. But our success has tended to produce a reaction; the younger climbers—guides and amateurs alike—show a disposition to flout and neglect the wisdom of their elders. They find that our precautions to a large extent eliminate the element of risk; they imagine that it is more completely eliminated than it ever can be, and so they go to work in their own way.   It has proved, and must prove, a disastrous way.

To preach caution to youthful ambitions and energies is too often a waste of ink, or breath.   It is better to provide them with a new outlet.   I follow the fashion of medical science in recommending change of air and scene.   A new playground is wanted for those of our countrymen to whom the first element of a holiday is to break away from their daily duties and habits, to live out of doors, to exercise their muscles, to freshen their minds by intercourse with human beings leading altogether dissimilar existences and in another stage of civilisation from themselves. There are Englishmen now, as there were forty years ago, who, without being travellers by profession — being indeed active members of learned professions—find pleasure and refreshment in rough travel among primitive people, in mountain scenery and in glacier air, in that sense of adventure and discovery which is best afforded by the virgin heights of a great snowy chain.   To such travellers—or Vacation Tourists—my friend Signor Vittorio Sella and I offer in these volumes the Caucasus.[1]

The finest portion of the range has, as I have shown, been brought within their reach.   The country is not only attainable ; it is ripe for travellers.   Since 1880 the Russian Government has tightened its control over the mountain tribesmen.   The good sense and patience shown by English and other mountaineers in their dealings with officials and natives—above all, our habit of paying for services rendered us, have borne fruit.   The dangers of travel below the snow-line are at an end ; its difficulties decrease yearly ; even its delays yield to practised persistence.   Caucasian exploration is a much harder game to play than Alpine climbing ; it calls for more varied qualities, much patience, and some endurance and experience.   But the game is emphatically worth the candle.

I cannot enforce my recommendation better than by echoing and enlarging on the advice given to the Alpine Club by my friend

---

[1] I have said nothing here of the Fauna of the Caucasus or of the attractions it may offer to sportsmen.   The subject has been recently and adequately dealt with in M. Mourier's *Guide au Caucase* and the *Big Game* volume of the Badminton Series.

Mr. Clinton Dent after his first journey in 1886. To those who have the strength, energy, and experience, the early explorers of the Caucasus would say:—' We have found at the other end of Europe a strange country, where giant peaks wait for you—remote, sublime, inaccessible to all but their most patient lovers. If you worship the mountains for their own sake; if you like to stand face to face with Nature where she mingles the fantastic and the sublime with the sylvan and the idyllic—snows, crags and mists, flowers and forests—in perfect harmony; where she enhances the effect of her pictures by the most startling contrasts, and enlivens their foregrounds with some of the most varied and picturesque specimens of the human race—go to the Caucusus. If you wish to change not only your earth and sky but your century, to find yourselves one week among the pastoral folk who once peopled Northern Asia, the next among barbarians who have been left stranded while the rest of the world has flowed on; if it attracts you to share the bivouacs of Tauli shepherds, to sit at supper with a feudal chieftain, while his retainers chant the old ballads of their race by the light of birch-bark torches—go to the Caucasus. If you can live without bed or board, without newspapers or *tables d'hôte*, if you can climb on boiled mutton, black bread and sour milk, get your tents ready and be off. You will never regret the exertion or the cost, for you will not only enjoy yourselves, you will bring back, for use in after years, a store of memories, of glimpses of another world, such as no Alpine journey has ever given you. And when home-keeping youths expatiate on the charms of "the old places," you will rejoice that among your "old places" are Betsho and Balkar, Dykhtau and Shkara, the new names of the Caucasus.'

CHAPTER IV

KASBEK AND THE OSSETE DISTRICT

"Εἰπέ μοι, ἔφη, ποῦ χθές ἦμεν; ὁ δὲ, ἐν τῷ πεδίῳ, ἔφη. Τήμερον δὲ, ὦ Δάμι, ποῦ; ἐν τῷ Καυκάσῳ, εἶπεν, εἰ μὴ ἐμαυτοῦ ἐκλέλησμαι· πότε ἐν κάτω μᾶλλον ἦσθα; πάλιν ἤρετο· ὁ δὲ, τουτὸ μὲν, ἔφη, οὐδὲ ἐπερωτᾶν ἄξιον. Χθὲς μὲν γὰρ διὰ κοίλης τῆς γῆς ἐπορευόμεθα, τήμερον δὲ πρὸς τῷ οὐρανῷ ἐσμέν· . . . τί οὖν ἡγῇ, ἔφη, παραλλάττειν τὰς ὁδοὺς ἀλλήλων, ἢ τι τήμερον πλέον εἶναί σοι τοῦ χθές; ὅτι χθὲς, ἔφη, ἐβάδιζον οὖπερ πολλοί, τήμερον δὲ οὖπερ ὀλίγοι." PHILOSTRATUS, *De vitâ Apollonii Tyanensis*, lib. ii. cap. v.

EW services across Europe are arranged every summer. At present, the shortest way to the Caucasus is by Vienna. A direct steamer, sailing from Odessa once a week, lands the traveller at Batum in five days from London. The voyage past the historical shores of the Crimea, the once familiar creeks of Sevastopol and Balaclava and the villas of Yalta, across the Straits of Kertch, and on under the forested hills and bays of the Western Caucasus, is varied, and generally agreeable. When rain has recently fallen, and the air is clear, it culminates, as the steamer traverses the last bay of the Euxine, in a superb panorama of the Abkhasian and Suanetian ranges. Below the white snows on the horizon the blue crests of the loftier spurs stand out pencilled firmly in the clear upper air, while the nearer foot-hills fade softly into the vaporous haze of the lowlands.[1] The view is similar in

---

[1] This contrast, often visible on the Pisan coast or the Lombard plain, was noted by Leonardo da Vinci in his *Theory of the Art of Painting*. See the very interesting notes, vol. i. pp. 299-300 in Dr. Richter's edition, in which the great artist describes his excursion to Monboso, now identified with the southern spur of Monte Rosa, which divides Val Sesia from Val de Lys and the Biellese.

character to that of the Dolomites gained from the sea approach
to Venice, but far grander in its proportions.

For a mountaineer, however, setting out about midsummer,
the quickest and surest way of making a good start is, perhaps,
to take one of the boats that call at Novorossisk, the new corn-
port of Ciscaucasia. In this way he may reach the Caucasian
Baths, at the foot of Elbruz, after eighteen hours', or Vladikavkaz
at the foot of Kasbek after twenty-four hours', railway journey.

It was by the Ciscaucasian line that I approached the mountains on both my last journeys in 1887 and 1889. For various
reasons, I came not from the Black Sea, but by land through the
heart of Russia, from Kiev or Moscow. Russian arrangements
allow any scenery through which the line may pass to be seen to
more advantage by railway passengers than is usually possible. The
first-class carriages are saloon cars fitted with movable armchairs
and wide windows, and the pace is extremely moderate. Unfortunately, there is seldom in Russia any scenery to look at. Forests,
cornlands, rolling downs dotted with few and far-off villages—
landscapes with endless horizontal lines but no marked horizons
—unfold themselves in endless succession before the eyes of the
semi-hypnotised traveller, as he rolls slowly day after day southwards towards the Caucasus through the summer heat and dust.
A famous Alpine guide, who was being taken out not long ago
by this overland route, became so much depressed at the persistent
flatness of Southern Russia, that on the second or third morning he
broke out into forcible remonstrance with his employers on their
folly in going farther in search of mountains in a direction in which
it was becoming hourly more obvious that the world was flat.

At a desolate junction, usually reached about midnight, known
as Tikhoretski, the trains from Rostov on the Don and Novorossisk unite. In the early dawn the line crosses the hardly
noticeable ridge in the downs which divides the waters that flow
to the Black Sea and the Caspian. Presently the bold lines of
Beshtau—the isolated group of porphyry hills of Piatigorsk, the first
outposts of the mountains, spring out of the long uniform undulations of the steppe. Then the vast white dome of Elbruz flashes

in the morning sunshine, and the snows rise slowly behind it along the horizon, until from end to end, not in a continuous line, but in clustered companies, the silver spearheads of the guardians of Asia gather against the southern sky. The train makes a halt at the 'Mineral Waters' station, where a crowd of omnibus and 'phaeton' drivers, eager for passengers for Piatigorsk, used to seem out of character with the desolate landscape which formed their environment. Then, as it approaches the base of the hills, the line swerves eastwards. The foreground resembles in its undulations rather the rolling uplands of Bavaria than the dead level of the Lombard plain. We cross formidable streams, the tributaries of the Terek, running between high banks, and half hidden in dense jungle, the home of the wild boar. After one glance at their grey, turbid waters, the mountaineer needs no further proof of the existence of great glaciers in the Caucasus. That professed 'scientists' should have been unable to interpret so obvious a natural indication is hardly creditable to their powers of observation or of inference.

On the right, the twin cones of Elbruz become more and more conspicuous. Slowly the western disappears, and the mountain assumes the simple lines of a typical volcano, a heavier and less graceful Fuji-san. There are no towns or roads in the foreground. Sometimes the train passes near the low cottages of a moated Cossack village, ranged in regular lines round a church, the white walls and green cupola of which remain visible for miles. Each hamlet is surrounded by sunflower-fields and ploughlands, a little oasis in the wilderness of pale weeds and waving grasses and broad muddy places where carts pass, which Russians call roads. We are here skirting the old military march, held till forty years ago by the Cossacks moved down from the Don in the last century to form a bulwark against the robber-tribes of the mountains. Their look-out posts have not all fallen to ruin ; one may still see the pigeon-houses or sentry-boxes on stilts from which they kept guard over the fords of the rivers, and gave notice of the approach of the marauders, who were ever lurking among the forests of the foot-hills. The border life which by its romance and adventure attracted many of the wilder and more adventurous spirits of the Russian nobility, has been vividly described, from personal experience, by a writer of genius, Count Tolstoi, in one of his early works, *Les Cossaques*, and some shorter tales, which every traveller should have in his book-bag.

As Elbruz is left behind, two of the highest peaks of the Central Group become conspicuous in front of the other snows. A Caucasian Jungfrau, a symmetrical pyramid, cloaked in snowy drapery, every fold and wrinkle in which is distinguishable, shines through the soft, lucid Caucasian air. A Russian officer says 'Koshtantau,' and our fellow-passengers look with increased interest at the noble mountain on which the Englishmen were lost in 1888. Presently a low ridge, crowned by the barrow of some forgotten chieftain, rises in front, and the railway joins the Terek, which traverses a narrow and shallow pass. As the line emerges into the plain of Vladikavkaz, two new snow-peaks, Kasbek and Gimarai Khokh, become conspicuous, and on the right the valley of the Ardon offers the first visible break in the vast mountain wall.

Slowly the weary engine pants up a long incline—a wide, fan-like slope, formed by the alluvial soil brought down by the Terek and other mountain-torrents from the flanks of Kasbek. Happy are those who arrive without accident at their far-sought goal! Twice I have found myself with unwelcome leisure to examine the landscape. In 1868 we sat for hours in the rain, watching our luggage, beside a broken-down and wheelless post-cart. Happily, we were not reduced to the position Alexandre Dumas has the audacity to assert he found himself in on a similar occasion —that of keeping off a horde of wolves by means of a box of lucifer matches. In 1889 our misfortune was comparatively slight, and would have been hardly worth notice had it not happened after an eighty hours' journey. But a traveller who has got into the train at Moscow on Thursday morning, by Sunday afternoon is apt to be impatient to arrive. Our destination was only half-an-hour distant when the engine broke down. The passengers sat on a bank and watched the white clouds play round the great peaks, the waves of air pulse, almost forming a mirage, over the undivided plain, Ossete horsemen, draped in their *bourkas*, canter between the distant farms, until at last a tiny puff of smoke on the line told them that our guard had not tapped the telegraph wires in vain, and that we might still sup and sleep at Vladikavkaz.

Vladikavkaz, though within a morning's drive of the base of Kasbek—as near as Interlaken is to the Jungfrau—is only 2300 feet above the sea-level. For those to whom Russian towns are already familiar, the place will offer little worthy of notice. It has grown immensely within my recollection, and the population has increased between 1865 and 1895 from 3650 to 44,000. But the place has still the usual Russian features, an air of space being no object and ground-rents inappreciable, a general mixture of pretentiousness and untidiness. The Station Road is full of holes big enough to swallow a perambulator ; the principal street has a stunted grove in the middle, and is called a Boulevard. The residential quarter consists of white-washed, one-storied houses, which stand back modestly among gardens, as if they felt out of place so near the large hospitals, barracks, stores and offices. The only local colour is to be found among the crowd in the streets, and in the bazaar or market, where Ossete fur-caps, daggers, arms, and red water-melons are the principal objects exposed. For the traveller there is an hotel, not inferior to those found in minor French provincial towns, with an excellent restaurant. Mountaineers are no longer the strange phenomena they were in 1868, when a waiter to whom I presented a silver medal of our Queen—in the shape of a sixpence —said he should preserve it always as a memorial of the English-men who had come to the Caucasus only to climb mountains. His point of view was Asiatic, and identical with that of the Japanese diplomatist who recently informed the Alpine Club that his nation were a 'serious people, who did not go up mountains without a religious object.'

In these volumes my business is with the exploration of the heights and byways, not with the comparatively well-known post-roads of the Caucasus. I shall not add to the already numerous descriptions of the great road to Tiflis. Is it not already included in the pages of Bradshaw ?

It may be well, however, to point out that the 'Darial Pass' is not a saddle in a chain, but a gorge like the Via Mala, a rent through the granite heart of the Caucasus. The pass over the watershed lies beyond it, and is properly known as the Cross Pass (7977 feet). A public carriage performs the service from Vladikavkaz to Tiflis in twenty-four hours, and it is easy to post over in a day and a half, sleeping in good quarters at Ananur, at the southern foot of the range. The scenery may, in my opinion, best be compared to that of the Col du Lautaret in Dauphiné. There is a very grand gorge, one unique view of a great mountain, then a bleak highland district and a dull pass. The descent to Georgia is interesting, but the southern valleys are neither so picturesque nor so fertile as those of the Italian Alps.

The impressions of awe and admiration reflected in the narratives of most of the travellers who have passed through the Darial are doubtless in some part due to the suddenness of the transition from the interminable steppe to the mountains—from the horizontal to the perpendicular. To me they seem, and I have traversed the Darial several times, somewhat excessive. It is true I have always come to it fresh from the more romantic and varied recesses of the central chain. The defile is extremely wild and savage. But its effect is somewhat reduced by the flat space beside the stream, and by the absence of the sudden turns and surprises found in many similar ravines. Its terrors have been perhaps further diminished by the construction of a new road on the left bank of the Terek, to avoid the destructive mud-avalanches brought down by a stream close to the village of Kasbek. It is a rare and happy accident when a frequented highway leads through that part of a range where the peaks are loftiest and the valleys most beautiful. Zermatt, Chamonix, Grindelwald, all lie far from the old tracks of pilgrims and travellers. The rule that the noblest scenery has to be sought out for its own sake, at a distance from the common and most convenient paths of men, holds good in the Caucasus as well as in the Alps.

The village and post-station of Kasbek owe their name to the Russians, who called them after a native chief, one Kazibeg. The

Georgians called it Stephans-zminda, or St. Stephen's. This has been
one of the spots where a quantity of antiquities, probably of very
various dates, from prehistoric to Roman times, from the end of the
Iron Age almost to the present day, have been found.   Many of
these curious objects, armlets, rings, knives, lance-heads, gold ornaments in the shape of bells or the horns of animals, are figured
in M. Chantre's volumes.   Near the church on the opposite hill,

ORNAMENTS FROM GRAVES IN OSSETIA

2000 feet above the station, other objects have been found, the
character of which, and possibly the name, Gergeti, of the nearest
hamlet, led M. Bayern, a Tiflis antiquary, to maintain this to
be the scene of the famous annual marriage of the Amazons
and Gergeretæ mentioned by Strabo.[1]   The evidence will, I think,

[1] M. Bayern was of much service to M. Chantre in his antiquarian researches, and
M. Chantre has repaid the obligation by an appreciative memoir of this hard-working and
ill-requited student.   M. Bayern was very successful as an excavator.   Unfortunately he
suffered from the Bible on the brain, and located in the Caucasus the home of Abraham and
his descendants.   See *Contribution à l'archéologie du Caucase par F. Bayern, précédée d'une
introduction biographique,* par M. Ernest Chantre. Lyon. Pitrat aîné, 1882.

satisfy no one but an enthusiast. Objects of a similar character are everywhere associated with primitive worship of the reproductive powers of nature, and are found in many other places in the Northern Caucasus.

The situation of the post-station has no beauty except when the great mountain is unveiled. Then the picture seen from the windows will not easily be forgotten. Again and again it has been painted and photographed : it is met with in every book of travel, even in the shop-windows of St. Petersburg. It is the keepsake view—the Jungfrau from Interlaken—of the Caucasus. Not that it has any likeness in detail to the Swiss landscape, or any of its charm of foreground. Austere and wild, the naked hillsides, when not relieved by atmospheric effects, appear ugly. But there is unique grandeur in the steep curves of the vast white dome, which fills all the sudden opening in the opposite range. Kasbek is a solitary classical mountain, not a Gothic pinnacled ridge. When the storm-wrack suddenly swirls apart and leaves the peak clear against the upper blue ; when it stands up at sundown, high above the vapours that fill the hollows about its base, cold and pure against a lemon sky, the passing traveller does not wonder at its fame. He may even enter for a moment into the spirit of genial amusement with which the Russian officials in 1868 looked on the modest equipment of the first party of young Englishmen who proposed to climb where colonels and even companies of Cossacks had found themselves helpless, and the equally frank and polite incredulity with which our hosts received, as a matter of course, our assertion that we had succeeded at the first attempt.[1]

Before the Russians came to it, the great mountain had half-a-dozen native titles. Mkuinvari, the 'Ice Mountain,' was the recognised Georgian name : it was also known as the 'White Mountain,' or 'Christ's Mountain.' All these titles are now superseded

---

[1] In the case of this, the first climb of any difficulty accomplished in the Caucasus, and the first complete ascent of one of its great peaks, I venture to repeat the account I gave at the time. I do so with the less hesitation, because the narrative was revised and in part written by my companion, the late A. W. Moore, and in some of the sentences I seem to catch an echo of his forcible way of putting things, of that combination of literal accuracy and effective emphasis which was characteristic of the man.

by that which has found a place in atlases. Its snows were hallowed by legends—obscure primitive fables of giants and hidden treasures, mixed with monastic tales in which the treasures became sacred objects—the tent of Abraham, the cradle of Christ. One belief was universal, and sustained by the best evidence, that the summit was inaccessible. The so-called 'ascents' of German travellers had been ascents 'to the lower limit of eternal snow.'

It was on the last day of June 1868 that our party left the post-station of Kasbek, bent on this novel enterprise. We had secured four inhabitants of the village to carry our provisions and a light tent. They were not Ossetes, but Chetchens, a mountain-tribe whose homes lie mostly east of the Darial. They are famous hunters; they are said also to be pagans, and to reverence only the spirits of the mountains and the ghosts of their ances-tors. The endurance beyond the grave of personal existence and the presence of mind behind the forms of matter appear to be almost universal instincts of the human race, and when we look closely, such sentiments may seem to be the basis of most in-digenous, or primitive, religions in the Caucasus and elsewhere. The beliefs and practices founded on these instincts have in the Caucasus, however, been overlaid with a varnish of extraneous morality or superstition, Christian and Mohammedan. Most of the so-called 'conversions' have been additions of new and half-understood superstitions, welded but imperfectly into the mental fabric of the tribes, and capable, as in the case of the Suanetians and Abkhasians, of being almost completely thrown off again.

We camped for the night on a mossy plot in a hollow, at a height of about 11,000 feet, under the moraine of the Ortsveri Glacier, which sweeps round the southern flanks of Kasbek. Our native porters went off to some shelter, probably an overhanging rock in the neighbourhood. We had left our interpreter, sick with fever, at the post-station, and our means of communicating with them were therefore naturally limited.

Next morning the porters were not forthcoming. The firing of a revolver produced no reply, and we started in the dark at

2.45 A.M., leaving our tent and luggage to the care of our missing troop. The sky was cloudless; the strange snows and rocky pinnacles that surrounded us soon caught the sunrise flush. Such rapid progress did we make up the frozen slopes that lead towards the base of the gap between the two peaks, that by 6.30 we were already (by aneroid) 14,800 feet above the sea, or 3700 feet above our sleeping-place.

From the height already attained the view was magnificent, and the sky was still perfectly clear; in the west some fine snowy peaks, afterwards better known to us as the Adai Khokh group, were conspicuous; to the south our eyes ranged over the main chain of the Caucasus and across the valley of the Kur to the Armenian highlands; behind the dark, rugged ridges east of the Terek valley the peaks of Daghestan raised their snowy heads.

FRANÇOIS J. DÉVOUASSOUD, 1895

At this point our difficulties began : the crevasses became large, and had to be avoided. François Dévouassoud resigned the lead to Tucker for forty minutes, during which the favouring snow-slope was exchanged for blue ice, covered with a treacherous four inches of loose snow. The work of cutting steps became laborious, and Dévouassoud presently again went to the front. An incident soon occurred which might have been serious. A *Bergschrund*—a huge icicle-fringed crack in the ice, three to four feet wide, of which the upper lip was about five feet above the under—barred our progress. Dévouassoud was first, I followed, Tucker was behind me, and Moore last. We had all passed the obstacle without serious difficulty when the rope, which in the passage had got somewhat slack, was discovered to have hitched itself round one of the big icicles in the crack. Tucker having, from the position in which he was standing, in vain tried to release it, began to cut steps downwards to the upper lip of the crevasse. At no time is it an easy thing to cut steps in ice beneath you; try to do it in a hurry, and what happened in this case is almost sure to occur. The step-cutter overbalanced himself, his feet slipped out of the shallow footholds, and he shot at once over the chasm. Of course the rope immediately tightened with a severe jerk on Moore and myself, who, though very insecurely placed, were fortunately able to resist the strain. Tucker had fallen spread-eagle fashion with his head down the slope, and we had to hold for many seconds before he could work himself round and regain his footing.

The escape was a narrow one, and we had reason to be thankful that neither the rope nor our axes had failed us at so critical a moment. So startling an occurrence naturally shook our nerves somewhat, but little was said, and our order having been re-established, we attacked the exceedingly steep ice-slope which separated us from the gap between the two summits. For the next four hours there was scarcely one easy step. The ice, when not bare, was thinly coated with snow. A long, steep ice-slope is bad enough in the first state, as mountain-climbers know: but it is infinitely worse in the second. In bare ice a secure step may be cut; through loose, incoherent snow it cannot. Dévouassoud went through the form of cutting, but it was of little use to the two front men, and none at all to those in the rear. In many places we found the safest plan was to crawl up on our hands and knees, clinging with feet and ice-axes to the slippery staircase. It has always remained a mystery to us how we got from step to step without a slip. The difficulties of the feat were increased by a bitter wind, which swept across the slope in fitful blasts of intense fury, driving the snow in blinding showers into our faces as we crouched down for shelter, and numbing our hands to such a degree that we could scarcely retain hold of our axes.

Time passes rapidly in such circumstances, and it was not

until 11 A.M., when Dévouassoud was again exhausted by the
labour of leading, that we gained the saddle between the two
summits. There was no doubt now that the eastern peak was the
highest. At this we were well pleased, as, in such a wind as was
raging, the passage of the exceedingly narrow ridge leading to the
western summit would have been no pleasant task. After snatching
a morsel of food, we left Dévouassoud to recover himself, and started
by ourselves, Tucker leading. The final climb was not difficult ;
a broad bank of hard snow led to some rocks ; above lay more
snow, succeeded by a second and larger patch of rocks (where
Dévouassoud rejoined us), which in their turn merged in the final
snow-cupola of the mountain. A few steps brought us to the edge
of the southern cliffs, along which we mounted. The snow-ridge
ceased to ascend, and then fell away before us. It was just mid-
day when we saw beneath us the valley of the Terek, and knew
that the highest point of Kasbek was under our feet. The cold
owing to the high wind would not allow us to stop on the actual
crest, but we sat down half a dozen feet below it, and tried to
take in as much as possible of the vast panorama before us.

Clouds had by this time risen in the valleys and covered the
great northern plain, but the mountain-peaks were for the most
part clear. The apparent grandeur of the ranges to the east was
a surprise. Group beyond group of snowy peaks stretched away
towards the far-off Basardjusi (14,722 feet), the monarch of the
Eastern Caucasus. Nearer, and therefore more conspicuous, was
the fine head of Tebulos (14,781 feet). On the western horizon
we eagerly sought for Elbruz, but it was not to be recognised ; the
summit was undoubtedly veiled by clouds, since S. Sella distinctly
saw Kasbek from Elbruz. Except in the immediate vicinity of
Kasbek, there seemed to be but few and small glaciers nearer than
the Adai Khokh group, on the farther side of the Ardon valley.

After a stay of about ten minutes we quitted the summit. It
was impossible to leave any permanent trace of our visit. We could
not spare an ice-axe to fix upon the snow-dome, and the rocks
were too big to use for building a snow-man. In a quarter of an
hour we regained the gap, and then held a council. From the

commencement of our difficulties our minds had been troubled as to how we should get down, though, fortunately for our success, they had been more pressingly occupied with the business of the ascent. Now, however, the question had to be fairly faced—how were we to descend the ice-slope we had climbed with so much difficulty? With a strong party—that is, a party with a due proportion of guides, and when good steps can be cut—there is no more delicate mountaineering operation than the descent of a really steep ice-slope. We were not a strong party, and on this particular slope it was practically impossible to cut steps at all. A bad slip must result in a fall or roll of at least 2000 feet, unless, indeed, our progress was cut short by one of the numerous crevasses on the lower part of the mountain. The exact manner of its termination might, however, be a matter of indifference when that termination came.

We were unanimously of opinion that an attempt to return by our morning's route would end in disaster, and that a way must be sought in another direction. This could only be on the northern flank of the mountain, and it was satisfactory to see that for a long distance on that side there was no serious difficulty. A steep slope of firm snow fell away from our feet to a great level _névé_, which we knew must pour down glaciers into the glens which open into the Terek valley below the Kasbek station. A very few minutes' consideration determined us to follow this line, abandoning for the time our camp and the porters on the east side of the mountain. The first hundred feet of descent down the hard snow-bank were steep enough. I was ahead, and neglected to cut good steps, an error which resulted in Moore's aneroid getting a jolt which upset it for several hours. Happily, the little thing recovered during the night, and told us our approximate heights for many a day afterwards. Very soon the slope became gentle enough to allow us to dispense with axe-work, and we trudged straight and steadily downwards, until we were almost on the level of the extensive snow-fields upon which we had looked from above. Here we again halted to consider our further course. We were on an unknown snow-plain, at a height of 14,000 feet above the sea, and it was most undesirable to hazard by any rash or hasty move our chance of reaching *terra cognita* ere nightfall. One plan suggested was to turn to the left and cross a gap west of our mountain which we had good reason to believe connected the plateau we were on with the *névé* of the glacier by which we had ascended. This course, if successfully carried out, would have brought us back to our tent and baggage, but its probable length was a fatal objection. Eventually we determined to keep nearly due north across the snowfield, towards a ridge which divides the two glaciers flowing respectively into the glens of Devdorak and Chach. We descended for some distance under the rocks along the left bank of the Devdorak Glacier, until the ice became so steep and broken that further progress promised to be difficult. We thereupon halted, while Dévouassoud climbed up again to the ridge and made a reconnaissance on its northern side.

After some delay, a shout from above called on us to follow, and we rejoined our guide, after a sharp scramble, at the base of a very remarkable tower of rock which crowns the ridge, and is visible even from the Darial road. It will be useful as a finger-post to future climbers. From this point the view of Kasbek is superb; its whole north-eastern face is a sheet of snow and ice, broken by the steepness of the slope into magnificent towers, and seamed by enormous blue chasms.

We were glad to find that there was a reasonable prospect of descending from our eyrie to the lower world without too much difficulty. The crest of the ridge between the two glaciers fell rapidly before us, and offered for some way an easy route. We followed it—sometimes crossing a snowy plain, sometimes hurrying down rocky banks—until we saw beneath us, on our left, a series of long snow-slopes leading directly to the foot of the northern glacier. Down these we glissaded merrily, and at 5.30 halted on the rocks below the end of the glacier, which was of considerable size and backed by two lofty summits. The view of the lower part of the glen was shut out by a rocky barrier, and before we reached its brow, mists, which we had previously observed collecting in the hollow, swept round us, and for the next two hours we were enveloped in a dense fog. A long snow-filled gully brought us to the bottom of the gorge, of which we could see but little, owing to the unfortunate state of the atmosphere. It must be of the most savage description. The torrent was buried under the avalanches of many winters; huge walls of crag loomed through the mist and pressed us so closely on either side that, but for the path afforded by the avalanche-snows, we should have been puzzled to find a means of exit. This aid at last failed us; the stream burst free and tumbled into a gorge. After a laborious scramble for some distance over huge boulders, we found it impossible to follow the water any farther, and made a sharp but short ascent to the right, where our leader happily hit on a faint track, which led us by steep zigzags into the same glen again at a lower point. After more than once missing and re-finding the path, we rounded an angle of the valley, and the fog having lifted somewhat, saw that we were close to the junction of our torrent with that from the Devdorak Glacier. On the grassy brow between the two streams cows and goats were grazing, and as it was now 7.45 P.M., we debated on the propriety of stopping for the night. The question was decided by the information we got from the herdsmen, an old man and two boys, who proved to be very decent fellows. All communication, except by pantomime, was of course impossible; but necessity sharpens the wits, and we gathered from them, without much difficulty, that the Devdorak torrent was bridgeless and big, and that they had fresh milk and would allow us to share their shelter. It was only a hollow between a low wall and a partially overhanging cliff, which was but a poor protection against the attacks of inquisitive sheep and goats, who invaded us several times during the night, and succeeded in carrying off and eating my gloves and gaiters. Despite these inroads and a Scotch mist. which fell pretty heavily from time to time, we managed, with stones for pillows and our mackintoshes spread over us, to snatch a good deal of sleep.

The preparations for our start the next morning did not take long. The chief herdsman accompanied us to the Devdorak torrent, which at this time of day was fordable; and one of the boys volunteered to go with us to the post-station. A well-marked path led us above the united torrents; on a neighbouring brow, we were told, stands a pile of stones, resembling an altar in shape, and covered with the horns of chamois and wild goats. This spot is held sacred by the Chetchen inhabitants of the neighbouring village, and once a year they repair hither, sing strange chants, and make offerings to the local deities. Ere long the defile of the Darial opened beneath us, and a short descent brought us to the Terek.

OSSETE SHEPHERDS

Our return did not create much excitement at first at the Kasbek post-station. The inmates seemed to take it as a matter of course that we had not really been to the top, but equally as a matter of course that we should say we had. We roused up our interpreter, who, still unable to shake off an attack of fever, was in a very gloomy mood, and through him despatched a messenger to look for our porters, whom we had left encamped at 11,000 feet the previous morning. The commission was quickly executed. In the evening the porters returned, bringing in safety all our belongings, including a pair of snow-spectacles, which had been mislaid in a start in the dark. The men had supposed us lost, and now, overjoyed to see us again, talked, kissed, and hugged us all simultaneously. The excitement among the villagers grew intense. The porters told them that we had disappeared up the mountain, and that our tracks were visible to a great height on the southern face ; the shepherd boy was a witness to our mysterious appearance on the other side the same evening : the two facts showed that we must have crossed the mountain, and we suddenly found ourselves installed as heroes instead of humbugs in the public opinion of Kasbek. Two of the porters after a time took courage to allege that they had followed in our footsteps to the top, but this bold fiction was not pressed on our acceptance.

In after years M. Muromzoff, a writer whose contributions to Caucasian travel and literature I have commented on sufficiently elsewhere,[1] set up for these two porters—Toto and Zogel, he says their names are—a serious claim to have followed us to the summit. The account, as he professes to have taken it down from their lips, is full of contradictions and impossibilities. But I would not attach too much weight to the defects of his version, if the story were otherwise credible. But it is not : no man in sandals, and without climbing appliances, could have got up by our route, and had the porters attempted it, we must have seen them in our tracks, during the hours we spent on the ice-wall or on our return to the gap. May Toto and Zogel long live to enjoy the honour thrust on them by the provincial or national feelings of the good people of Tiflis, who twenty years later were ready to hail the first Russian ascent of the peak as its first ' authentic ' ascent !

As usual, our successors have escaped most of the difficulties and perils that beset pioneers. Some details of subsequent ascents are given in the Appendix. Recent climbers have altogether avoided our ice-wall ; they have either climbed the rocks of the eastern face, or followed the obviously easiest route—the line of our descent. Nothing is wanted but a hut on the rocks, high above the Devdorak Glacier, to make the expedition as practicable as the ascent of Mont Blanc.

---

[1] *Alpine Journal*, vol. xii. p. 320.

The glen which we had traversed in our descent from Kasbek, that of the Devdorak Glacier, is almost as famous as the mountain itself. It has been the source of catastrophes—known for many years as the 'Kasbek Avalanches,' by which, prior to 1832, the

THE DEVDORAK GLACIER

gorge of Darial and the Lower Terek valley were frequently inundated. Now it is obvious that no 'avalanche,' in the ordinary sense of the term, falling from anywhere near Kasbek, could reach the highroad. There is a long, comparatively level, glen between them. The inundations were clearly similar in character to those of the Swiss Val de Bagnes. Blocks of ice as well as boulders were carried down by the raging torrent. The origin of the mischief has never, however, been authoritatively or exactly explained. The sudden bursting of a sub-glacial lake, as in the St. Gervais catastrophe, the creation and subsequent destruction of a dam, caused by the fall of an avalanche from some lateral ravine across the glacier torrent; these are among the obvious hypotheses that have been brought forward. But the bursting of a sub-glacial reservoir is, in the Alps and elsewhere, a very rare event. The Kasbek disaster, early in the present century, was of frequent recurrence, and was believed to recur at periods of seven years. There should, therefore, be something exceptional in the local conditions. Now, as every experienced mountain explorer will note on looking at the photograph here reproduced, the peculiarities of the Devdorak Glacier are its narrowness, steepness, and thickness. The terminal slope is of almost unparalleled height. Is it not probable that the upper and central layers of ice, moving according to the law that governs glaciers, faster than the lower layers, sheer over and fall, temporarily burying and blocking the cave from which the stream issues? Such accounts as I have found of the conditions preceding a flood speak invariably of an advance of the glacier, and assume it to be the main cause. Dr. Abich expressly attributed the disaster to a fall in the front of the glacier. I put forward, however, this suggestion tentatively. Further local inquiries are very desirable. Bad weather has prevented me from making any detailed examination of the ground myself, but those who desire to do so can now obtain lodging in a house, erected by the Government near the foot of the glacier.

Two glens, those of the Lagzdon and Gezeldon, run up to the northern glaciers of Kasbek and its neighbour Gimarai Khokh, a summit of the height of Mont Blanc. For a full description of them the reader must turn to the forthcoming volume of Herr Merzbacher, who was successful in scaling Gimarai Khokh, and also Kasbek, from this side.

Close to the glacier at the head of the former glen the German traveller found a curious and primitive bathing establishment. It consists of a few rude stone huts, grouped round a mineral

spring, which is much visited in summer by the Ossetes. The
habit of making medical use of mineral springs, both for men and
animals, is of very early origin. I doubt not that in the Alps, in
Roman times, the waters of St. Moritz and Bormio were resorted to
by shepherds and their flocks. In the Middle Ages we know them
to have been extremely popular. St. Moritz Water was even stated
to be ' an excellent substitute for wine'; a belief not encouraged by
the modern innkeepers of the Engadine. The most popular of the
mountain baths of the Caucasus are situated a few miles above Oni,
near the head of the Rion valley. Here in summer there are said
to be several hundred visitors, camping out or bivouacking in the
most primitive manner. Families also may be found here and there
established in tents upon some solitary pasture round an iron or
sulphur spring. These are very abundant in the Caucasus, and are
always pointed out with great interest by the inhabitants, who show
a strong sense of their importance. Gebi is blessed with a peculiarly
powerful spring, there is another near Karaul, another in the
picturesque valley of the Garasu at the northern base of Tiktengen.
These are the health-resorts of the future, waiting to be opened
up by some 'Caucasian Spas' Company.' Railroads have not penetrated the Caucasus without bringing new notions with them. A
mountain Prince once offered me a lease of all the minerals, and
the exclusive right of keeping hotels, in his territory, on certain
conditions. A company promoter might find an opening even in
Suanetia; but I should be sorry to promise his shareholders that
they will make their fortunes.

The Kolota Pass (10,633 feet) is the only one practicable for
horses across the Kasbek Chain. It crosses a saddle connecting the
main mass with a small glacier group, of which the most conspicuous
peak is known as Tepli. The pass and the peak both await their
explorers. It is probable that a grand defile will be discovered in
the Fiagdon valley, which leads to the pass from the north.

As has been already pointed out, the Kasbek and Tepli Groups
form no part of the Caucasian watershed. They are linked to it
by a high grassy ridge, which divides the sources of the Terek and
Ardon. Over this our route led us in 1868. The Tyrsui Pass, which

crosses it, ought to be, and doubtless is, practicable for Caucasian horses, but at that date we could not procure any to carry our baggage. Nothing can well be more tame than the upper valley of the Terek above Kobi. The rocks are friable, the slopes uniform, and the scenery is dreary and monotonous. The summit south of the pass, Zilga Khokh (12,646), is notable as having been used by General Chodzko as a trigonometrical station. On the descent there is more variety in the landscape. The slate peaks of the ridge which divides the Nardon sources from the tributaries of the Kur rise in bold shapes from broad platforms, separated by grassy gaps, which form passes over the main chain. The almost treeless valleys consist of alternations of deep basins, and often impassable gorges. On high perches, or defensible ridges, stand the rude walls and towers of fortified farms and villages, the most remote fastnesses of Ossetia.

This district has been approached by travellers, Dr. Abich and Professor Hahn, from Gori on the Tiflis Railway by the valley of the Liakhva and the Bakh-fandak or Roki Passes. Hitherto no English mountaineers have followed these tracks, which are interesting in scenery, and particularly interesting to geologists as leading near one of the most important volcanic centres of the Caucasus.

Since the prospect scarcely pleases—at any rate, does not absorb the traveller's attention—he may turn with interest to the people into whose inmost territory he has penetrated. The Ossetes,[1] who in 1881 numbered 111,000 souls, are one of the most important of the Caucasian tribes. They have dwelt in the same region, under slightly different names, from the dawn of history. They had their golden age when their communities spread north and south of the chain, when the steppe was whitened with Ossete flocks, and the vintages of the Georgian hills were gathered in by Ossete labourers. But they remain essentially a primitive and a mountain people. Queen Thamara, the Charlemagne of the Caucasian isthmus, at the close of the twelfth century spread Christianity among them and dotted their heights with churches; the Kabardans from the Crimea drove

---

[1] Ossi is the Georgian, Assi the Russian appellation: the people call themselves Irons. See Hahn's *Aus dem Kaukasus*.

them from their northern pastures; Turkish tribes supplanted them in the valleys of the Cherek and Chcgem, and introduced Mohammedanism in their borders.   But the Ossetes still held their own central highlands ; they had in their hands the keys of the Caucasus, the grass-passes leading from the sources of the Terek and the Ardon to those of the Rion and the Kur, by which alone the range is traversable in summer by horsemen and troops.   They gave Vladikavkaz, the Key of the Caucasus—as its name implies—to Russia.

In appearance they are a prepossessing and a martial race ; their dress and accoutrements are cared for and often costly, their daggers and cartridge-pouches are silver-mounted.   They adapt themselves easily to civilised ways, take service readily in the Russian army, and even outshine their Russian comrades in the ballroom. Coming from a country where the males are as naturally given to dancing as certain birds, this is only natural.   Hence the Russians have called them 'the gentlemen of the mountains.' But it is in virtue of their ancient laws and usages that the Ossetes have most interest for the world.   To students of primitive institutions and the origins of law they are exceptionally attractive.   A

Russian scholar, Professor Kovalevsky, has made them the subject of his special inquiries.[1]

Their earliest habitations, known as *kaus*, were the fortress-farms, clusters of buildings and out-houses, enclosed by high walls and

AN OSSETE VILLAGE

dominated by a rude tower—many of which still dot the slopes of the upper valleys.   It was apparently at a later stage that

[1] See an abridged translation of Professor Kovalevsky's ' Memoir,' by Mr. Delmar Morgan, in the *Royal Asiatic Society's Journal*, vol. xx.   On the dancing propensity of Caucasians see a capital story in Mr. F. C. Grove's *Frosty Caucasus*, p. 14.

they formed villages. These consist of two-storied stone houses, with flat wooden roofs and balconies, not altogether unlike those found in many of the ruder hamlets of the Italian Alps. In each of the old fortress-farms lived a family, or *gens*, who held all property, even their personal earnings, in common. They owned slaves, prisoners taken in war or the offspring of female captives. Blood-revenge produced terrible feuds between the clans, and it is only in comparatively recent times that crimes have been allowed to be atoned for by payments in cattle.

Funeral feasts form a great part of Ossete religion. In Ossetia a man has to feed not only his descendants but his departed ancestors. There is no greater insult to an Ossete than to tell him that 'his dead are hungry'! They have no less than ten Feasts of the Dead, some of which last several days, in their calendar. By a pious fiction the food consumed is held to benefit not him who eats but him in whose honour it is eaten; thus greediness may cloak itself in filial piety. The prayer that is recited with the New-Year offering to the departed is not without local colour and character : 'May he be at peace and may his grave be undisturbed ; may he be famous among the dead, so that none may have power over his sustenance, and that it may reach him untouched and be his for ever, that increasing it may multiply as long as the rocks fall down our mountains and the rivers roll over the plains, neither growing mouldy in summer nor being frozen in winter ; and may he divide it according to his goodwill among such of the dead as have no food.' The Ossete idea of a future world is clearly one where ' daily bread ' still continues the first and chief care.

It would take too long to repeat the various and interesting details given by Professor Kovalevsky of Ossete rites and customs, their peculiar reverence for sacred trees and groves, for the hearth and the great chain that holds the cooking-caldron, their beliefs in the visits interchanged between the visible and the invisible world, in heroes who return to fight, like Castor and Pollux, side by side with the living. It is, I think, impossible not to recognise that we are here in the atmosphere from which classical legends sprang, among stay-at-home relations of the more brilliant people who, stimulated by the climate, the contact with other races, and the town life possible on the shores of the Ægean Sea, developed Greek Mythology. Of architecture or of art, beyond jewellery and metal-work, there is indeed little in Ossetia. But what there is bears out this suggestion. In several places in the district groups of tombs are met with. They are quadrangular edifices, with sloping roofs, and furnished with external ledges, on which are laid votive offerings, generally weapons or antlers.

The Ossetes appear to be quicker in temper than the neighbouring tribesmen. Twice I have nearly come to open quarrel with them. On the first occasion, in 1868, a skirmish arose over an exorbitant demand for payment, and was to some extent, perhaps, our own fault. We were young, and our interpreter, who had been accustomed, in the service of the late Mr. Gifford Palgrave, to see his master treated with the respect due to a British Consul in the East, was brusque in his ways.

Such passing unpleasantnesses are not, in my experience, frequent, and I have never heard of one that resulted in any harm to a traveller. M. Levier, however, tells a story of a Russian officer who, being attacked by a sheep-dog, shot his assailant. He was thereupon attacked also by the Ossete shepherd with such violence that he only owed his safety to his revolver, which he was compelled to use a second time. It may be inferred that it is judicious to avoid petty wrangles with Ossetes, and to tranquillise their sheep-dogs with ice-axes rather than to dismiss them with fire-arms. I have on many occasions followed the former course with complete success.

CHAPTER V

THE MAMISON PASS AND GEBI

'Αστρογείτονας δε χρὴ
Κορυφὰς ὑπερβάλλουσαν ἐς μεσημβρινὴν
Βῆναι κέλευθον.

ÆSCHYLUS.

THE passes of the western portion of the Central Caucasus are barred by glaciers. It is not until we come to the eastern source of the Rion that we find that Nature has provided any facility for the passage of the main chain. At this spot, the frosty crest, that has stretched uninterruptedly from the Klukhor Pass, above Sukhum Kale, turns suddenly into a grassy ridge, easy of access from either slope. On the south side the road accomplishes the last climb by a series of zigzags, but there is no need for any heavy engineering, such as is common on Alpine Passes of much less elevation. On the north side, the 7000 feet of ascent from Alagir to the top is effected with only one zigzag. If proper Refuges and a staff of labourers, charged with the repair of bridges and embankments and the removal of snow-drifts, were provided by the Government, the pass might be kept open for wheels during at least four months in the year. Its importance as the only direct access from Ciscaucasia to Kutais would seem to make it worth while to incur the needful expenditure. To half-construct a road and then let it fall to ruin seems to us Western Europeans bad economy. Not so, however, to Russians. Throughout the Empire the tradition of road-making is absent. The national road is a track deep in dust or mud, and barely passable, except when sledges supersede wheels. The stamp of Russian road-work is its imperfection. In the Caucasus, where so much work of this kind has been called for, the peculiarity is conspicuous. With prodigious effort, and at enormous expense—it is said £4,000,000, or more than five times the cost of the Simplon to Napoleon—the Pass of the Caucasus has, indeed, been brought to a condition equal to that of Alpine highroads. A Swiss canton or an Italian commune looks after its contractors very differently. But the Mamison Road remains in part an un-metalled track, liable to be broken by every winter snowfall or summer rainstorm. On the Klukhor Road, the bridges are built only to be carried away or disregarded altogether by a playful stream, which waits until they are finished, and then either sweeps the whole structure down to the Black Sea or adopts a new channel a few yards away, leaving the arches high and dry. The visitor who drives eastward along the coast from Sukhum Kale soon finds, like Io, his road barred by a violent torrent, and his horses forced out to sea to ford it by the bar.

To return to the Mamison. Where a commercial highway ought to exist and to be maintained, a track has been secured which, at any sudden emergency, a few regiments might render practicable, without any great delay, for troops and artillery. In the mean-time it furnishes mountaineers with a convenient approach to the chain; and it can be recommended to travellers who are not in a hurry and can afford to run the risk of finding the road interrupted, and no relay of horses or vehicles procurable beyond the break.

In variety of scenery the Mamison Road, in my opinion, far surpasses the more famous Pass of the Caucasus. There may be nothing so *horrid*, as a last-century traveller would have said, —so '*duris cautibus horrens*,' in Virgil's phrase—as the Darial defile, no single view so strangely impressive as the glimpse of Kasbek from the post-station of the same name. But the Kassara

gorge is singularly picturesque; the view from the pass itself along
the great chain is magnificent; the upper valley of the Rion offers
many most lovely combinations of snows, flowers, and forests.   In
the suddenness of the transitions from the romantic gloom of the
gorges to the stern nakedness of the mountain basins, and again
from these to the idyllic beauty of the Rion forests, the drive
is, as a whole, typical of Caucasian scenery.

It was on this track that we set out in 1889 for the mountains.
We were a party of nine, including four Swiss and a Jew, our
cook and interpreter, whom we had picked up at a post-station
on the Darial road.   Our departure lacked the usual cheerfulness
of a start for the mountains ; our errand was a sad one, and our
guides had been greatly discomposed by the stories they had heard
from German colonists in the wine-shops of Vladikavkaz.   According
to local belief, our friends Donkin and Fox, and their Bernese guides,
Streich and Fischer, whose fate we had come to ascertain, had
all been the victims of treachery on the part of the mountaineers.
In venturing into the same region without an escort, and with
only a Jew for leader, we were pronounced to be courting a
similar fate.   These worthy citizens knew nothing whatever of
what they were talking about, and consequently were so picturesque and eloquent in assertion that they thoroughly convinced
their audience.   The occupants of the two hindermost post-carts
during the next two days wore an air of woful anticipation of
the worst.

As far as Alagir—that is, until the mountains are entered—
there is nothing but an unmetalled track across the broad treeless
steppe.   The torrents descending from the northern glaciers of
Kasbek and Gimarai Khokh, very considerable streams, have been
left bridgeless, and the fords are sometimes deep enough to astonish
a traveller new to Russian recklessness.

Our tarantass, drawn by four horses harnessed abreast, proceeded
at a leisurely pace across a sea of wild-flowers, amongst which, in
late July, the pale mauve hue of the mallows predominated.   To
the south the mountains rose in broad slopes, dark with forest.
Behind the first range the snows were seen from time to time,

mingling with shadowy clouds that had crossed the Mamison and hung about the heights.[1]

The road, or rather the absence of anything like a European road, seemed, however, in keeping with the wild and primæval air of the landscape. The homes and works of Man were wanting : Nature reigned supreme. I have already compared the steppe to the Roman Campagna. But there civilisations have come and gone ; the sadness of decay and far-off things overtakes the wanderer. Here he finds the freshness of a virgin country, of which mankind has as yet taken no formal possession, or only such passing possession as leaves little permanent mark behind.

The second stage ends at Alagir, a large Ossete town, situated close to the spot where the Ardon leaves the hills. We drove up the street, a broad lane of mud, on either side of which low wattled and plastered huts hide behind a luxuriant growth of sunflowers and rampant vegetables. I class the sunflower with vegetables, because its seeds are a common article of diet in the Caucasus. Half or quite naked children play in the dirt ; furcapped, long-robed men, armed with goads, lead creaking carts, drawn by oxen, through the lanes. A disused fort above the town stands as a monument of the old border warfare. Near it is a large house constructed for the officials who superintended the making of the Mamison Road. Here we found quarters among billiard-tables, gilt mirrors, and decayed sofas. The deserted orchard-close at the back of the house would have delighted a pre-Raphaelite painter.

At Alagir a road, in the European sense of the word—a metalled track—begins. It immediately enters a limestone defile. Every northern stream of the Central Caucasus has a similar gate to pass before it reaches the plain. Here the crags are fringed with ferns, and clothed in hanging woods of elm, lime, maple, oak and alder. This is part of the forest-belt which covers the outskirts

---

[1] The Meteorological Records show that the vapours of the Black Sea, intercepted farther west by the unbroken rampart of the Caucasus, take advantage of the trench of the Ardon to reach the northern steppe. The rainfall at Alagir exceeds that at Piatigorsk, although, as a rule, the figures grow less from west to east in the isthmus.

of the Northern Caucasus, lying along the outward slopes of the
limestone range that turns its precipices to the snows. It was
one of the main defensive resources of the tribes in their struggle
against Russia.   Beyond it lie the first of the 'longitudinal
trenches,' the bare basins between the limestone and the crystalline schists. Presently the valley widens, and the traveller sees
on either hand smooth green buttresses, dotted by grey human
nests and broken by tawny spurs. The landscape is dull and
ineffective, and a gleam of snow here and there fails to vivify
it. The eyes are gladdened when, at the point where the
stream from the silver mines of Sadòn and the path to the
Urukh over the Kamunta Pass join the Ardon, the granite
mountains close in on the river. Above the hamlet of Nukhal a
low precipice, overhanging the entrance to the gorge, is pitted
with fortified caves. These were the main defence of the Ossete
population of the upper valley of the Ardon in former days.
The country-side is full of memorials of 'old, unhappy,' but
not as yet 'far-off things.'   A Russian bayonet may often be
seen serving as a spike to the native hunter's staff.

The ascent is steady to a meadow, in which stands the Cossack
post of St. Nikolai (3950 feet), sheltered by walnuts and pine-
woods at the entrance both of the Zea Valley and of the Kassara
gorge. Here we found a substantial cottage, containing one or two
rooms furnished with tables and sofas, the last tolerable sleeping-
quarters on this side of the pass.

The mountain sides slope up with extraordinary abruptness,
and on all sides the highest crags are snowy. St. Nikolai lies in
one of the great clefts which rend from top to bottom the central
ridge of the Caucasus. Within three miles east and west the cliffs
tower 8000 to 8500 feet above the Ardon. The average slope of
the hillsides, therefore, is about 1 in 3 : an angle of at least 30°.
Compared to the Darial, the scenery of the Kassara gorge is less
savage, but more romantic. Broken tiers of granite, or porphyritic
buttresses, spring up into the air in noble curves. White peaks
shine between them ; glaciers send down waterfalls among their
hollows. The river tumbles in a succession of cascades and rapids ;

the road runs close to it. The Kassara is an open defile, not a water-cut cleft like the Via Mala. The rocks are fringed with fir-forests, which recall the giants of Corsica rather than the meagre stems of the Alps. So romantic a portal raises high expectations. But as above the ravine of the Averser Rhein, which shares on a smaller scale some of the characteristics of the Kassara, the road emerges into an upland basin, destitute of forest, where wide pastures rise in uniform slopes, over which the higher summits appear only at intervals. The valley of the Nardon, the eastern source of the Ardon, up which runs the path to Kobi—trodden by my party in 1868—and that to the Georgian valleys, falls in on the left. The highroad turns westward, and mounts steadily to the village of Teeb, the chief place of the upper valley.

The scenery on the ascent to the Mamison Pass is as dull as that of any Graubünden carriage-pass, except when the heights of the Tepli Group are thrown up against the early morning light. The road, terraced along the northern side of the valley, rises steadily but not steeply. Near a ruinous Refuge we met some bullock-carts drawing stones. A four-horse tarantass was so far beyond the experience of the animals that the leading pair dashed violently down the hillside. After a few yards the cart and cattle turned a wild somersault, and were brought up in a confused mass against a great boulder. To our amazement, the bullocks shook themselves free of their broken harness, and rose to their legs apparently little the worse for the adventure. Had the drivers been Italian peasants, they would have owed a votive tablet to the nearest shrine. On the walls at Crissolo, in the Po valley, I remember a very vivid representation of a similar catastrophe.[1]

Soon after this enlivening incident we crossed the infant Ardon, less than a mile from its parent glaciers, two small ice-fields enclosed in a rocky cirque, and then by one long zigzag mounted

---

[1] Since there are next to no roads in the Central Caucasus, there are naturally few vehicles. The cart of the country is a rude, large basket placed on runners, which form a sledge in winter. In summer a low pair of wheels are attached under the forepart of the runners. They travel about two miles an hour, and creak horribly.

the final slope to the Pass. A few yards before reaching it the road traverses a spring avalanche track, where, for want of a short gallery, it is apt to be blocked for several weeks after the snows have left it elsewhere free.

The ridge of the Caucasus is here a smooth flowery bank, the direction of which is north and south, or nearly at right angles to the general direction of the chain. The height of the pass is 9282 feet, or about 200 feet higher than the Stelvio. In the immediate foreground a slender rock-pyramid dominates the small glacier which feeds the eastern source of the Rion. To the left the eye rests upon a maze of green hills, ringed by the dark pikes of Shoda and its neighbours. Far away to the west the mountains of Suanetia, the giants of the Central Group, raise their pale crests through the golden haze. The distant prospect is much extended by following the gently rising crest southwards for a few hundred yards.

The first zigzags lead down into a narrow glen; where this opens on the lower valley the woods begin, not to cease again before Kutais is reached. Beside the torrent, and perhaps half a mile from its glacial source, is a substantial building, which was constructed for the use of the engineers of the road. I understood on seeing it what one of them had meant when he informed me that he had lived for four months 'on a glacier'! It had been allowed—à la Russe—to fall to ruin, and we found in 1889 bare boards and broken roofs. In 1895 the house had been restored, or a new one built. It will be of no small service to travellers, who should use it as headquarters while they explore the neighbourhood. From all the high green ridges or pastures, from all the glades where the creamy rhododendrons blossom between stately pines, delightful prospects of rock, snow and forest are enjoyed. Perhaps the most varied views are those gained in a stroll over the hill west of the Hospice, a spur of which is called Zitelta (9254 feet) on the new map. Above the last birches —the Caucasian birch grows to stately proportions and far out-climbs the pines—the grass is enamelled in July with mountain flowers. Snowdrops and crocuses pierce the still brown turf in the hollows, from which the snow has but just disappeared. Gentians—new species, most of them, to the Alpine climber—forget-me-nots, cowslips, and pink daisies adorn the brows. To the north rise the peaks of the central chain : the tower of Burdjula ; then the long wall, behind which lies the Karagom Glacier ; close at hand a broad double-peak and a rock-pyramid—not unlike a steeper Piz Zupo and Piz Bernina. At our feet spread the pastures and beech-forests of the Rion. Through the trench by which the river escapes from its mountain prison there is a glimpse of the sunny hills beyond Oni, shimmering in vaporous sunshine. Troops of horses and a few heifers are pasturing on the hills, but otherwise there is no sign of life or habitation. The humble huts of Glola and Gurshevi lie buried in the woods. No brown cluster of chalets marks the summer lodgings of herdsmen ; no tinkle of bells announces the whereabouts of the herds. Yet the landscape is too brilliant to be melancholy. There is no waste visible : fertility begins where the snows cease. Fed by their bounty the streams pour forth from the hills, the flowers and forests spread themselves out in glowing luxuriance. Nature is solitary, but self-sufficing. The keynote of the landscape is struck in the lines of the opening chorus of *Faust* :—

> ' Alle Deine hohen Werke
> Sind herrlich wie am ersten Tag.'

As I have said already, there are those who pretend that frequent traces of Man's presence are essential to the enjoyment of scenery— that Nature unadorned cannot satisfy souls in search of the Beautiful. These critics range from the most eminent mountaineers down to the frequenters of tea-gardens. No doubt there is a truth in their contention. The incidents man adds to scenery are often very essential. There are many landscapes which owe their beauty in great part to such incidents, which would lose their effect and sense of size without them. Lake and river scenery—Como and the Rhine— depend to a great extent on human habitations. But there is also scenery which is sufficient in itself, and the sentiment of which—the appeal it makes to the mind—is not only independent

of any artificial decoration, but depends on the absence of human
adjuncts. An analogy may, perhaps, be found in poetry : some of
the noblest poetry represents the feelings produced by the direct
reflection of Nature on man's consciousness, without reference to
human interests or passions.

On our return from these untrodden pastures to the highroad
we found a second series of zigzags to lead us down from the
bare upland glen of the Hospice to the woods. For several
miles the road accompanies the torrent down a deep valley. Snow-
peaks flash between tall pines, beeches and alders, which frame
between their branches frequent vistas of side-glens. The ruined
towers and brown cottages of Glola are passed on the opposite
bank. Presently a stronger torrent, flowing from the opposite
direction, meets ours. This is the Rion, the ancient Phasis, coming
down from its source, some twelve miles to the west among the
snows, still known as the Pasis Mta.[1] The united streams turn
at right angles to their previous courses, and the road follows them
through the narrow trench that here divides the slate range.

As the elbows of the mountains retire, and the woods leave
place for open and cultivated fields, where maize and vine
mark the approach to a milder region, we come to a road-side
dukhan, or drinking-shed, and a few cottages. This is Utsora
(3500 feet), one of the ' Baths ' of the Caucasus. Here in early
summer come families from the lowlands, to drink the iron springs
and shake off their fevers. Dr. Radde was informed that there
have been as many as six hundred to one thousand visitors in a
summer. I suppose I was too late to see the fashion of Utsora.
There are only a few sheds for its accommodation. The bathers
lodge, as our ancestors did on Tunbridge Wells Common, in
temporary booths or under canvas, bringing with them often their
own provisions and poultry.

Through fields of barley and maize, and under a burning sun, we
approach Oni, the only assemblage of buildings having any pretence

---

[1] This name was applied by Dubois de Montpereux to the high peaks of the Central Group,
which he saw from the lowlands only. Hence Pasis Mta has been treated as the name of a
great mountain. It is really the designation of a pass.

THE MAMISON PASS AND GEBI

to the title of a town in this region. It is the capital and centre
of the Racha, or middle valley of the Rion. This is a broad and
spacious basin, which lies geologically between the slate range and
the outer limestone belt, through which the Rion has carved a series
of comparatively shallow gorges. The condition of the country up
to the middle of this century was that of Europe in the Middle
Ages. Feudal princes ruled a population of serfs, bandits haunted
the roads, every man went armed, and every nobleman was accoutred
in the gayest colours and resplendent with the precious metals.
Even in 1868 a gentleman did not ride into Kutais without sword,
dagger and pistol at his waist and a gun over his shoulder. He
wore a tall Circassian sheepskin hat, or wound round his head a
bashlik twisted into a turban, with the tails flapping over his
shoulders in a fashion made familiar to us in old Flemish pictures
and stained-glass windows.

Oni itself is a farmers' and a peasants' town without dignity
or picturesqueness. The ordinary houses are two-storied wooden
shanties with balconies ; Swiss cottages devoid of style or ornament.
The low, white-washed Russian bungalows have nothing to recom-
mend them to the seeker for the picturesque. The inns are no better
than drinking-shops, where you can spread a mattress on bare boards.

We spent a tepid August night on an open balcony. The
gaiety of the inhabitants and the quarrels of their dogs gave little
chance of sleep, and we were astir hours before the old Jew who
was to find us horses for the ride to Kutais had brought together
our cavalcade. That Jew still haunts my memory. Tall and
spare, with wild hanging locks, gestures of the most primitive and
tragic force, and an expression in which avarice and contempt
and longsuffering in turn predominated, he strode in front of us,
for the best part of a long summer's day, the 'Wandering Jew'
in the flesh.

The Jews of the Caucasus—Mountain Jews, the Russians call
them—are a race apart.[1] They are found in small communities

---

[1] See in Hahn's *Aus dem Kaukasus* a most interesting sketch of this race, based on the
Russian work of M. Anisimoff, himself a member of it. In the whole Caucasus there are
reckoned to be 38,000 Mountain Jews.

or separate villages; their customs and beliefs—described at length by Professor Hahn—are peculiar and primitive. They are possibly a remnant of the Jews of the Captivity, banished more than two thousand years ago by the Babylonian monarch, as Russian Non-conformists are banished to-day, to a frontier-land. There are many of them in Daghestan; they have occupied the lowest hamlet in Suanetia from time immemorial; a small colony is found at Urusbieh.

Beyond Oni true mountain-scenery is left behind. The hills are lofty, their slopes are well wooded, the timber and under-growth indicate the approach to a more temperate climate. Wal-nuts surround the villages; lime-trees spread a broad shade; poplars grow beside the water. The road when I last passed was unfinished. A more motley crowd than the labourers—it scarcely seems the right word for the peasants who were lounging in a leisurely way with inefficient implements over their work, or chatting noisily over the most frugal meals—would be hard to find. Persians in skull-caps were mixed with every variety of needy peasant from the valleys that send their streams to the east end of the Black Sea.

A long morning's ride brought us to the point where the ridges that form the outer zone of the Caucasus close in on the river, and serve as a picturesque gate to the Racha. Here, not far from a large church of the last century, the old direct horse-track leaves the new road and the valley of the Rion to cross the limestone ridge of the Nakarala by a pass of 4000 feet. The slopes on the ascent to Nikorzminda, celebrated for an eleventh-century church that rivals that of Gelati, are bare, and the land-scape is unattractive. It is, however, a region of natural curio-sities. There is an ice-cave similar to those found in the Jura, whence Kutais is supplied in summer. The river, after the fashion of streams in limestone districts, disappears for miles underground. Presently, after passing a deep blue pool reputed to be bottomless and inhabited by fabulous trout, we entered a most romantic wood. The broad limestone upland is clothed with great pines and beeches, box-trees and alder, evergreen-oaks and wild fruit-

trees. Creepers hang from the branches; underneath spreads a
tangle of rhododendron and laurels. As we rode through it in
the late hours of a perfect summer evening it seemed an enchanted
land, a fitting home for high romance. Now and again between
the tree-tops one of the distant Adai Khokh peaks flashed a red
signal from the skies; then as the light faded we came out on
the crest, and looked far westward over solemn, vaporous folds
of blue and purple hills, into the heart of the fiery after-glow.

A FARM NEAR KUTAIS

It was strange next morning, on waking at the foot of the hill
in a shanty dignified by the name of the 'Gostinitza London,' to
find oneself confronted with rails. The coal-mines of Khibuli have
brought a light line to the base of the forest ridge.

The Nakarala range is the last effort of the mountains. The
rest of the ride to Gelati and Kutais lies over low foot-hills.
On the spurs, fringed with oak and chestnut copses, the landscape, spacious and sunny, is illuminated by distant glimpses of

the Suanetian snows, the horn of Tetnuld or the white walls of Shkara and Janga. The valleys are featureless and tame. In the neighbourhood of Kutais they are enlivened by hamlets and the farms of the old Mingrelian gentry, low one-storied dwellings, embowered in vines, figs, peaches, and pomegranates. Great oxen, goaded by peasants in long grey frock-coats, drag enormous earthen wine-jars across the azalea commons. Groups of tall men and comely women, sharing their meals under the shelter of the pine and plane, or of orchard trees, recall Horatian measures. Mingrelia has fairy tales ; it has perhaps poetry. But it required the contrast and stimulus of a great capital, the

'Fumum et opes, strepitumque Romæ,'

to create those admirable pictures of country life and country pleasures, which Eton stamps into the memory even of her dullest pupils.

What will the travellers of to-morrow care for these things ? They will take the train. And how long will it be before the nymph of the Nakarala has to lament the fall of her forests ? how long before her tallest pines are converted into sleepers, and her box-trunks cut up into blocks, to suit the purposes of civilisation ? The best one can wish for them is that they may serve to commemorate the glories of their native heights, to carry back the memories of a few, and to stir the imaginations of many, with shadowy outlines of noble scenery. But there is yet hope. Railway construction advances but slowly in Russia, and wood-engraving is on the decline.

Thinking of days and companions past and present, I rode slowly down from the shrine of Gelati. Those white points on the horizon, nameless twenty years ago, were now as familiar and friendly to me as the Pennine peaks. Shkara and Tetnuld have taken their place among the glories of the world that men love and go on pilgrimages to visit. It was with a sad heart and lingering eyes that I waved them what I then thought would be a last farewell. But on the opposite bank of the Phasis rose, close at hand, the acropolis of Kutais, 'the ancient city of Æa' of Apollonius Rhodius—and we hoped to catch the evening train to Batum.

I have described without digression the road of the Mamison as far as Kutais. But before leaving the mountains to follow the Rion to the verge of the lowlands, travellers of any enterprise will arrange to pay a visit to the true source of the river, and to the former centre of Caucasian wayfarers, destined perhaps to become a future centre for mountaineers, the village of Gebi, which lies only two hours' ride from the highroad.

The courage shown by a mountain population in facing difficult passes, and in particular glacier passes, depends to a great extent upon their necessities. Peasants travel for business ; when a good and safe track exists they will go a long way round to find it. The opening of the Simplon for wheels closed to commerce the Gries and the Monte Moro. Yet there are limits to the circuits of mountain people. Where the snowy barrier is extensive, as in the Pennine Alps, the natives of the adjacent valleys will commonly traverse glaciers which would be looked on with horror by the dwellers under a less continuously lofty chain, such as the Tyrolese Tauern. In the Caucasus the natural barrier is an unbroken rampart of snow and ice, not—as between the Great St. Bernard and the Simplon—fifty, but a hundred miles in length. Moreover, until quite recent times, other dangers had to be taken into account by travellers. The easiest pass might lead to a hostile village or under the towers of some predatory noble. Hence glacier-travel has been developed among the Caucasians to a point beyond that it had ever reached in the Alps, even in the Middle Ages. They drive their flocks and horses, they bring their cattle to market, over passes comparable to the St. Théodule and the Col d'Hérens. They will cross the ice for a seven or eight hours' journey in order to procure salt, or even to enjoy a few days' feasting on southern fruit, and to make such small gain as the basket they can carry home on their shoulders may bring. They have, if legends are true, even chosen a glacier, the Tuiber, about the size of the Aar, for a battlefield.

Besides the Mamison, there are no less than four passes which four-footed beasts can be forced over from Gebi to the northern side. Of these, two lead to the Urukh, and two to the Cherek and Karaul.

In old times another track of much importance led through Gebi. One of the easiest approaches, and the direct road from Georgia, to the wilds of Suanetia, lay across the grassy ridges that divide the sources of the Rion, the Skenis Skali, and the Ingur. The old tracks have now been overgrown by forest, and the towers that guarded them, or perhaps served for fire-signals, are in ruins. But if all roads no longer lead to Gebi, there is still plenty of life and traffic in the old place, and the inhabitants have not lost their traditional position as the pedlars of the Caucasus. If I wanted a story to be spread—with variations—throughout the Caucasus, I should tell it to the Club that meets, on most days of the week and at most hours of the day, on the village green.

The part played in similar institutions near Pall Mall by newspapers and tape-messages is taken at Gebi by the constant and various new arrivals. Now a tall, blue-eyed, tawny-bearded Mingrelian noble rides in with his servants from the Racha, his long *bashlik* (a Phrygian hood) hanging loose over his shoulders, and his sword, dagger and pistols clattering on his belt. Now a party of Karatshai Tartars, or Mountain Turks, in black sheepskin bonnets and cloaks —the *bourkas* of the Caucasus—arrive over the passes of the main chain, bringing their herds and horses from the pastures of Balkar or Chegem, or the more distant downs under Elbruz. Here a ragged company of Mingrelian peasants, armed with scythes for the hay-cutting, are bargaining for the provisions that will sustain them on their tramp to the meadows of the northern side. For in the Caucasus, as in the Alps, it is the southern peasant who meets any demand for extra labour.

At a little distance the maidens of the place, adorned with necklaces of sea-shells, pieces of amber and many-patterned beads, clad in bright red robes and crowned with turbans, made up of a parti-coloured cotton handkerchief fastened on the top of a long white cloth that falls down the back, gossip round the fountain, or, ranged in a circle, pass the time in songs and dances. Smaller children, more or less naked, play with sticks and rags, or carry home on wooden platters portions of the ox that has just been slaughtered in the churchyard, pursued by large, wolf-like dogs, dis-

posed to claim prematurely their share in the harvest-feast.   Many
of them stop to cheer—or jeer—an individual confined in an enclosure
close at hand.   The villagers will explain that he has been 'drunk
and disorderly,' and in consequence had to be punished.   It is our
old English plan, with a Pound substituted for the Stocks.

Between my two visits in 1868 and 1887 Gebi had made considerable progress, but the manner of receiving strangers remained
the same.   The traveller dismounts under the balcony of the wooden
court-house.   A peasant,
distinguished   from   his
fellows by wearing round
his neck a chain of office,
comes   forward   from   the
crowd.   He   introduces
himself as the Starshina,
or   mayor.   These   func-
tionaries   are   elected   by
popular suffrage, with the
approval   of   the   Government, and are responsible
to   the   Nachalnik,   or
Priestav,   the   Russian
district-officer,   for   public
order.   Keys are brought,
doors   unlocked,   and   the
traveller's luggage stacked
in   a   corner   of   a   bare
boarded   room,   furnished
only   with   a   fireplace,   or
rather   hearth.   Opening
out   of   it   is   a   smaller
room.   On my last visit,

PEASANTS AT GEBI

one of the oldest and dirtiest inhabitants established himself on a
still dirtier sheepskin in one of its corners, and announced his
intention of remaining as guardian of the village archives, which
he asserted were stored in an old box.   In a Suanetian village

we once found the archives to consist of letters from the Russian Priestav to the Starshina, of which, as the latter was ignorant of any language but a Georgian *patois*, not a word had been read. The Master of the Rolls at Gebi was somewhat obstinate, and had finally to be ejected by the door, while his sheepskin went through the window. Much impressed by this summary eviction, he soon came back to offer to serve as our caterer.

The new church, though a poor enough specimen of modern Georgian architecture, gives an air of civilisation to the village. A

NEW CHURCH AT GEBI

priest has been appointed, who talks Russian, and addressed me constantly as 'Professor.' An influential native desired me to visit a sparkling iron spring close by, said not to be inferior to the famous Narzan or Giant's Spring at Kislovodsk, and suggested that I should start a bathing establishment. Here was gratifying evidence of the march of ideas. Let the proprietors of Apollinaris beware. Materially, too, we were excellently provided. In place of the interminable bargaining required of old to get a dozen eggs, and the necessity of paying the owner of each hencoop separately in exactly the right number of kopeks, we were able to procure beef and fowls, potatoes and vegetables, flour, sugar and capital wine, at fair prices. Horses were at our disposal when wanted, and I believe we might even have secured porters with less than two days' discussion. Yet there was one luxury, as of old unobtainable, one point on which the manners of the men of Gebi were still the same. This population of pedlars have no mean idea of their own merits or of the value of their opinions : their time and other people's they value less. They are, in their own estimation at least, the Athenians of the Caucasus, and there is no new thing

which they do not make it a duty to investigate and discuss
exhaustively; other duties they—the males, at least—appear to
have none.   Hardly has the traveller arrived than his first efforts
to make himself comfortable are watched by an audience of at
least a hundred, of whom as many as possible squeeze into the
little room, while the rest jostle in the balcony, or gather on any
neighbouring roof or wall from which a glimpse of the performance may be obtained.   Except perhaps at our Law Courts on a

SILVER EIKONS AT GEBI

sensational trial, I have never seen such emulation for a good place.
The first scene, the unlacing of boots, will be favourably received.
Since no Caucasian ever wears anything but leathern sandals stuffed
with dry grass, it has the merit of entire novelty.   Moreover, the
counting of the nails in the soles affords a problem that engages
and baffles the highest mathematical intellects of the new
village school.   The use of a sponge or a pocket-handkerchief
is a certain success, and seldom fails to draw a roar of appreciation from the gallery.   When the spirits are lighted under a

self-cooking soup-tin, there is a subdued murmur of amazement at
the evident miracle. To empty the house on a night when such
attractions are offered is no light matter. Even dumping the
toes of the front row with ice-axes is not always effective. When
at last the floor has been cleared, eager eyes still gaze through
the window till that too is shuttered up; then they betake themselves to the chinks between the boarded walls. On my last visit,
however, my popularity as a show, I was glad to find, did wear
off somewhat on the second day. I was able to stroll about the
village at leisure, to have some talk with the priest, and to witness
the interesting ceremony of blessing the first-fruits of the harvest.
Sheaves of corn, baskets of apples and other vegetables, were brought
into the church and laid on tables. An ox was slaughtered at the
church door, and the joints distributed among certain of the

villagers—a pagan cere-
mony, for which the priest
apologised. Here, as we
shall find again in Suanetia,
when religion died out,
the old church pictures,
Eikons, plated with silver
and studded with coarse
turquoises and other
stones, were guarded with
superstitious reverence.
Some of those still pre-
served at Gebi are figured
in Signor Sella's photo-
graphs.

The inhabitants occupy
the first place in one's
memory, but the situation
of Gebi has great pictur-

ANCIENT CHURCH PICTURES AT GEBI

esque attractions. The village stands 4400 feet above the sea,
where a green knoll projects and bars the valley, below defaced
by torrents, above smiling with corn-fields. It is surrounded

by forested slopes, golden and fragrant through the early summer
with sheets of azalea blossom, by pastures fringed with delicate
birches and low thickets of the creamy Caucasian rhododendron.
Snow-crests look down from all sides over the shoulders of the
lower hills. There are few signs of prosperity in the dark, stone-
built, windowless cottages, crowded closely together about a group
of ruinous towers. But of the peace that the Russian Government
has given to the country in the last half century we may note
a trace in the extension of the use of timber in external architecture. So long as hostile flames were to be feared, as at Ushkul
till twenty years ago, all was of stone. Now the gloom of Gebi
is broken by many brown wooden balconies and barns, similar to
those found south of the Alps.

There are many yet undiscovered and uncatalogued 'excursions' from the village within the reach of anybody who can
walk, or ride uphill on a native saddle. The beautiful pastures
on the way to the Gurdzivsek offer themselves for a morning's
ramble. For a panorama of the great chain the snowy dome of
Shoda (11,860 feet), conspicuous in the range south of the village,
can have no rival. Moore in 1868 had been most anxious to
climb it. Weather then was adverse; and it was not till nineteen years later that it was trodden by Dévouassoud and myself.
It has since been visited and the view photographed by Signor
Sella.

A path crosses the Rion, and then traverses open corn-land
and the scattered rivulets of the water that descends from the
small glacier that hangs high on the brow of Shoda. Leaving
to the right the glen from which this stream emerges, Dévouassoud and I climbed a zigzag path through a great beech-forest.
Some 2000 feet above the valley we turned a corner, and entered
another glen to the north-east of our peak. From this point
there is a noble view of the snows of the main chain, while
Burdjula rises as a bold tower immediately opposite. Farther
east the clustered summits of Adai Khokh come into sight.
Here for the first time I saw and recognised behind the two
peaks of the Rion Valley a double - fanged crest and a more

distant comb of ice.   The last held the sunset longest, and subsequent explorers have proved it to be the Adai Khokh of the five-verst triangulation.

The near scenery carried my memory to the Dolomites : here too were craggy peaks, beech-forests broken by flowery glades, steep slopes dotted by hay-cocks : but for the dark colouring of the rocks we might have been in one of the side glens of Val Rendena. We took up our quarters in a deserted shepherd's shelter, a tent-shaped hut of boards, well lined with hay.

At daybreak grey mists were driving about the higher peaks. Still the weather did not look by any means hopeless.   The chief fatigue in the ascent was a tiresome gully—tiresome only because

A FRONT DOOR AT GEBI

it was filled with loose, small fragments of slate, which sank under the feet like shingle on a sea - beach.   Above this a rocky buttress, where Signor Sella found many crystals of great size, gave easy access to the snow.   On our right the *névé* ended in broken cliffs, fragments of which formed a small *glacier remanié* at the bottom of a dark precipice far below us.   On our left the mountain sloped in an enormous mass of absolutely smooth slate, pitched at a very high angle. At this point the clouds covered us, and all distant view was lost.   Twenty minutes' tramp up snow-banks brought us to the long level ridge that forms the summit.   Sheltered on the southern side from the cold wind by the rocks, we waited long but vainly in the grey fog.   The skirts of the veil were from time to time lifted just enough to show us the basin of Oni and the rough bare slopes that lead down to the forests of the Racha. But not a glimpse of the great chain, of the immense prospect, extending from Kasbek to Ushba, which Signor Sella has added to his panoramas, was granted to me. It was a mischievous freak of the weather-clerk, for by sunset the sky was again cloudless, and the two following days were superb.

At last we gave up hope. We varied our track, making straight for some white rhododendrons near a snow-bed at the head of the glen where our camp was. Our Gebi porter had made ready for us afternoon-tea, and then, watching with mingled feelings the mists melt away one by one from the bright crests of the great chain, we sauntered home together in the beautiful evening light. Gebi had become quite a home to me.

CHAPTER VI

THE ADAI KHOKH GROUP

Illa sub horrendis praedura cubilia silvis,
Illi sub nivibus somni, curaeque, laborque
Pervigil.

CLAUDIAN.

THE traveller who crosses the Mamison Pass has frequently in sight the broad glaciers and closely clustered summits of a mountain group which rises steeply above the sources of the Rion. This block of mountains and glaciers is situated on the main chain, near the spot where it ceases to be the watershed, and about half-way between Kasbek and the Central Group—that is, some forty miles from either. The upper valleys that almost enclose it run roughly parallel to the main ridge of the Caucasus. The Rion and Ardon valleys are best represented by two T's, the Urukh by a Y. In the Kassara gorge the Ardon makes a clean break through the granitic axis. Its main sources are derived from the southern range of slates, to which the watershed has been transferred. So gradual is the slope of its bed that, as I pointed out in the last chapter, in an ascent of 7000 feet from the town of Alagir to the top of the Mamison, there is only one zigzag on the road.

The scenery of this portion of the range is very varied. The open basin of the Rion, filled by low, broad, green spurs, has many of the charms of Suanetia, though all on a smaller scale. Glorious forests, in which lofty, smooth-stemmed beeches mingle with the dark cones of gigantic pines—pines that are to those of the Alps what Salisbury spire is to a village steeple—clothe the river banks. Rolling downs, fringed with birch-groves and carpeted with flowers, spread along the base of the frosty chain, itself a succession of bold buttresses, snow-peaks, and tumbling bays of ice. But there is no Ushba behind Gebi, and the southern summits of Adai Khokh are 2000 feet lower than the giants that overhang the sources of the Ingur.

On the north side the upper valley of the Urukh, parallel to the main chain, is picturesque in comparison with the stern troughs up which the mists course before they gather round the feet of Dykhtau and Koshtantau. The scenery of the Zea valley is unique in the northern Caucasus in its rich variety of foliage and romantic wildness. The great glaciers, the Karagom and Zea, end under bristling rock-peaks and among luxuriant forests. The upper snowfields of the Karagom produce an overwhelming impression of vastness and purity, different from, but not inferior to, the effect of the stupendous and apparently perpendicular mountain-walls that confine within narrower limits the sources of the Bezingi Glacier. The Adai Khokh group has been called the Monte Rosa of the Caucasus, and in some details the comparison may hold good, but I should prefer to compare it to the Bernese Oberland—an Oberland with the points of the compass reversed and its Aletsch Glacier, a little below the 'Place de la Concorde,' plunging suddenly in an ice-fall as high as that of the Ober Grindelwald Glacier towards the fields and forests.

It would be easy, at this point, to encumber several pages with a laboriously compiled statement of orographical facts, to point out the exact position of the chief ridges and their relations to the great snowfields. But all this information can be better procured by those who care for it from the map, where it is, in my judgment, in its proper place. To decompose a map is a short way of making an article appear solid, much favoured by a class of Continental writers who pretend to be scientific, and generally succeed in becoming unreadable. I shall be content to summarise only some of the chief indications of the new survey. In this group it shows one peak over 15,000, nine over 14,000 feet. The lowest pass over the main chain falls just under 11,000 feet. About sixty-five square miles are covered with snow and ice. The Karagom Glacier is ten miles, the Zea Glacier six, and the Songuta Glacier three and a half miles in length.

In 1868, when the three young Englishmen whose travels are recorded in my *Central Caucasus* undertook to examine *ambulando* the nature of the chain between Kasbek and Elbruz, the second object of their journey was the exploration of this Adai Khokh Group. We had no trustworthy map to guide us at that date. Our information was limited to the notes, mainly archæological, of Brosset, to a very confused notice in Klaproth of the snow-passes between Stir-Digor and Gebi,[1] and to the vague indications and blue smears of the five-verst map. The excursions of Dr. Abich and Dr. Radde had been limited to the lower ends of the two great frozen streams which, issuing from far invisible and unknown fountains in the recesses of the range, stretch their icy tongues down into the forest region. One of these, the Zea Glacier, flows into a glen some ten miles long that opens on the Ardon valley at St. Nikolai. Beyond the paths of men or the tracks of hunters all was obscure.

Our intention in 1868 was to have gone up the Zea valley, and crossed from its head to the Mamison. But the difficulties we experienced with the inhabitants in traversing the deep and isolated basins that hold the sources of the Nardon made us give up a project which involved separation from our baggage. Consequently we carried out but half our plan, and were content, in the first instance, to cross the Mamison to the southern side. We found ourselves at Chiora in the Rion valley, at the foot of a native glacier pass, leading to the north side of the chain.

---

[1] The best explanation that has been given of Klaproth's very curious description of the passage with horses of the Gebi Passes—the Gurdzivsek, and Gebivsek or Gezevsek (new map)—is that he took down hearsay information and turned it into a narrative in the first person.

It seemed, according to the map, to descend by a side glen on to the great glacier referred to by Abich. At that time passes were still as much in vogue with climbers as peaks. We saw pleasing prospects of adventure and discovery in crossing the native pass, and finding a way for ourselves back over the unknown snowfields farther east. Our interpreter and luggage were abandoned, and we started in the lightest marching order.

Leaving Chiora before daybreak, we wandered over pastures where the birches waved their delicate branches in the first breath of dawn, while the moonlight still shone on the upper snows. Shepherds' fires shone at intervals through the dusk, and the native who was carrying our provisions up to the snow led us a long circuit in order to visit some of his friends who were camping out with their flocks. In the Caucasus the peasants take far less pains than in the Alps to make themselves at home in their summer quarters. They have more sheep and horses, and far fewer dairies. It is only rarely, and on the north side, that huts answering to an Alpine chalet are found. In general, the herdsmen are contented with a slight shelter; an overhanging crag, a hollow under an erratic boulder, or a few boughs with a sheepskin thrown over them. Close at hand a forked stick is thrust in the ground, on which the owner, when at home, hangs his gun. Two more sticks and a crossbar support a pail. This is a Caucasian Kosh, a place where men sleep or rest, the *gias* or *gîte* of the Western Alps. That in so moist and variable a climate as that of the Central Caucasus the shepherds should not suffer more from exposure says much for the general healthiness of the highlands. Not long ago, similar natural shelters were used by Bergamasque shepherds in the Engadine. There are two, close to the Club-huts of Boval and the Roseg Glacier, where names or initials and ancient dates are carved on the rocks.

Up and down, or along ridges, our track led us, till it descended into a beautiful meadow, surrounded by trees, where a bright spring bubbled up amongst flowery grass under a clump of alders. This spot, called on the one-verst map Notsanzara, served as a camping-ground for the English mountaineers who explored the snows in 1890. It lies not far from the foot of the steep zigzags that lead up on the side of the glacier that flows out of the basin west of Burdjula.

Flocks of sheep, led by men in sheepskin hats and long grey coats, and escorted by savage dogs, were hurrying down from the pass. After entering on the glacier, we missed, or rather abandoned, the tracks of the shepherds, which turned sharply to the left.

THE KARACOM GLACIER

Walking straight up to a gap at the head of the *névé*, we crawled equally straight down a snow-wall, which seemed to me at the time of appalling steepness. Photographs have since confirmed my first impression. But the snow was in such perfect condition that the descent proved neither dangerous nor difficult. From the top we had the amusement of watching a second flock of sheep leap the *Bergschrund* on the true pass, which lay at some distance on our left.

A level glacier and a rocky glen received us on the north side.

The glen soon opened on the great ice-stream we had come to encounter. The first view of it, admirably reproduced in Signor Sella's photograph, was exciting, but hardly encouraging. The ice - falls of the Karagom equal in beauty, in breadth and in altitude any that I know : not so steep or so formidable as the frozen cataract of the Adish Glacier, they are more singular in their surroundings, and the noble gateway in the mountains through which they pour adds to their scenic effect. We camped—if to

KARAGOM KHOKH

light a fire and spread a mackintosh can be called to camp—in the fir-wood above the moraine. Nineteen years later I revisited the spot, coming up from the valley of the Urukh on the north side. The native track crosses the broad ice-stream, and in the hollow under the moraine, on the right bank, a substantial log-hut offers unexpected shelter to travellers.

The position of our 1868 bivouac, with regard to the glacier, was similar to that of the Montenvers Inn with regard to the Mer de Glace. Looking northwards over the great frozen billows,

we could see, beyond the point where they plunged out of sight,
the fir-forests and corn-land of the Urukh. In the opposite
direction the great ice-fall closed the view, and gave no hint of
the mysterious region from which it flowed.

Next morning at daybreak we set out on our adventure.
For two hours a shepherd's track helped us as far as the highest
grass on the west bank of the ice. Here we were close to
the foot of the last and loftiest of the frozen cascades, and
the work of the day began. At first all went smoothly; we
found corridors between the great ice-blocks, and were able to
avoid the chasms that seamed the slope. But when these chasms
became more and more continuous and, running across the snowy
dells, forced us right or left into the intricate labyrinth and among
the crystal towers, our prospects of success began to look very
questionable. We had to encounter in an aggravated form all
the familiar difficulties and perils of an Alpine ice-fall. The aggra-
vation consisted chiefly in the constant repetition. No sooner had
one turret-staircase been hewn out in a crack of some imposing
barrier than another castle appeared behind it. The glacier was
something more than a mountain dragon : it was a very hydra.
But our motives for perseverance were strong. To retreat meant
a long tramp down to a distant village, where we should have
to trust to signs to get provisions, and to run the risk of being
arrested as suspicious characters, and sent down two days' journey
to some Cossack outpost on the northern steppe.

I renounce any attempt to depict the individual difficulties—
the 'bad places'—we encountered during the next few hours :

> ' The moving accident is not my trade,
> To freeze the blood I have no ready arts,'

to quote Wordsworth—and climbers suffering under no such dis-
ability have frequently depicted their feats and those of their guides
in similar emergencies, both with pen and pencil. One particular
snowbridge or causeway remains pre-eminent in my memory. It
was long and narrow and rotten, and it ended in nothing. The
leader had to lean across and cut a precarious foothold in the

opposite bank of ice, and then make a bold leap into his pigeon-holes. Dévouassoud leapt, and we followed. The rest was not quite so bad, but there was a great deal of it. We wearied of the exquisite beauty of the icicle-fringes and the blue ravines, of the fantastic forms of the sun-smitten towers and pinnacles. There was not a moment's pause in the battle; we halted neither for food nor rest. At last the clear ice turned to more opaque *névé*, the surface was less tormented, and we began to count on victory. But the final moat, at the point where the steepening of the slope caused the most severe tension, had still to be overcome. It held over us an upper lip which was not mastered at the first attempt.

It was half-past one, and we had been six hours in the fall, and nine hours from our bivouac, before we sat down on the level snows to consider our further course through the undiscovered country no human eye had ever before seen.

We were on a great snowfield, sloping gently towards us from the south; more steeply from the east. A low rocky mass divided the branches; to the right rose a conspicuous and welcome landmark, the crest of Burdjula. Behind us were wild rock-peaks, the Karagom Khokh of my map: the highest summit of Adai Khokh and its neighbours were no doubt seen to our left, but I did not identify them till long afterwards. We chose the southern bay, and again set out. The surface at this late hour of the day was soft, and it was not till after three hours of steady and heavy wading that the monotony of the white and blue world into which we had broken was suddenly relieved by the appearance, above the level snows that had hitherto formed our sky-line, of the purple line of the mountains on the Turkish frontier.

The view from the pass towards Asia was of surpassing beauty. The whole basin of ancient Kolkhis, Mingrelia and Imeretia, the Racha and Lechgum, lay at our feet. Flashes of reflected sun-shine showed where the waters of the Rion forced their way through a labyrinth of green ridges and dark forest-clad ravines to the pomegranate gardens of Kutais. Far away in the west we saw for the first time the snows of the Laila, the range that encloses Suanetia on the south. The mid-day vapours had disappeared early: it was a perfect late summer afternoon, and the rays of the sun, which was already sinking towards the west, transfigured parts of the landscape with a golden glory, heightened by contrast where the shadows thrown by the dark pikes of the range south of Gurshevi and the tower of Shoda fell across the lower slopes. One of the reasons that a want of picturesque effect is so generally complained of in high mountain views is that they are rarely seen early or late enough in the day. I have never been on a peak or pass more than four hours before or after mid-day without being astonished at the beauty of detail and colour, of light and shade, added to landscapes that, in the noonday glare, are apt to be impressive only by reason of their vastness. Thus, for example, the view from the Wetterhorn becomes superb when the great peaks of the Oberland fling their shadows towards the spectator who watches from that lonely pinnacle; the prospect over Suanetia from the Laila is exquisite when the first sunbeams touch its corn-fields and towered hamlets.

Over the details of the descent into the Rion Valley I need not linger. As first-comers generally do, we got into some needless difficulty, but before nightfall we had gained turf, and, conscious that Glola might be reached by breakfast-time next morning, lay down beneath the highest birches, with ice-axes driven in below us to prevent our rolling down the slope, as heedless as any Caucasian shepherd of the absence of supper or the showers that passed over us. We were conscious of having lived a day which would never fade from our memories.

In the expeditions just described we had gained a general idea—but only a general idea—of the character of the group. It was obvious that its chief feature was the gigantic *névé* of the Karagom Glacier; that this was ringed on the east by a semicircle of lofty peaks, while to the west Burdjula stood comparatively isolated. From the Rion basin we had seen two peaks, the Eiger-like summit overhanging the Mamison, and a double snow-crest; we had seen also two great rock-peaks beside the Karagom ice-fall: what lay on the connecting ridge had been partially masked from us as we traversed the snowfields by lower spurs.

Years passed without any further exploration of the Adai Khokh Glaciers. It was not until 1884 that a traveller undertook, with the help of the famous guide, Alexander Burgener, to climb the rocky pinnacle above the Mamison Pass, which had in 1868 attracted our particular admiration.

M. de Déchy, the traveller in question, is a Hungarian gentleman. From his Russian connections and his mastery of the language, he had exceptional advantages as an early explorer in the Caucasus. He had, moreover, obtained in the Alps the mountaineering qualification requisite for membership of the Alpine Club, together with such photographic experience as enabled him to produce technically excellent, as well as topographically interesting, illustrations of Caucasian landscapes and people. In this branch of Caucasian exploration he was the forerunner of Signor Vittorio Sella, Mr. Donkin, Mr. H. Woolley, and Mr. C. Dent, and it is to him that we owe the initiation of the admirable and now almost complete series of photographs of the Central Caucasus executed by members of the Alpine Club. These photographs assuredly deserve the praise given to some of Mr. Donkin's earlier Alpine work by Mr. Ruskin :—'Anything more beautiful than the photographs now in your printseller's windows cannot be conceived. For geographical or geological purposes they are worth anything.' The scientific value of such work must be appreciated by all who are genuinely interested in the exploration of mountains, however low it may stand in the estimation of certain foreign critics who seldom venture above the horse-level.

M. de Déchy chose the Zea Glacier as his mode of approach. He took photographs, explored the glacier, and climbed a peak at the head of it, which he at the time believed to be the pyramidal summit conspicuous from the Mamison Pass, which both he and I had erroneously identified with the Adai Khokh of the five-verst map, the highest triangulated point in the group. The weather was broken, and clouds interfered with the explorer's examination of the local orography; but on the third day from St. Nikolai

he gained the top of a double peak. Questions have been raised
in his own and others' minds as to which summit he ascended,
but after very careful consideration of all the evidence contained
in M. de Déchy's narrative and Mr. Woolley's photographs, I feel
very little doubt that he attained the peak he aimed at.

In *Petermann's Mitteilungen* (1889, Heft 9), M. de Déchy
published a map on a large scale of the Zea Glacier.   His carto-
grapher, with excellent intentions—for it is a hard thing to persuade
cartographers that a Government Survey may be worse than useless
—tried to extend it to the Karagom Glacier, using for the latter
the five-verst map.   Not unnaturally the result was most unsatisfactory.   There was obviously 'something wrong somewhere.'
We have now, I believe, found out where.

From officers of the Topographical Bureau at Tiflis—whose
invariable courtesy to foreigners and readiness to communicate all
scientific information relating to the Caucasus call for my warmest
acknowledgment—I obtained the points from which the triangulation of the Adai Khokh of the five-verst map—made in the
Fifties—was taken, and found that they were very distant points.
Obviously General Chodzko and his surveyors had triangulated
the highest peak of the group from afar, and on nearer approach
had wrongly identified the summits, and distorted their topography
in order to reconcile them.   The Adai Khokh Group resembles, as
I have pointed out, in several respects the Oberland ; the Karagom
corresponding roughly to the Aletsch Glacier.   What had happened
was equivalent to the Finsteraarhorn having been triangulated from
Bern, and the Schreckhorn or Eiger wrongly identified with it in
filling in the topography.   But the Finsteraarhorn of the Caucasus
still remained to be discovered.

It was not until 1887 that, as has been described in the last
chapter, when half-way up Shoda, the isolated peak south of Gebi, I
saw once more the Adai Khokh Group, and looked over our old pass
to the mountains that encircle the Karagom Glacier.   There, sure
enough, was the peak I wanted.   There were indeed two mountains ;
a rock-peak with two blunt heads, close behind the double snow-
peak of the Rion, and, farther back, a long comb of snow and ice on

which the sun's last rays rested longest. Clouds spoilt my panorama from the summit of Shoda, but this short glimpse had been enough to suggest a solution of the problem.

In 1889, before undertaking the search for traces of our friends lost in the previous year on Koshtantau, we gave our Swiss guides a training walk in the Adai Khokh Group. We forced the glacier pass I had planned in 1868, between the Zea Valley and the Mamison Pass. We left the half-ruined refuge on the south side of the Mamison at 2 A.M., and knocked up the Cossacks at St. Nikolai at 9 P.M. The ascent was by the glacier which gives birth to the Ardon. We had a very extensive view over Ossetia to the south, a region of isolated mountains and high grass-passes, where the main chain changes its character, as the Alps do beyond the Simplon. What we saw on the farther side was more limited and less agreeable. Four hours were spent in descending a very difficult rock-wall, only 400 feet high, on to the Zea snowfields. There was seldom foothold and handhold at the same time; and, as all the grooves and hollows were sheeted with ice, there was much of that interminable work known to climbers as step-cutting. We were a party of eight, on two ropes it is true, but still more than twice too many. Our Ober-landers were somewhat out of condition and heart; they had not yet taken the measure of life in the Caucasus. We on the last rope were hampered by the terror of sending down stones on those in front. Wherever it was possible to find a perch we halted till they were out of range, and I succeeded in utilising such leisure moments in making rough outlines and notes of the peaks and ridges that encompassed us. Opposite was the Mamison Peak, or Khamkhaki Khokh. From this side it loses its symmetry and exhibits a long rib of rock and ice, running down to sepa-rate the two basins of the Zea. The northern snowfield is by far the more extensive. Over this appeared the double peak of the Rion Valley, masking the summits beyond it. To its right,[1] hemming in the head of the invisible Songuta Glacier, rose a

---

[1] I doubt if there be any direct pass from the Zea *névé* to the Songuta Glacier.

splendid fence of splintered granite pinnacles, 14,000 feet high, a Gymnasium which may some day serve as a rival of the Chamonix Needles. The ridge on which we were fell to the east of us in most formidable precipices towards the Zea ice-falls : there are two, one from each snow-reservoir.

We had mastered the orography, and were beginning to get tired of marking time, when a happy thought struck Kaspar Maurer. He seized a stone and heaved it out a certain distance into the centre of the ice-gully we were skirting, where the surface was less glittering. There was enough snow, we judged from the result, to venture on a direct descent. Down this snow, as on a ladder, we crept backwards, moving one at a time, and driving in the staffs of our axes to the head at every step. The *Bergschrund*, or great moat below the wall, might have been impassable later in the season. As it was, we had each in turn to take a flying leap into the feather-bed of fortunately soft snow that lay beneath it. For the light-weights it was a pleasant drop,

THE LOWER ICE-FALL OF THE ZEA GLACIER

but at least one climber imbedded himself so deeply that he had to be tenderly dug out, like a precious, newly-found Greek statue at Olympia, from the superincumbent material. Then we lunched luxuriously, under the shadow and shelter of the over-hanging upper lip of the snow-trench, secure from all that might fall from above. The southern ice-fall of the Zea Glacier we did not find formidable, nor did Mr. Mummery, in the following year, meet with any serious obstacles in the northern. M. de

Déchy, however, had a bad time, and it must be remembered by all Caucasian climbers and critics that the snow and ice conditions vary in different seasons far more than in the Alps. In 1887 and 1889, I found the snows greatly altered, and in 1890 again, on the Laila, Herr Merzbacher's experiences were very different from mine of the previous year.[1]

After a very enjoyable halt we set out, but by keeping entirely to the left of our ice-fall, we almost completely evaded its *séracs*, and soon found ourselves at the spot where the two cascades unite. The rope could now be thrown off, and we were able to run along the broken glacier and slide swiftly down the snow-banks beside a last fall, where the ice bent slightly to the north. Here we came on a meadow and water, a fine site for a bivouac. But we had more ice and moraine before us. Some of us clung to the glacier, others tried the moraine; I do not know which fared worse; at any rate, the moraine party came in last.

The two who first reached smooth ground were suddenly aware of a white tent pitched a few hundred yards from the terminal moraine. We hastily assumed it must be Signor Sella's camp; visions of afternoon-tea rose before us. I trust I shall not mention tea too often. If I do, may it be remembered that tea of necessity takes the place in a Caucasian journey that 'Bouvier' occupies in the records of mountaineering nearer home. We hurried on, counting on a cordial reception from our comrade or his Italian followers, whom we had met at Vladikavkaz. But the tent proved empty; its furniture was not European; there was no sign of a photographic outfit. Presently an elderly Ossete came in sight, hurrying up in the greatest alarm. He obviously looked on us as a party of unusually dare-devil robbers, on his property as lost, and on his own days as probably numbered. His face did not recover its composure so long as we were in sight. Captain Powell ascertained from him that he was there for his health, undergoing a 'cure'

[1] Our pass is seen in the illustration (from a photograph of M. de Déchy), immediately east of a rock-tower on the skyline. A more practicable passage may possibly be found a few hundred yards farther west.

of glacier air and milk diet.   His servants had gone down to
the villages, two hours' distant, for provisions.

The scenery throughout the descent had hitherto been of the
most stern magnificence.   The Zea Glacier rolls its billowy flood
between rocky walls and spires hung with fantastic, frozen draperies.
But the most charming hours and landscapes of the day were still
before us.   The valley we were entering is one of the few northern
glens of the Central Caucasus which are wooded to their heights.

Overhead shot up crags like the Engelhörner of Rosenlaui,
but granite in place of limestone; a second great glacier poured
in a broad sheet from a recess in the right-hand range.   The
foreground was occupied by a forest of beech, birch, and fir, with
an undergrowth of laurels, golden azaleas, cream rhododendrons,
and roses—not *Alpenrosen*, but single wild-roses.   That evening
walk, the gleam of the white and blush roses under the forest
trees, the faint delicate colours of the tall mallows and Canterbury
bells on the open glades, the fragrance of the fading azaleas,
live among the most vivid of my Caucasian day-dreams.   There
was hardly a track through the wood until we came suddenly
on the ancient and famous shrine of Rekom, a place of pilgrimage
from time immemorial for all the country side.   On a little
clearing stands a low wooden building about the shape and size
of an ordinary Alpine chalet or hay-barn.   The logs of which
it is constructed are unsmoothed, and the only external ornament
is some curious carving on the projecting beams of the roof.   The
interior is now ruinous, and contains nothing but a few sacred
pictures in decay, heaps of iron arrowheads, and piles of bones of the
Caucasian ibex (*Ægoceros Pallasii*).[1]   In ancient times it is reported
that many offerings were made by the devout, but since the
Russian occupation any one has been allowed to exchange the old

---

[1] Mr. Clive Phillipps-Wolley, the author of *Savage Svânetia* and editor of the 'Big Game'
volume in the Badminton Series, kindly supplies the following note :—

'I make no pretension to being more than an unscientific field naturalist.   But in what I
say about the *tur*, I have, I believe, the authority of Dr. Radde, the curator of the Tiflis
Museum, as well as my own opinion.   The *tur* is not the *steinbock*, which I take to be the
German for ibex.   The *tur* (*Capra caucasica*) has the horns thrown out laterally from the
head instead of being crossed right back towards the quarters as in the ibex.   There are, Dr.
Radde holds, two varieties of the *tur* in the Caucasus, chiefly distinguishable by their horns,

coins—many of them, it is said, of at least Roman antiquity—
for new. We saw no trace of any coins whatever; the treasury
appeared to be entirely empty.

The wood of which the chapel is built has been stated to
be a pine that does not grow on this side of the chain. We

did not verify the asser-
tion, which has been used
to support a legend that
'once upon a time' there
was a frequented pass
where the Zea Glacier
now pours its frozen
billows through the steep
mountain - walls. 'Once
upon a time there was
and there never was,'—
to quote an original and
very charming formula
common in Mingrelian
fairy - tales. The story
involves a physical im-
possibility, but is worth
recording as a parallel to
the Alpine legends of a
similar nature which have
been convincingly, and I
should hope finally, de-
molished by Dr. Richter
in a paper in the *Zeit-
schrift* for 1891 of the

AN OSSETE GRANDFATHER

German and Austrian Alpine Club. The time of pilgrimage is

which are in one case deeply serrated white horns of an ibex, in the other, smooth. The *tur* is
pretty general throughout the Caucasus, but the ibex, I believe, is only found on Ararat and in
the eastern Caucasus. I have never seen or heard of ibex in Suanetia or any of the neighbouring
districts, although I was looking carefully for signs of its existence for some months.'

M. Dinnik confirms these remarks. See *Petermann's Mitteilungen* for 1884. The *tur* of
Daghestan is *Ægoceros Pallasii*.

August, and as on the Rigi in old days the pilgrims have a double object, bodily as well as spiritual advantage. The Ossete we had found camped by the Zea Glacier seemed a solitary survival of the old habit, unless, indeed, a party of young women, whom we discovered bathing in a clear spring, were also pilgrims. But on this point I can say nothing certain, for they disappeared among the bushes with a promptitude equal to that of our first parents, and for a similar reason. From the corn-fields of Zea we saw the sun set behind the higher of the double-headed peaks, we nearly missed the cart-track below the villages in the gloaming, and an hour after dark were being warmly welcomed by the friendly Cossacks of St. Nikolai.

Clouds vexed us, as they have other travellers, in crossing the Kamunta Pass, and we felt bound not to put off the search we had set before us by lingering about the magnificent mountains of the Karagom. The next, and last, instructive view I had of the Adai Khokh peaks was from Donkin's bivouac on the rocks below the Ulluauz Pass. The peaks were seen in outline at a distance of from thirty to thirty-five miles, and I summarised what I saw in a sketch-map issued in the *Proceedings* of the Royal Geographical Society for 1889. But this sketch, though since confirmed in essentials, was, to a certain extent, hypothetical and without detail. It was a means and not an end. In 1890 the end was attained. The orography of Adai Khokh was made clear, its highest peak and its finest belvedere, Adai Khokh itself and Burdjula, were climbed, and the scenery was illus-trated by the superb photographs of Signor Sella, and by some views, very valuable from a topographical standpoint, taken by Mr. Holder.

I must briefly summarise the work thus done by mountaineers. Signor Sella has given, in the *Bollettino* of the Italian Alpine Club for 1892, a very clear and instructive account of his expedi-tions and discoveries. He and his caravan descended from the Kamunta Pass (8000 feet) to a bleak pastoral basin on the head-waters of a tributary of the Urukh. Here they ascertained that the Skatikom of the natives is the glen west of that so named on the five-verst map. The latter is locally known as Songuta and its important glaciers remain unexplored. Like all its visitors, S. Sella was overcome with admiration at the picturesque splendour of the scenery round the lower part of the Karagom Glacier, in the vicinity of which he camped for many days, and made several expeditions. He climbed the two summits, Zikhvarga and Burdjula, on either side of the Gurdzivsek Pass; and obtained photographs revealing all the secrets of the Karagom snowfields. About the same time two English mountaineers, Mr. Holder and Mr. Cockin, starting

THE MORAINE OF THE KARAGOM GLACIER

from a camp in the Rion basin, climbed Burdjula by its southern face, and after traversing the great snowfields reached, without difficulty, the triangulated peak of Adai Khokh. They satisfied themselves of its predominance, and ascertained the existence of a curious twist in the watershed (see map), which allows the western slopes of the peaks south of the highest summit of Adai Khokh to drain towards the Rion. Clouds hindered more minute observations. Mr. Mummery also, from the Zea Valley, penetrated into the hitherto unexplored north-western *névé* of the Zea.[1] He describes

---

[1] Mr. Woolley in 1895 photographed Adai Khokh from this side.

the gaps leading from it to the Karagom as steep, but not inaccessible. Its relation to the Songuta Glaciers has not yet been ascertained.

Meanwhile those very energetic and competent officials, the surveyors and engravers of the Tiflis Topographical Bureau, had not been idle. They pushed up their new survey into the basin of the Zea and all along the northern glaciers of the chain, venturing as far as the ice-fall of the Karagom; they measured numerous peaks; finally in 1891 M. Kovtoradze, the head of the local survey party, paid a visit to Mr. Holder's stone-man on the summit of Adai Khokh. In the sheets he has prepared the local names have been revised and added to. In this important matter of nomenclature, the surveyor differs everywhere, I think, from Dr. Radde, while Signor Sella in most places differs from both. In fact each village, sometimes each individual, has a separate nomenclature, and it is always a question which shall be adopted Add to this that to no two Europeans does the same uncertain sound, a Georgian sneeze, or a Turkish grunt, suggest a similar representation in a Western alphabet, and the consequent confusion is obvious. When, as sometimes happens, a Caucasian traveller of one year's standing tells me that my nomenclature is quite wrong, I am always ready humbly to admit the justice of his criticism, subject to my own liberty to say the same of that which he desires to substitute. For, in point of fact, I am embarrassed in too many instances by the possession, not of one but of several sets of names: one for each time I have been in the country, and one for each separate native or each official map I have consulted. Consequently, as regards accuracy in Caucasian place-names, I am somewhat both of a sceptic and an opportunist. Until the survey is issued in a definitive form discussion may in certain cases be profitable. But as a general rule the final decision of the Government officials, right or wrong, must, I hold, as a matter of convenience, be allowed to prevail. I have yielded in the matter of Dykhtau and Koshtantau, although by transposing these names the surveyors have inflicted on Western map-makers and geographers an inconvenience almost as great as that which historians suffer when a British statesman changes his name on taking a peerage late in life. Smaller grievances seem to me hardly worth talking about, much less arguing over.

Before I leave this embarrassing and unsatisfactory subject I ought, perhaps, to define further my own position, and the principle on which I have acted. It must not be assumed, because I have acquiesced, except in a few instances, in the decisions of the Surveyors, that I accept the place-names inserted on their new maps as the most suitable or accurate that might have been chosen. No doubt, as a rule, names travel upwards; a glacier is called after the valley or pasture at its base, and hands on its name to the ridges or peaks above it. When Tyndall first wrote, Monte Rosa was known at Zermatt as the Gornerhorn. But the Russians have carried this practice much too far, especially on the Upper Baksan. Again, their names appear in many instances to be arbitrarily imposed, and not to correspond with local usage. This discrepancy is not uncommon when the language of a country is foreign to its officials. It is conspicuous in the Austrian maps of the Trentino. In that district, geographers and the people of the country have agreed to accept the majority of the mountain names imported by travellers or map-makers. Despite objections, the weight of which I recognise, I believe that in the Caucasus a similar course will be found to be attended with fewer practical inconveniencies than any other, and I have therefore generally adopted it.

CHAPTER VII

THE VALLEY OF THE URUKH

Lectus, culcitra, plumae, pulvini desunt. O mollem et effeminatum hominem, omnium instar tibi foenum erit !

C. GESNER, A.D. 1555.

THE Urukh Valley is the only great valley north of the main elevation of the Central Caucasus that runs for any distance parallel to the chain. It is to this fact that it owes the distinctive character of its scenery. The mountains at its head, crystalline schists, are comparatively tame in outline, but the granitic ranges on either flank are bold, lofty, and clothed in glaciers.

When we study the map closely we find that from the Nakra Valley in Suanetia to the Mamison Pass the crystalline rocks which form the central elevation of the Caucasus constitute not one but two or three parallel ridges. A crest starting from Dongusorun serves as the watershed as far as Salynan Bashi, and then continues in the Koshtantau-Dykhtau Spur and the mountains north of the Urukh. Another ridge, starting from Shtavler, passes south of the head of the Betsho Valley through Bak and the peaks immediately above the Mujalaliz, and then becomes the watershed at Gestola. In neither of these ridges is the granite continuous; it alternates with the schists. Schists crop up east of Dongusorun and about

146

Salynan Bashi ; they are found also between the Rion and the Cherek sources, and wherever the rock is schistose, practicable passes exist. But what I want to emphasise here is the result of this ridge-and-furrow arrangement in producing internal basins which are filled, according to their elevation, either by vast glaciers or pastures. North of Suanetia the great *névés* of the Leksur, Tuiber and Zanner, the Bezingi and Dykhsu Glaciers, occupy such basins. The assertion in popular works that there are no great snowfields in the chain is consequently contrary to the facts. But when we look farther east we shall find the upper basins unoccupied by ice. They are represented by the pastures of Karaul and the broad trench of the Urukh. Laboda rises as directly above the head of that valley as Ailama does over the Dykhsu Glacier, or the Wetterhorn above Grindelwald.

To the Caucasian tourist of the future the Urukh Valley will be important for its own sake, and also because it offers a very convenient way between Vladikavkaz and a spot destined to be one of the centres of Caucasian mountaineering. Karaul— the meadow said to owe its name to the guard posted there in olden times to keep in check the forays of the cattle-robbers from the south—is only a day more distant from the railway by the Urukh than by Naltshik, and this day is occupied in crossing one of the finest passes in point of scenery in the whole chain. My sketch of the panorama from the Shtuluvsek, published in 1869 (which has happily borne better than I could have hoped the test of comparison with photographs), was the first pictorial representation of the group. It was by a happy inspiration that we went to this spot, for after all the experiences of recent years I cannot point out a better viewpoint. From Vladikavkaz there are three roads, or rather mountain tracks, to the upper Urukh.

Let us, since it unites this district with the Mamison road, follow that we used on my last expedition in 1889. As far as the silver mines of Sadon there is a road for wheels. Here we had to organise our transport for the mountains. A great deal of energy went in the task. We were eight English and Swiss mountaineers, with three tents—tents of the lightest make, it is true—provisions,

and camp-utensils. Six horses carried the load ; on a seventh
rode our temporary attendant, a Vladikavkaz Cossack.   On the
top of the pots and kettles was perched the melancholy Finkelstein,
a Jew, whom we had picked up in Vladikavkaz, and who served us
faithfully, and on the whole efficiently, as cook and camp-manager.
Great was the talk, loud and long the argument, over the distribution of burdens, each owner striving to secure the lightest for his
own animal.   At last, amid the barking of curs and the grunting

THE INTERPRETER AND BAGGAGE TRAIN

of human beings—the Caucasian grunt is a special accomplish-
ment—our Exodus was accomplished.   At the moment of departure
Captain Powell was laid hands on by a native, who, simulating a fine
frenzy, gesticulated violently and flourished his broad dagger.   His
words, being interpreted,. proved to be to this effect :—' I, your
post-boy, have driven you here ; it is off the post-road ; it must
be reckoned two posts, and I have only the payment for one :
if I do not receive double fare I shall be dishonoured, and my
family will be covered with perpetual shame.   Let me receive
what I ask, or I will kill myself on the spot, and my spirit shall

pursue you through the mountains.' We preferred the sacrifice of a few kopeks to the psychical manifestations with which we were threatened, and bloodshed was happily avoided. These sudden outbursts of temper are not uncommon in Ossetia, but as a rule no harm comes of them.

Our first night in camp was spent under damp mists and drizzle. The near scenery was of the dullest. The landscape was of a type not uncommon north of the Caucasian chain in the schist zone between the granite and the limestone. The mountains are no better than monstrous downs. There is nothing quite so tame and featureless in the Alps, though the ascent to the Furka Pass from Hospenthal comes near it. But the scale in the Caucasus is larger, and the result more monotonous.

We saw nothing from the pass but clouds above, interminable green slopes below. The first noteworthy object on our track was Kamunta, the centre, or township, of this unattractive pastoral region. As seen in M. de Déchy's photograph (p. 101), it may remind Syrian travellers of the type of village common in that country. It represents one of the simplest orders of human architecture in a stone district. North of the Caucasus the Ossetes and Tartars have alike adopted it for ordinary domestic purposes, where defence was not the primary object. Seen from above, the chief signs of habitation are flat, grass-grown terraces, out of which protrude rude wicker baskets. From one or two of the baskets smoke issues. These are the chimneys ; occasionally a pig or a child tumbles down one, and is fortunate if it does not fall into the cooking-pot. If a cow strays incautiously the results may be more serious. In local nursery songs the 'Little Boy Blue' is warned not that 'his cows are in the corn,' but on the roofs. Seen from below, a village is represented by a series of low rough walls, like those of olive-gardens in Southern Italy. The houses are half dug out of the ground. Kamunta is not quite of the most primitive type ; many of its houses have four walls, and stand clear of the hillside, while some have even rude wooden balconies. On the hilltop may be noticed a small chapel and some ancient tombs.

On the north the basin of Kamunta is shut in by a high crest of the limestone ridge known as Kion Khokh. This should be a fine panoramic point; it is interesting also to the glacialist, for on its shoulders, at a height of 10,000 feet, M. E. Favre found granite erratic boulders.

Kamunta stands on a tributary of the Urukh. A path leads along the stream, down the valley. As the weather improved, we caught from time to time glimpses of the great Songuta Glacier. We determined, therefore, to take the hill-path which leads to Zinago, a hamlet close to the foot of my old acquaintance, the Karagom Glacier. We camped in a narrow valley, the true Skatikom, between two grass-passes. Signor Sella gave some days to the exploration of the higher ridges which separate the glaciers of this glen from the Karagom. He found the Kosh owner a person of strong commercial instincts. He was selling his sour milk to some families who had come up for a ' cure ' after the local fashion I have already noticed. He even made a charge to Signor Sella for each day his horses were turned out to pasture.

The climb to the next pass was over an interminable meadow, glorious with unmown and unpastured flowers. Loud were the lamentations of our Swiss followers on the waste of natural wealth involved in the absence of herds. When at last we gained the ridge, we saw far beneath us the open valley of the Urukh, framed between its granite walls and shadowed by the cliffs and glaciers of Laboda. Clouds had not yet obscured the distant heights : beyond the broad saddle of the Shtuluvsek the great peaks of the Central Group met our eyes. The descent brought us into a most picturesque region. Waterfalls dashed down the crags on our left, forests climbed up from the valley, glaciers gleamed in the hollows above the deep trench where the frozen fiord of the Karagom still lay hid. Even in the villages conspicuous towers shot up above the horizontal grass-roofs.

We halted at Zinago to examine the curious group of tombs here figured. They are small oblong edifices with convex curved roofs and ledges along the sides, on which trophies of the chase are laid as offerings. They thus resemble, on a small scale, and

with less ornament, the classical tombs of Asia Minor, and differ
entirely in type from the elongated Tartar headstones found elsewhere on the north side of the Caucasus, on which the horse,
arms and accoutrements of the deceased are often depicted in
low relief.

These tombs may perhaps be taken to represent a transitional
stage between the simple heap of stones or pyramid which
formed the first human monument and the elaborate edifices of
later civilisations. The shelf which serves to support the trophies

OSSETE TOMBS AT ZINAGO

of the chase—chiefly horns of the Tur or Caucasian ibex—left as
offerings to the departed, may have suggested the carving of
animals' heads as an ornament on the structure itself in after times.

The district of Digoria, named from the Ossete tribe who
inhabit it, was at one time a debatable land.   After the Turkish
hordes had occupied the steppe and driven in the borders of the old
Ossete dominion, they proceeded to take possession of the valleys
of Chegem and Balkar and to spread their influence into Digoria.
The people are now mixed, and their religions are confused, though
the Ossetes and a nominal Christianity still prevail.

The arrival of so important a caravan drew the usual Caucasian crowd. The children offered good subjects for the photographer; the elders had, more than usual, the air of peasants in a comic opera. This they owed in great part to their headgear: soft, shapeless felts, such as were largely sold under the name of lawn-tennis hats in this country about the same date (1889). One such I had brought with me for camp use, and on its first appearance I was at once greeted with a shout of 'Ossetinsky' from the boys on the wall. Ossete boys are at least equal to Etonians in their capacity for sitting for hours on a wall.

Few things can be more trying to the temper or more

OSSETE WIDEAWAKES

destructive to enjoyment than to be treated as part of a travelling show. There are, unfortunately, not infrequent occasions when the Caucasian explorer must submit with as good a grace as he can to share the penalty of princes. In a Mohammedan village he is a guest, and must conform to some extent to local customs and his host's habits. But there are also occasions when evasion is admissible. We ordered our train to move on, and finally pitched our camp in a lovely spot among firs and copses, a mile beyond the hamlet, on the path to the Karagom. Our tents soon enlivened the glade; beside them, and almost as speedily, was raised an arbour for the camp-followers. Caucasians excel in such extemporised structures. Four stout posts forked at the end are stuck in the ground, cross-bars are laid over them, and a roof and walls wattled in closely with beech-boughs, until with the aid of a *bourka* or two a snug and almost weather-tight retreat is provided.

The following day was one of unmixed enjoyment. We mounted through a romantic wood beside the tongue of the great Karagom Glacier. In the hollow under the eastern moraine we found a substantial empty hut, constructed for the people of the country on their way to the Gurdzivsek, the pass to Gebi. Then we crossed to the wooded bank under the ice-fall, where I had camped twenty-one years before. The scenery was sublime, the weather perfect ; old memories were vividly called up, the strange seemed familiar ; I could hardly believe I had only been for a few hours so long ago amidst these shining ice-falls. I seemed to hear once more old François's cheerful verdict as we first looked up at the great *séracs*, ' On passera toujours, mais avec beaucoup de travail.'

Our next halting-place was Stir-Digor, a large Ossete community, surrounded by corn-fields, and lying in a broad valley closed by the singularly graceful mass of Laboda. In front of the Tana Glacier rises a low, wooded, conical hill, which adds much to the effect of the landscape. The weather had turned rainy, and we were quartered in a room which in an English farm might have been called a shed, and would have been declined by any respectable horse as a stable. The floor was moist mud, only made tolerable by comparison with the slush outside. The villagers were unattractive. Our Cossack secured us reasonable civility, but hardly reasonable prices.

From Stir-Digor there is a good horse-path up the valley. The views of the peaks of Ziteli and Laboda, the Wetterhörner of the Caucasus, with their glaciers, are very striking. Mr. Dent and Mr. Woolley, who climbed the former peak in 1895, were delighted with the region of flowers and fruits they passed through on the ascent. Over the glaciers east of these summits, there is a second pass to Gebi. The path to the Shtuluvsek mounts through a ravine, above which lies one of those long, level, smooth-sided troughs often left behind by ice. The great cliffs of the north-western face of Laboda, best seen as the track begins to mount the slopes leading to the Shtuluvsek, are a very imposing feature of the scenery.

The Shtuluvsek is a pass of the character of the Monte Moro. If the snow is soft on the east side, it is almost impossible to get laden animals over it. We found it in this state on my second visit. I had hurried on to the top in hope of finding the view clear. But clouds had already covered the highest peaks, and I was reduced to botanising on the loose rocks of the crest, which were covered with a delightful and very varied high alpine flora. Presently shouts in the rear indicated that our caravan was in unusual confusion. Looking back, I saw that all the loads had been taken off. Our horsemen were energetically arguing that the pass was impracticable for their animals; our Jew was distracted and dolorous; Powell was issuing vigorous orders; Woolley, Dent, and the guides were shouldering the heavy loads the horses could not carry through the soft drifts. The scene was extremely picturesque, and it was with regret that I at length ceased to be a spectator and took my part in helping to heave some of the bundles up the final slope. That day there was no distant prospect to the west. It was a grievous loss; the panorama of the Shtuluvsek is one of the finest in the Caucasus. The basin of the Dykhsu is admirably displayed, and the great peaks that rise in a ring round it are fully seen. On the right, above the ice-fall of the Tiutiun Glacier, the Ulluauz Pass and the site of Donkin and Fox's Bivouac are easily distinguishable.

The descent towards Karaul is steep but easy. At the point where the valley is first reached a glacier comes down from the black friable schistose range south of the pass. The ice has been in retreat lately, and the accumulation of rubbish on its snout has protected the frozen mass beneath, so that there still remains a great shapeless mound of earth and stones, the inner substance of which is only here and there visible under the black pall of moraine, while the main glacier has retreated several hundred yards and is quite disconnected with it. In the Arctic regions such a phenomenon is not rare, many of the glaciers in their retreat leaving behind them buried tracts of ice.

Two strong mineral springs are passed. The first is near the pass, the second bursts forth in a pleasant pastoral basin—an old lake-bed, overhung by the skirts of the Fytnargyn Glacier. The stream from it breaks out at present from the flanks of the ice; its old channel is deeply carved in the rocks at a lower point. A final descent leads into the wide bowl of pasture, hemmed in on all sides by high ridges, a less arid La Bérarde, in which the torrent from the Dykhsu Glacier joins the Cherek. This is Karaul, the centre of a new district.

There are two other routes from Vladikavkaz to the Urukh country, and a path thence to Balkar, which is often preferred by native travellers in early summer before the Shtuluvsek is free from snow. From Ardonsk, or Urukhski, on the Cis-caucasian Railway, horse-tracks lead up the gorge of the Urukh, or across the hills and forests that separate it from the plain of Vladikavkaz, to the lower villages. M. de Déchy has taken the former; I, in 1868, followed the latter track. The beauty of the forest scenery, the picturesque detail of crag and water, of hanging woods and ferny dells, delighted the Hungarian traveller. On the hill-track I found a succession of the noblest landscapes. As far as a village called Tuganova the way lies across the bare steppe. At this point a track begins to climb along the ridges of a range of foot-hills. After entering the forest zone, it loses itself for hours in dense beechwood or under thickets of the purple rhododendron, brightened by frequent copses of golden and fragrant azaleas. On the occasional grassy brows, fringed with walnuts and wild fruit-trees, parties of peasants, in white wideawakes, may be found mowing. Then the track, striking more deeply into the primæval forest, leads the traveller to a sudden corner, whence he overlooks the deep wooded gorge of the Urukh. Old Tartar headstones, tall monoliths, capped by a stone-wrought turban, and decorated on the face with rude carvings or mouldering inscriptions, stand beside the path. Hamlets hang like swallows' nests on the lime-stone cliffs that rise 5000 feet above the river. To the north spreads a wide tract of forest, wave upon wave, where the only signs of man are the hay-cutters' fires, which rise in some distant clearing. The spires of Adai Khokh indent the southern sky. The horizon is wide and open. Nature makes her appeal to the imagination in a key that great artists are often fain to imitate— not by overwhelming masses but by aerial gradations, subtle lines, and suggestions of infinite variety, combining to produce unity.

Of the rest of the lower road to Balkar I can say nothing. It is unknown, except to the Russian Surveyors and the natives, who consider it a fair horse-path. It crosses no fewer than four passes between the glens of the streams that drain the great glaciers which descend from the northern flanks of the as yet untouched Bogkhobashi Group, north of the Urukh. Here are three peaks, of over 14,000 feet, waiting for their conquerors. The finest in form, though not the highest, Giulchi, was figured in my *Central Caucasus,* and is well shown in Signor Sella's photographs. The more accessible side of these summits is probably displayed in the views gained from the main range south of the Urukh. Before long, doubtless, we shall hear of their investigation.[1]

---

[1] See the plate opposite p. 30. Signor Sella climbed the eastern spur of this range, Dashi Khokh, which rises behind Stir-Digor.

CHAPTER VIII

BALKAR AND BEZINGI

Cold, insipid, smouchy Tartars.

CHARLES LAMB

HE limits of the Central Group, the heart of the Caucasus, have been defined very conveniently by Nature. The geologist as well as the topographer finds a .clear boundary laid down for him. The granite stretches from the Agashtan Pass westward to the Zanner; on both these tracks the traveller finds crumbling slopes of crystalline schists. The Central Group comprises the main chain from Fytnargyn to Gestola, with the great spur which circles horse-shoe-wise round the Mishirgi Glacier and includes Dykhtau and Koshtantau.

In 1868 nobody knew anything about these mountains, except that two of them had been measured and called Koshtantau and Dykhtau by the Russian Surveyors. The first English mountain explorers were puzzled, and we naturally made some serious mistakes. So did Mr. Craufurd Grove and Mr. Clinton Dent, who followed us. The Koshtantau of the old five-verst map (now called Dykhtau) we identified with Shkara; our successors confused Gestola with Tetnuld. It was not until 1887 that I was able to show positively that the gigantic Shkara had been ignored by the earlier survey, and that Mr. Dent's

'Guluku' was the five-verst Koshtantau, since renamed Dykhtau. Slowly we worked out the nomenclature and topography with the imperfect means at our disposal. Mr. Donkin's map, published in the *Alpine Journal* for 1888, was the first-fruits of the revival of interest in the Caucasus; my map in the *Proceedings* of the Royal Geographical Society followed it at a year's interval. Soon afterwards the results of the new one-verst survey began to come in and we found in many districts our preliminary investigations corroborated, extended, and made more precise, by the work of a government staff. It is only fair, however, to point out that several of the sheets of the new map, printed—the Elbruz sheet alone has yet been published—before the Surveyors and Alpine explorers came into close and friendly contact, were far from correct in the upper regions. The Austrian map of Tyrol had to be revised in accordance with the knowledge of mountaineers. Without the example of Mr. Adams Reilly, the French map of Mont Blanc might have been no better than other mountain portions of the contemporary survey. It is no discredit to the Caucasian Staff if it has to some extent profited by similar communications.

In my first visit in 1868 to the Central Group we climbed no snowy heights. Nor were Mr. Craufurd Grove and his companions more successful in 1874. To that expedition the public owes a work which has long been scarce, and deserves to be reprinted. *The Frosty Caucasus* is a lively and at the same time very accurate series of sketches of Caucasian travel and Caucasian people. But, though it includes the story of the first ascent of the highest peak of Elbruz, it is in the main a record rather of travel than of climbing. It is possibly on this account that it has proved so generally attractive. There is, it must be confessed, a certain monotony in the innumerable pages in which we Jacks and Jills of the day record our experiences on uneven ground.

In the preceding chapters the traveller has been brought from the east to the foot of the great peaks. The man in a hurry —the traveller who has only six weeks to give to the Caucasus —will probably wish to go straight to its most characteristic scenery, to Karaul, the Bezingi Glacier, Chegem, and Suanetia. Should he come from the south by way of Batum and Kutais, he will cross one of the Rion passes. This plan has advantages, as he can easily despatch provision cases from Kutais to Suanetia to meet him. But should he land at Novorossisk, and take the Ciscaucasian Railway, Naltshik is his nearest starting-point for the mountains.

At Kotlarevski, a station or two beyond the Mineral Baths, he will see the daily train with its luxurious cars disappear into the distance, while he is left surrounded by a heap of the more or less shapeless boxes and bundles that a Caucasian tour necessitates. The station itself is not much behind a country station in England. Tea may be had, or red water-melons and loaves of Russian bread; there are leathern sofas in a waiting-room. But at its door the luxuries of travel end. The post-road to Naltshik, an important administrative centre, is the part of the steppe where carriages pass. The vehicles are not the commodious tarantasses or phaetons of civilised Russia, but the cruel carts called telegas, shaped like broken-down tub-boats, and set upon wheels with no intervening springs. The steppe, however, is less stony than the wilds of Armenia, and six hours of slow jolting, during which, in clear weather, the view of Elbruz is some consolation to the mountaineer, will bring him and his baggage to the gates of Naltshik.

Perhaps Naltshik has no longer a gate. On my first visit it certainly boasted of a wooden barrier, guarded by a sentry, while a stockade surrounded the settlement. Under the influence of less troublous times the old military cantonment has developed into a quiet country town. The broad streets or roads are shaded by trees and bordered by one-storied,

AT NALTSHIK

paint-brightened, green-roofed cottages or bungalows, each standing detached in its own garden plot. There are several stores, where the Russian or German colonists supply their wants, or the hill-men purchase such simple implements or luxuries as they can afford. The local architecture might remind the traveller of rural Holland, were it possible to imagine an untidy Holland.

As an administrative centre Naltshik has considerable importance, for here lives the official, or Nachalnik, who is responsible for the peace of all the Turkish tribes between the Urukh and Elbruz, the men of Balkar and Bezingi, Chegem and Urusbieh. Hither the village chiefs, or Starshinas, come down to render a periodical account of their stewardship, to be instructed as to new forest regulations, or to discuss some moot point of rights

THE MOUNTAINS FROM NALTSHIK

of pasturage between their communities. Russian administration of Asiatic mountaineers, as far as a traveller sees it, is in many respects the opposite of our own in India. Contrast, for instance, Captain Younghusband's account of how we bewildered the folk of Gilgit at first by our activity, our demands for labour for public works, our insistance on public order. The Russian civil servant in the Caucasus, as a rule, does little he can help, unless it conduces to his own immediate amusement or advantage. The idea of developing his district, of adding to its natural resources, seldom seems to occur to him. The national talent for doing without roads naturally disinclines him to any efforts in their construction. I am afraid the national tendency to jobbery comes in also. No other explanation of the dozens of broken and useless bridges, the roads paid for by distance, which take a fatuously circuitous course, suggests itself to the Western mind, or has been offered to me by Russians themselves. On the other hand, if little is done for the mountain people of the Caucasus, comparatively little is required of them. They have never yet been systematically called on for military service, domestic disorders are easily overlooked, taxation is light, and in the mountains almost nominal. The Turkish tribes are not disaffected, but they might easily be persuaded to emigrate to some country whence the pilgrimage to Mecca would be made easier to them, and where they would feel less cut off from the Mohammedan world.

It would be a pity. I trust that we may never hear of this fine race, so well suited to the highlands they inhabit, being driven, through misunderstanding with local officials on matters of administrative detail, to follow their Circassian neighbours in seeking a new home outside Russia, and thus to add a new element of disorder in lands where the nations of Europe, and England in particular, have too long supported that effete and barbarous system of extortion and misrule which is called the Turkish Government.

The two main avenues of approach from Naltshik to the great glaciers at the sources of the Cherek are naturally the valleys of that torrent. Its two branches unite some miles above and to the east of the town, in a depression between the outer or cretaceous chain and the northern belt of limestones. To reach Bezingi a short cut over the lower hills is generally used. To Balkar the track strikes at once eastward to the Cherek, through a rolling country, the edge of the steppe, garnished with dog-roses and wild fruit-trees, and but sparsely inhabited. This formed part of the Kabarda, so named after a race said to have come from the Crimea, who made themselves masters of this part of Circassia. The villages are long ranges of simple wooden huts or sheds, and gardens surrounded by wattled fences. They lie in the open country. The hills and woods are the old debatable ground, and no human habitation except a shepherd's hut is met during a long day's journey and till after the great limestone gorges have

been left behind. In 1868 we rode up from Naltshik to Balkar in
two days. A Cossack will reach Karaul in the same time ; but
mountaineers new to Eastern travel may find the days long enough ;
for Turkish saddles, if difficult to be thrown out of, are irksome
to remain in—though habit may do much.

After the river has been crossed the forest becomes beautiful
enough to call forth enthusiasm, even from those who are no novices
in the Caucasus. Crags jut out from the green slopes and afford a
home to delicate ferns ; moss-cradled brooks pour down out of secret
hollows. The tall smooth trunks of elm and alder are festooned
with the long streamers of creeping plants, the common rhododendron and golden azalea grow to an immense size. A tarn, fringed
with grasses, reflects on its surface the overhanging crags and boughs,
and suggests a mid-day halt. We camped not far off in 1868.
In 1847, this neighbourhood was the scene of a more imposing encampment. The famous Schamyl, the leader of the tribes of
Daghestan, penetrated to this point in an attempt to raise the
Central Caucasus, having with him a formidable host of Chechens
and six cannon. His immediate object was to establish himself
in the basin of Balkar and hold it as a citadel whence he might
sally forth into the Kabarda, the inhabitants of which would, he
hoped, make common cause with him. But the Tauli, or Mountain
Turks, in place of welcoming their co-religionists, barricaded the
great gorge against them ; the flocks sent from the Kabarda
were cut off by the Cossacks, and one night the armed host
suddenly struck camp and hurried back by forced marches to the
forests of Chechnaya beyond Vladikavkaz. It was a critical
moment in the history of the Caucasus when the Moslem host,
with its banners and its knights in chain armour, such a host as
we read of in the tales of the Crusades, retreated to its native
fastnesses ; and the Russian Government owes no slight debt to
the Balkar chiefs who prevented the flames of revolt smouldering
on the shores of the Euxine from bursting into a blaze which would
have spread from sea to sea.[1]

---

[1] I owe these particulars to Dr. Abich's *Reisebriefe aus Kaukasischen Ländern*, vol. i. p. 457.

The valley above our camping-ground was completely closed by precipitous limestone cliffs, which seemed to form a barrier against all further progress. The path—already at some height above the Cherek, glimpses of which could only be seen from time to time at the bottom of a deep ravine—turned abruptly upwards, and climbed rapidly through the forest. Having reached a height of at least 1500 feet above the bed of the river, it struck boldly into the heart of the gorge, circling round ravines, and winding over the top of the perpendicular cliffs, where a fall from one's horse on the off-side would have led to a short roll, followed by a sensational header of many hundred feet. The vegetation, where-ever it could find room to cling on the shelves and crannies between the precipices, was magnificent ; pine and beech still predominated, though there was a sprinkling of other foliage. Single trees crowning some projecting crag, where, destitute of any apparent source of sustenance, they yet contrived to maintain a vigorous existence, added much to the beauty of the defile. Alpine flowers for the first time showed themselves in company with the most delicate ferns, and even the grandeur of the surround-ing scenery did not make us forget to welcome such old friends.

We could best appreciate the magnitude of the precipices immediately below us when a bend in the hillside enabled us to look back on some portion of the road already traversed; the cliffs on the opposite bank were even more tremendous. Half-way through the defile, a spur of the mountains on the eastern side of the river juts out straight across the gap, and in fact does at one spot actually touch the opposite mountain, leaving the water to burrow underground as best it may. The path descends on to the saddle connecting the rocky crown of this spur with the hillside from which it springs. This brow, from its position, commands a view both up and down the defile, to which there is nothing similar, or in the least comparable, in the Alps. The gorge of the Cherek is no mere crack in the lower slopes of the mountains, like those of Pfeffers and the Via Mala ; it is rather a trench dug down from their very summits to a depth of 5000 feet or more. Behind us forest trees clung to every available inch of ground ; looking upwards, the character of the defile was more savage. The foaming waters of the Cherek, crossed three times by bridges, filled the bottom of the trench, the sides of which were perpendicular walls, succeeded by shelves capped in their turn by a loftier tier of precipices. The path, a mere ladder of broken stones, brought us by

a rapid series of zig-zags to a most extraordinary spot, where the overhanging cliffs meet and form a natural bridge over the river, which can barely be seen at the bottom of its deep bed. Seen from this point, the torrent to all appearance plunged directly into the heart of the mountains, and it was impossible to discover how it found a way out. The savage grandeur of the scenery here attained its height, and so far as my own and my companions' experience goes, there is no gorge in the Central Caucasus of equal grandeur.

Henceforth the cleverly contrived rock-staircase which connects Balkar with the outside world finds room—now on one

THE GORGE OF THE CHEREK

side, now on the other—to creep along the base of the cliffs at the river's edge ; until at last, just when the careless observer would think it was hopelessly defeated, it crawls across the face of an overhanging bluff by a gallery, partly cut into the rock, partly built out from it. We next wound over barren and disintegrated slopes, broken occasionally by stone-capped earth-pillars, similar to those we had seen before on the Ardon, in the Caucasus, and to the well-known examples in the Val d'Hérens in Switzerland.

At last the difficulties are left behind, the cliffs draw back in two grand curtains, and the cultivated basin of Balkar, studded with human habitations, opens in front. A castellated farm or fortress watches the exit from the defile. The lower slopes—no longer cliffs, for we have passed from the zone of limestone to the crystalline schists—are bright with corn; but not a tree is visible on the vast, monotonous green downs. The only incidents in the landscape are stone boundary-walls and stones in heaps or scattered. The heaps are villages, the scattered blocks mark graveyards.

The people of these villages belong to a race numbering in all about 13,000 souls. They describe themselves as Mountain Turks, and claim to be a branch of the tribe who conquered Constantinople. In olden days they were ruled, in a more or less patriarchal manner, by chiefs whose authority was hereditary in the family and whose policy was directed by travelled Mollahs, who in their turn got their ideas from Stambul or Mecca. Stambul was their world's centre; thither went adventurous youths, in the hope of ending their lives as pashas, and occasionally adventurous young women, not averse to becoming pashas' wives. Now these avenues for ambition are closed; orders have to be taken from Naltshik or Vladikavkaz, and the native appointed Starshina by the Government may exercise authority over the old village chief. Their home-life and occupations are little varied. They are rich in flocks and herds, cultivate much barley and brew an abominable substitute for beer, which an infatuated German (Klaproth), famous for his inaccuracies, once described as equal to the best London stout! One of their chief occupations is to collect brushwood for fuel, for which purpose they employ innumerable donkeys. They hire southerners, Mingrelians or Suanetians, who come in crowds across the glacier-passes to mow their hay-crop and for other labour, while they themselves enjoy sport and society after the manner of the country. Capital walkers, keen hunters, they are still keener conversationalists. Subjects for conversation being naturally limited, they make the most of what material they have. Their legends extend from Prometheus to the first climbers of Elbruz. If travellers' tales are not always exact, tales about travellers never are—at least according to my experience. I am said—so it has been reported to me—to have paid some Suanetians 80 roubles to declare I had ascended Ushba. I did pay this sum—for porterage in 1868 at Urusbieh. The disappearance of Mr. Donkin's party in 1888 was naturally a subject for much invention, and the German interpreter who was with the mountain-climbers was, I believe, made the subject of many quite groundless calumnies. Clubs and newspapers are still unknown to these secluded mountaineers : they have to manufacture their own gossip, and—like their beer—it is but an inferior article.

I have already described an Ossete village. The Turkish villages are of the same type, only while the Ossete house is more of a building, the Turkish is more of a burrow. The timber of which the roofs and porticos are made, axe-cut without the aid of a saw, is more massive ; the windows are even smaller ; they have no glass, only wooden shutters ; the greater part of the house is dug out of the hillside, so that the flat roof hardly interrupts noticeably the general slope. A great field of the dead, thickly planted with immemorial tombstones, surrounds the houses of the living. The tombstones are rough blocks, or in the case of men of note tall slabs, sometimes capped by a stone turban or covered with inscriptions, sometimes engraved with representations of the horse and accoutrements of the deceased. Thus is preserved the memory of the earlier time, when the horse was slaughtered and the arms buried for their owner's use in another, but not a better, world. The Mosques may easily escape notice. Except at Chegem, where one has been designed under external influences, they are low large halls, without architectural ornament, and it is from a house-roof or low platform and not from a minaret that the Muezzin's voice wakes the echoes of the hills.

As our cavalcade files along the muddy lane that serves as a street the roofs are crowded with women, clad in loose, red robes, with rows of coins hanging from their caps, over which and their faces they forget, in the unwonted novelty of the event, to draw their veils. In the doorway gather companies of tall, bearded, grey-frocked men, with daggers and pistols at their belts and swords dangling from their girdles. One, taller than the rest, in an overcoat of inverted sheepskins, steps forward and salutes the interpreter. He is the Starshina, or village chief, responsible to the Government for the peace of the district. In the old days he received strangers in his guest-house ; now they are sometimes invited to find lodging in the generally bare and mouldy room of a so-called Cancellaria or court-house. They may often do better for themselves by making inquiries for the storekeeper of the valley, the man of enterprise, who, with a painful disregard of local colour, has put a tin roof and a boarded floor to his house, and keeps a small store with the goods he fetches up once in three months from Naltshik.

I will describe here a native house of the ordinary type. The room into which travellers are shown has a mud floor ; a raised wooden dais serves as divan ; trays are perhaps ranged on the walls ; pegs stuck in between the unmortared stones hold miscellaneous odds and ends of saddlery or dress. The visitors are at first left to their own devices, as far as men can be said to be left who are surrounded by an eager but respectful mob, the grown-up members of which have not the least hesitation in fingering any article of dress that strikes them as novel and interesting. They seldom steal, and generally only trifles. But they will do their best to open all the blades of an English knife and then try their edge in a leisurely way on their beards. Should a boy attempt similar liberties he is cuffed. But these Turks are very fond of their children, and the cuffs they administer are quite inadequate for the main purpose of punishment, the prevention of a repetition of the offence. Presently there is a stir, and the Chief, who has absented himself, reappears, followed by a servant bearing a stool and a tray, on which—welcome sight !— is the steaming samovar, the one Russian invention that has added to human happiness. Around it are ranged brown cakes smeared with honey, and if the Chief is a very wealthy or liberal man a few lumps of sugar, a luxury which the traveller should not forget to replace from his own store before leaving. The Chief, on being pressed, takes a seat, and over a great many glasses of tea—we drink it in the Russian fashion and without milk—courtesies are interchanged and plans discussed. The hours pass, the day is spent, and darkness already fills the room. At last the word 'repose' is suggested, and the company, some of the leading members of which have come in for the dregs of the tea-drinking, file out to discuss the new arrivals out of doors.

Afternoon tea is no doubt the pleasantest meal in the day, but it is hardly adequate as a substitute for dinner for men in hard exercise. About 8 P.M. the travellers begin to repeat this truism and to appeal to the interpreter, who will suggest that it is probable the Chief has sent for a lamb to the pastures, but that he does not know how far off they may be.

At last, about 10 P.M., just as one of the party, after munching philosophically a kola biscuit, has rolled himself in the coverlets provided, the notables re-enter. First the Chief, then the Chief's brother and his favourite son, then a small table covered with a cloth and supported by two Tartars. The cloth is raised, and underneath are displayed many hunches of boiled mutton, arranged on the flat, thin loaves common in the East. In the centre is a shallow bowl of *airam* or sour milk, meant to serve as sauce. The Chief selects a choice fat morsel, dips it into the sour milk, and offers it with his fingers to the guest, whom the other strangers have been successful in leading him to regard as the most distinguished of their party. Water or sour milk is generally the only drink. The meal is abundant, so much so that the more distinguished heads of families—the Village Council, perhaps—come in for their turn, and it is midnight before the entertainment comes to a close and the cushions and pillows are brought in.

I am quite unable to explain how, in a district where the interiors are obscure, where until the last few years artificial lights were difficult to procure and birch-bark torches are still in use, this habit of late hours should prevail. The fact is noteworthy.

To make an early start in the Caucasus you must get your men away from villages and into camp.

The traveller bound for the glaciers at the head of the valley soon leaves the level cornfields of Balkar. The scenery again undergoes one of those startling transformations peculiar to the Caucasus. The bare, rounded, crystalline schists are left behind; we enter the great trough which divides the granite of Kosh-tantau from the granite of the Bogkhobashi range. Grey cliffs,

THE CHEREK VALLEY AND FYTNARGYN

the foundations of the mountains, rise too steeply for the summits close behind them to be visible. Pines cluster on the rocky shelves. The path is alternately a terrace on the face of the cliffs or traverses the fan-shaped screes brought down by lateral torrents. The scenery is more Alpine in its character than is common in this region : it may remind an Oberlander of the approach to the Grimsel : the fine snow-crest of Fytnargyn, used as a panoramic point by Signor Sella, closes the vista. A roaring glacier stream, the Tiutiunsu—(Smoking-water, we were told, the word means)—bursts out of a wooded gorge on the right. It comes from the very heart of Koshtantau, and from a glacier which has now a tragic fame in the annals of the Caucasus. After an hour's further steady ascent up bare slopes the mountains retire and leave space for a great level meadow—a mile, perhaps, in length by half a mile in breadth. Two torrents—the milky stream from the great Dykhsu Glacier and the darker torrent from the schistose glens that lead to the Rion Passes—meet in it, but their beds are deep and the turf is not ravaged by their streams. Cattle and horses are feeding on the plain; flocks of sheep can be seen high on the hills. The scene is primitive, pastoral, peaceful: it has the peculiar charm of every secluded level surrounded by steep mountains. This, however, is its chief merit. Like Zermatt, only without any visible Matterhorn, Karaul lies too much under the hills for picturesqueness, and the new-comer may view it at first with disappointment. But he will grow to regard it with different eyes when he has learnt what stupendous mountains are close at hand, what sublime views are to be gained by a short uphill stroll! And he will end by feeling a kind of affection for the friendly meadow beside the river, where the white tents promise quiet nights and the broad turf invites to hours of well-earned rest in the pure mountain air.

The only permanent summer inhabitants of Karaul are two not unamiable old Tartars, who dwell in a stone-hut close to the bridge over the Dykhsu. In old days this was a post or frontier-guard against the robbers who came over the passes from the Rion or Skenis Skali. Now the guardians of the bridge appear to levy a toll on passers-by, and are very ready to act as purveyors in the matter of milk and mutton to any travellers who may camp in the neighbourhood. In 1889 Karaul was the home of the Search Party for nearly a week. Beneath us, in close proximity, stood the three tents of M. Bogdanoff, the Russian Surveyor. Never before had Karaul harboured so many guests.

The camping-ground is a grassy terrace between the rivers. Grey granite screes, partly cloaked in azalea bushes or dwarf birches, rise behind it. Three vistas open in the mountain circle, that close at hand is up a deep gorge, the mouth of which is not a hundred yards off. The crags above it bend forward in great beaks and fantastic profiles; a snow-peak towers high above them. This is the last gorge of the Dykhsu, the inner gate of the mountain sanctuary, and it leads directly to the great glaciers which flow from the northern slopes of Ailama (the Koreldash of the south side) and the western flank of Shkara. To the east rises the noble peak of Giulchi—the corner-stone of the North Urukh or Bogkhobashi Group—one of the many ridges that confute the old idea that the Caucasus is a narrow, single range. To the north the deep defile already traversed leads down to Balkar, and at its angle a patch of white boulders, the pale granite brought from Koshtantau, indicates the entrance to the valley of the Tiutiun.

The Riffel Alp of the district is a level-topped spur south of Karaul. It is wooded with birch and fir, hazel and alder, rhododendron and azalea. On one side it looks straight up the Dykhsu Glacier, which flows down in singularly graceful curves, marked by the lines of its medial moraines, from beneath the massive crest of Shkara; on the other the broad Fytnargyn Glacier descends from the main chain in gentle slopes until it ends in a tapering snout within a few hundred yards of the travellers' standpoint. This is the ice-stream which overhangs the Mineral Spring [1] on the road to the Pasis Mta and Shtuluvsek. Its meltings escape from its side in several waterfalls, leaving the snout dry, but with a deep water-cut gorge beneath it to show that it has not always been so. On this charming spot M. Bogdanoff, the Surveyor, was 'at home' one afternoon. His Tartar Cossack brought up the samovar, and we enjoyed a rare combination of luxuries—Russian tea, Caucasian cakes, and English marmalade.

Toppfer, the Genevese schoolmaster (whose charming *Voyages en Zigzag* should find a place in every Alpine library), insists somewhere on the delights in travel and in life of 'les petites

---

[1] See *Central Caucasus*, p. 414. The glacier has retreated considerably in the last twenty years.

haltes'; of the ten minutes by the wayside, when we can enjoy conscientiously the luxury of repose, and appreciate to the full its contrast to the exertion to which it is but an interlude; of the happy moments which we leave behind before we have exhausted their charm. There are no halts equal to those in the Caucasus, for nowhere is the contrast between the hardships and worries of travel—of ' doing,' and the pleasure of mere ' being,' as the poet says —more trenchant. On that ' perfect day ' on the heights above Karaul the Dykhsu Glacier flowed in majestic curves round the mountain spurs, the river flashed into life from its icy cave at our feet. Wherever we looked our retreat was fenced off from the world by snowy walls and towers of primæval rock. The delicately iced air was fragrant with the scent of the fading blossoms of the highest azaleas, the lights and shadows played softly on the faces of the great peaks as the afternoon vapours from Suanetia streamed up across the cliffs of Shkara. The landscape was sublime, with a sublimity beyond that of the Alps. The samovar in our midst completed it. It had a Caucasian character, a modest and refined local charm, far beyond that of the proverbial hotel in the foreground.

Karaul is a natural centre for a mountaineer's headquarters camp. There is no similar spot at the head-waters of the Bezingi Cherek. But the western flanks of the great group offer even more striking snow-and-ice scenery than the eastern. An artist may prefer to draw Shkara from the brow near the Fytnargyn Glacier, or Koshtantau from the belvedere north of Karaul: those peaks are more symmetrical on the Balkar side. But he will make his companion picture of Dykhtau—as Signor Sella has done—from the slopes of the Zanner. And for unearthly magnificence in mountain architecture, for sheer height of cliffs, enriched with frozen incrustations— with slabs and bosses of veined snow and crystal ice, with cornices of pendent icicles—there is no scenery in the Alps or Caucasus to compare with the amphitheatres of the Bezingi and Mishirgi Glaciers.

The ride from Naltshik to the base of these glaciers is rather shorter than that to Karaul. I traversed the distance from

Bezingi[1] to Naltshik in 1887 in a day without difficulty. From the start the road is different from that to Balkar. In place of following the cart-tracks running eastward the traveller canters—if he has learnt to canter in a Tartar saddle—for several miles over open ground like an English common, with a long, low, wooded range on his left. The snows of Dykhtau and Koshtantau disappear behind the green line of the foot-hills: at a ford over the Naltshik stream the forest is entered. If it is the first specimen of a Caucasian forest-path the rider has encountered, he will view it with mixed feelings—admiration for the forest, dismay at the nature of the track. He will, however, meet with many worse in the mountains. Weather makes a good deal of difference, and one should not be benighted. Long circuitous wanderings in the mazes of the beech-woods, or through the alders of the glens and among the stones of their torrent-beds lead at last to a broad unmown hayfield, gay as is every glade of the northern forest with golden flowers, which botanists tell me are those of the *Telekia speciosa*. A slope, the timber of which is disposed by nature in the style man imitates—on a very small scale—in an English park, leads down to the clear waters of the Karasu,[2] a tributary of the Bezingi Cherek. The limestone gorge of that stream opens in front, a narrow gate in the mountains; behind it rises Ukiu, a summit north of the Mishirgi Glacier, which I climbed in 1887. The view is one for a landscape painter. Turner might have done it justice.

The gorge is shorter and less wild than that of the Balkar Cherek; it too has a stone fortress at its head. The pastoral basin beyond is not so extensive as that of Balkar, and its human burrows are even less conspicuous. It is difficult for strangers to appreciate fine social distinctions; but the chiefs of Balkar and Chegem consider, I think, the giant of Bezingi several

---

[1] The first mention of Bezingi in English literature is in *A Memoir of the Various Countries comprehended between the Black Sea and the Caspian, etc.*, J. Edwards, London, 1788 : · ' Besnighi, near the Tsherek : about a hundred families.'

[2] Kara or Garasu (Blackwater) is a common name in the Caucasus for the streams which are not at all, or comparatively little, discoloured by glacial mud.

degrees beneath them in the Caucasian nobility, and his villagers
are certainly held in low estimation by their Russian masters.   I
do not see my way to label them in a block.   'Simple, curious,
dirty and lazy,' Mr. Dent calls them : so far I agree.   'Their
favourite exercise is talking,' he goes on : again all travellers must
acquiesce.   'Not thieves, but born liars, with a talent for petty
swindling': the verdict sounds too harsh, formed from a mental

BEZINGI

standpoint too remote.   'Truth,' even among ourselves, is a term
that can cover much scandal ; 'swindling'—that too is not readily
to be defined.   The Tauli or Mountain Turk says what he thinks
you will like to hear, or what he at the moment intends.   He tells
you horses are forthcoming, or that they will be ready to-morrow
at 6 A.M.   If the facts do not correspond with his words, so much
the worse for the facts.   He has done his duty as a host and
as a member of polite society.   Again, he mentions a sum as an
appropriate payment for his own and his horses' services : it is
appropriate to your exalted station, and if he asked a smaller

sum there would be less room left for a pleasant day's bargaining such as gentlemen in the Caucasus enjoy. Can we throw the first stone? Have we never wrangled over the price of a horse or an estate?

There are two excuses to be made for the rapacity displayed by some of the Bezingi folk. A strange company of Franks (all Europeans, other than Russians, are still Franks to the mountain people) came among them. In place of taking what they wanted for nothing they paid what they were asked. It became obvious to the meanest Tartar mind that the part of a wise man was to ask as much as possible. Then these strange Franks required things done in a hurry, as if the years and the days of man's life were not long enough, or one week was not as good as another. Those who go to Bezingi, the natives consider, should do as Bezingi does; strangers have small reason to complain if called on to take a part in reasonable preliminary conversation. A bargain seems to them what a financial scandal is to Parisian idlers, something that ought to last at any rate twenty-four hours. If the traveller is in a hurry the least he can do is to submit to be imposed upon—it is the penalty due for this selfish luxury. Not so long ago a noble-man in our own country complained of an energetic Chairman, who had a habit of tapping on the table and exclaiming, ' Let us get on to the next point.' ' Committees,' remonstrated the peer, ' are called to consider, to talk, not to "get on"; he is not a man of business.' The villagers of Bezingi entertain, I doubt not, exactly the same feeling with regard to their English visitors; they do not look on them as ' men of business,' in the local sense of that term.

Perhaps the secret of some of the difficulties travellers have met with in Bezingi lies in the fact that the village wants a ruler. The gigantic stature of the old chief is his only force; his son is a gentle but limp youth; the family have none of the authority exercised elsewhere by the Turkish chiefs. They are less well-to-do : this at least is the only excuse for the detestable, damp, dark dungeon which they call a guest-house. Yet even the old chief was thawed by the geniality of Mr. Mummery. ' I became

great friends with him,' our countryman writes, 'and he gave
me several dinners in his private apartments. I, in return, provided tea and sugar for himself and his numerous friends and
relations.'

Happily, on my last visit, we found a clean wooden shed,
belonging to a householder at the upper end of the village, where
we were lodged decently, if not sumptuously. Bezingi has been
very unreasonably called the Caucasian Chamonix. There is no
resemblance whatever between the two places. It is at least three
hours from any glacier; no peak can be climbed from it. Such
limited celebrity as it has attained is not due to any picturesque
attractions. An ugly hamlet in a barren landscape, its only
importance for mountaineers is from the point of view of the
commissariat. I must not say its only importance, for Mr.
Mummery and others have proved that it breeds hardy hunters,
the raw material of the Caucasian guides of the future, men of
unselfish and chivalrous habits, with a talent for climbing, and
even some feeling for mountain beauty. Such was the Turk
whom Mr. Mummery has described as disappearing, without a
word, for an hour's tramp in order to bring him a cup of water,
or that other who shouted 'Allah! Allah!' when, with Signor
Sella, he saw the splendour of the snows from the crest of
Fytnargyn.

To go from Balkar to Bezingi it is not necessary to ride round
by the gorges. There is a hill-path which leads directly over the
wide pastures that spread between the granite and the limestone.
The pass is high, 10,111 feet, but the horse-track is easy though
ill-marked. In cloudy weather the vast downs are dull and featureless; under a clear sky the great peak of Koshtantau, supported on
one side by Ulluauz Bashi, Signor Vittorio Sella's conquest, and
my more humble Ukiu, on the other by the Kashtan crest, rises
on the south. The two gaps of the Mishirgi and Ulluauz Passes are
conspicuous on its flanks. Many years ago, in 1849, Dr. Abich
followed this path, and was perhaps the first traveller to mention Koshtantau and its neighbours, for which he obtained the
names of Dumalu Bashi, Djülü and Rzuaschikibaschibyk (*sic*).

It seems strange that it should not have occurred to Dr. Abich at that time, or afterwards, to describe in any detail the splendid scenes he was the first traveller to visit.

The ride up to the glaciers from Bezingi is curious in its ugliness. It is as dull as a ride in a mountain country can be. The features of the scenery are large but not beautiful; the colour is monotonous; brown rocky slopes and treeless turf alternate. The contrast of the brightest sunshine with afternoon shadows is needed to make the landscape in the least impressive. To those who see it under the shroud of mist to which these valleys are peculiarly subject it is depressing in the extreme.

This singular form of bad weather calls for particular mention. After a fine morning a single grey mist is seen, *racing*—no other word expresses accurately its apparent speed—up the valley. It is followed in a few minutes by a company of these children of the steppe. They 'are lost in the hollows, they stream up again,' closing their ranks as they advance. To those who are on high the advance of this cloud-army may be a glorious spectacle. But to those below it is a disaster. The climber on the heights may look down on a smooth silver floor of moving vapours; but the travellers tented in the valley are soon enveloped in a dripping mist. This fog sometimes lies for days at an elevation of 6000 to 8000 feet, leaving all above clear. But more often it develops into normal bad weather. On the south side these persistent valley mists are unknown, nor are they common in the Urukh Valley, which is less open to the direct draught from the steppe. Fog of the same kind is common in the Alps only in late autumn and winter. In January I have sat on the top of the Faulhorn, basking in sunshine and looking across at the grey Jura, while below me the plain of Switzerland was covered by a sea of mist through which portions of the lakes glowed like patches of an inverted blue sky.

The immediate approach to the Bezingi Glacier raises expectations. A vast mound of grey rubbish and discoloured ice fills the valley. Behind it stretches a white precipice or curtain, the skyline of which rises and sinks in gentle undulations between the crests of Janga and Katuintau. On the left a prodigious slope runs up 8000 feet to the icy comb of Dykhtau; as we advance the mountain-side to the east suddenly breaks open, and a second large glacier, backed by a serrated snowy range, appears in the gap. This is the Mishirgi Glacier, hitherto neglected by travellers for its more important neighbour, but not less remarkable in its scenery. It fills all the great and deep horseshoe between Koshtantau and Dykhtau. The Bezingi Glacier, on the other hand, must be pictured under the figure of a T. Fed by the snows in the trough which lies parallel to the great chain and beneath its highest peaks, its stream escapes at right angles through the deep rent or hollow at the western base of Koshtantau. The junction of the arms of the T is obviously the view-point to aim for. Thither, accordingly, in 1874, tramped the first travellers to visit these fastnesses—A. W. Moore, Craufurd Grove, Horace Walker, and F. Gardiner. There Dent and Donkin set up their camp in 1886, and climbed Gestola, the first peak of the Central Group to be trodden by human feet. Later travellers have put up at a Kosh under Dykhtau, described to them by the natives as the Missess Kosh. It is a hole under a great boulder, which every thunderstorm turns into a dripping well. It has no recommendation over the better situation selected by Donkin and Dent except as a starting-point for the northern ascent to Dykhtau. I trust it may be feasible in the future for the Alpine Club, in conjunction with the Russian Government and Scientific Societies, to erect a substantial shelter at this or some still more suitable point, similar to the club-huts of the Alps, or to the native hut already existing beside the Karagom Glacier.

The crest of the chain at the western extremity of the upper basin of the Bezingi Glacier, between the two Zanner Passes, which lead to Mujal in Suanetia, is easy of access to any travellers provided with a rope. The great peaks, on the other hand, without exception, demand skill, and—still more—experience and sound judgment, in their climbers. Mishirgitau and Dykhtau from the south are both hard and long rock-climbs; but the crests of the main chain, Shkara, Janga, Katuintau, Gestola, are to be attained only by traversing frozen slopes, often found in a condition in which no prudent mountaineer would venture on them, and where at all times the choice of a route, free from the risk of falling *séracs*, is a matter calling for discrimination. But I must reserve for later chapters any detailed account of the exploits and adventures of English mountaineers in this district.

The scenery surrounding the site I propose for the Mountaineers' Home of the future has been described in detail by one of the first Englishmen to visit it, and I gladly conclude this account of the northern approaches to the Central Group by an extract from Mr. Grove's volume.[1]

'The wonderful sight which we now looked on I despair of being able in any degree to render in words. It was not merely the beauty and majesty of the great mountains which caused wonder and admiration; it was even more the utter wildness and strangeness of the valley over which they rose; its complete unlikeness to anything I had ever seen in the course of many years' wandering in the High Alps. It was indeed a mountain fastness so secluded and so stern that it seemed not only as if man had never entered it, but as if man was never meant to invade its beautiful but terrible solitude.

'To our right was Gestola, a "tall pyramid with wedge sublime," towering over a broad glacier, which descended in an undulating ice-fall between it and a rocky barrier opposite. Uniting Gestola to Shkara was the great curtain of Janga, a vast wall of rock and snow, looking as we stood in front of it almost vertical. Of course it was not so, but standing there under its shadow the cliffs seemed to rise with a marvellous abruptness, which was all the more striking that they sprang straight from the level glacier at their base unbroken by slope or shoulder. Literally it seemed as though a man standing on the glacier might put his hand against the wall which rose straight some four or five thousand feet above him.

'At the end of this barrier, bearing south-east from us, rose Shkara, and even as we were looking the mist which had clothed the upper part of the mighty mountain cleared away, and it was revealed to us in all its grace and nobleness of form. Tier after tier of steepest escarped cliffs rose on its side, and above them was a fan-like ridge, so thin seemingly

---

[1] In order to prevent confusion I have modernised the nomenclature.

that its huge rock articulations looked to me from below like the delicate fibres and veins on a leaf. Above these was the crest of the mountain, a sharp *arête*, marked by a series of gentle curves of great length covered with a new garment of fresh snow. Shkara shone with dazzling brightness under the eastern sun, and I think the eye of man could hardly rest on a more noble and beautiful mountain than we looked on that summer morning.

'And will the master ever come for the virgin so clad in bridal array? Is the great peak accessible? Will cragsman ever stand on the highest point of that keen ridge and look down from it on lovely Suanetia on the one hand, and the wild Cherkess country on the other? Well, of mountains yet unattacked, as of ladies yet unwooed, it is exceedingly difficult to predict anything, but certainly going up Shkara will be no work for the timorous, or for those weak of limb or unsure of foot. From a col to the east of where we stood, to which snow-slopes of small difficulty lead, rises the north-eastern *arête* of the mountain, for some distance not impracticable. This then could, with much step-cutting, be climbed up to a certain point, and a considerable height on the mountain reached, but the higher part of the *arête* is irregular and broken, looking altogether impossible for human feet, while the slopes below are of terrible steepness, the final ridge being also apparently of extraordinary difficulty. Owing to its gentle curves, it might be very hard for a man to know when he had reached the summit of the mountain. We certainly could see no way thither, but still ways have been found over places which, from below, seemed quite impassable, and there are peaks in Switzerland now frequently ascended which, no very long time ago, were deemed altogether beyond the powers of man, so I am not prepared to say that, with two first-rate guides, a good mountaineer able to give plenty of time to the peak, willing to sleep out many nights, and to persevere after unsuccessful attempts, might not, if blessed with perfect weather, reach the summit of Shkara; provided always that he could get supplies of food sent up from the village, which he would find by no means a very simple or easy task.'

Travellers who are in no sense of the word climbers, but have sufficient energy and endurance of rough life to be able to camp for a day or two in this mountain sanctuary, may walk without difficulty to the crest of the Caucasus at the Zanner Pass, or to the ridge under Shkara that overlooks the Dykhsu basin. They may see many strange sights during their sojourn among the glaciers. The starry stillness of night will be broken by the crash of tumbling ice-cliffs, and their fall made visible by a sudden sparkle as of innumerable lights.

Such luminous avalanches were witnessed by Signor Sella, Mr. Donkin, and other travellers. Signor Sella, in search of a scientific explanation of the phenomenon, quotes the experiences of the observers on Pike's Peak in Colorado, and his own in a storm at one of the cabins on Monte Rosa. It seems that, in certain states of the atmosphere, the friction of snow and hail is capable of producing these curious phenomena.

Of interest in a different connection is the circumstance that, after bad weather, both Signor Sella and M. Jukoff found the upper region of the glacier strewn with the bodies of birds of passage which had perished in the attempt to cross the chain. In July the travellers came upon the skeletons of ducks, larks, and quails, besides many that were not recognisable; in September Signor Sella met with quails, alive but too feeble to escape from the fatal prison in which they found themselves. These observations establish the fact that the migratory birds do not, as had been supposed, make the circuit of the range, but boldly, and even blindly, face the snowy barrier at its loftiest point.

Another phenomenon, more wide-spread in the Caucasus than in the Alps, is the 'red snow,' which is due to a small vegetable growth, the *Protococcus nivalis.* This is, according to my experience, less noticeable in some years than in others. A large extent of surface thus coloured has often been observed on the slopes above the Bezingi Glacier.

CHAPTER IX

THE PATHS TO SUANETIA

Die ganze Majestät des wundersamen Kaukasus findet in Hochsuanien ihre Spitze, und Niemand wage zu sagen, Er kenne den Kaukasus, wer jene hehren Regionen nicht betrat.

ABICH.

IN many of the following chapters my readers' attention will be kept steadily directed to the very heart of the Caucasus, the cluster of superb summits which forms the true centre of the chain. We shall live in camps near the snow-level, or lodge in holes of the rocks beside

> 'The firths of ice
> That huddling slant in furrow-cloven falls
> To roll the torrent out of dusky doors.'

But for the present we may turn to a region of wider horizons and softer landscapes, to the forests and flowers of the Asian slope. We must direct our steps to that unique district, which combines all the most characteristic splendours of the Caucasus—Suanetia. The mountaineer need not bid farewell to his mountains and glaciers; he will find himself still at their very feet. But the landscape-lover may rejoice with me to escape for a season from between the monstrous walls which seem to shut off the sources of the Cherek from the habitable world, from under the roof of trailing mists that too often hang for days obdurately across the narrow span of sky left between the mountains that overshadow

the burrows the Tauli shepherds call their homes. From the treeless
downs and impending ridges of Balkar and Bezingi we shall pass
into a country of comparatively open valleys, where the villages are
not sordid burrows but clusters of rustic castles, and the native
sledge-paths wander amidst woods and copses and natural flower-
gardens; where, beneath the icy precipices of the great chain, the
lower hills spread out in gentle horizontal curves; where distance
succeeds distance in soft gradations of blue and purple, where the
atmosphere is full of moisture, and sunlit armies of clouds roll
up and disappear with a frequency which delights the eyes, if
it sometimes defeats the best-laid schemes of the mountaineer.

The poet Tennyson would sometimes describe to the companions
of his walks on the Downs of Freshwater a landscape he had
seen in dreams, in which, from a mountain range loftier than any on
this Earth, lofty as the great banks of clouds that are piled up
in summer skies, the pale rivers of ice streamed down into valleys
where the vines ran riot in the forests and the torrents flashed
seawards amidst flowers of the wildest luxuriance. There is little
or nothing in the Alps to suggest or realise this poet's dream. The
utmost luxuriance that is attained in any close proximity to the
glaciers is where the pines and sycamores of Rosenlaui frame the
peaks of the Wetterhörner, or the Glacier des Bossons raises its milky
spires among the cornfields and cottages of the Chamonix valley.
The chestnuts of Val Anzasca are divided by many miles of rock,
pines, and pasture from the snows of Monte Rosa. Mr. Ruskin,
indeed, once went so far as to suggest that the Maker of the Universe benevolently inserted a waste zone between the snows and
the habitable world, in order to secure mankind from the dangers
of living too immediately under structures in the dangerous state
of decay of most of the great ranges. Suanetians, it would seem
to follow, were not held worthy of any such divine protection. But
let us not endeavour to discover the designs of Providence. It is
enough for us that we are about to penetrate a region where that
close union of sublimity with softness, of sky-piercing snows with
vast fields of flowers and luxuriant forest scenery, which in the
Alps is an unattainable ideal, is found as an every-day reality.

Along the whole southern face of the mountains, westwards from the Rion sources, the frosty Caucasus and the flowery Caucasus join hands. In Suanetia the ice-avalanches of the Laila fall upon beds of yellow lilies; the terminal moraines of the Chalaat and the Zanner Glaciers are cloaked in dense copses. But if there is one region where, more than elsewhere, the forest giants raise their heads to an 'unbelievable height,' where the field-flowers break forth under the summer sun with almost fabulous luxuriance, it is round the sources of the Skenis Skali. The general verdure of the southern side finds an adequate explanation in the climate : in summer the perpetual moisture of the English Lakes, combined with Pyrenean sunshine, in winter the protection afforded by a prodigious snowfall. The depth of alluvial soil in the bottoms, the richness of the vegetable mould formed by the decay of immemorial woods thinned by no woodman's axe, account for the unusual dimensions of both trees and plants. The total absence for centuries of in-habitants or traffic in the upper glens of the Skenis Skali has pre-served the woods from the clearances wrought by the recklessness of the natives, who have no scruple in setting fire to the dry mosses on a gigantic pine, and turning the tree into a pillar of flame, for no other motive than the childish pleasure of seeing a good blaze.

From another and a different point of view the forests of the upper Skenis Skali are a surprise to the European mountaineer. He, for the first time, finds himself in a region where difficulties begin at the point at which he is accustomed to find them end— that is, below the snow-level. In the valleys, the beds of torrents or the tracks of bears are the only practicable paths, and the traveller wades knee-deep, not in snow, but in fields of lilies and campanulas ; knee-deep do I say—rather over head and shoulders. A man on horseback is only just visible to his companions among this extraordinary vegetation. To Alpine guides the southern valleys of the Caucasus are an abomination ; *Es gefällt mir nicht*, is the burden of the Oberlander's discourse, and his occasional utterances are apt to be of a far stronger description.

There are climbers nowadays, other than guides, so dead to the beauty of the green things of the Earth that they grudge every hour they are not 'at work' above the last moss and lichen. Such was not the spirit of my early companions. A. W. Moore, one of the keenest of the founders of the Alpine Club, held it as an axiom that the true mountaineer explored every valley as well as every crest of his favourite mountains, and in the case of the Oberland and Monte Rosa he carried this principle into practice. The traveller who goes to the Caucasus and confines his curiosity to the 'frosty Caucasus' shows himself a degenerate mountaineer, a creature physically specialised, perhaps, but intellectually maimed. There may be over-specialisation in sport, as much as in science and industry. Have we not heard of climbers who cannot bring them selves to waste time on snow and ice, so devoted are they to perfecting themselves in the gymnastics of rock-climbing; of men who can scale a boulder or a rock-tooth, but cannot find the right way up a great mountain?

The subjugation of Suanetia has been a boon to the Suanetians, and also to the wanderer, to whom it opens the Paradise of the Caucasus. The peak-hunter may be attracted thither chiefly by the virgin southern crest of Ushba. For the rest, he may prefer Karaul, or the Missess Kosh. But the mountaineer who can be satisfied with summits of 13,000 to 15,000 feet, or who appreciates passes, may find in the ranges that encircle this great valley occupation for several summers.

I have myself been in and out of Suanetia eight times, by seven different tracks. I have been twice through the Skenis Skali forests. I have also penetrated the still wilder forest of the Kodor, and wandered among the scarcely less tangled woods that cover the northern slopes of the Laila. The Kodor forest is the greatest in extent, and its canopy of foliage is denser. The traveller who scarcely sees the sky for days, or finds his way barricaded by an unfordable river, gets some hint of the difficulties of travel in Africa or New Zealand. The Suanetian woods are more scattered, and admit frequent open glades. The special quality, or charm, of the Skenis Skali forests lies in the superb proportions of individual trees—above all, of the pines and beeches, and in the extravagant —I can use no other word—growth of the flowers. I have for

years felt a certain hesitation in insisting on the marvels I have
seen. It has been the fashion for 'specialists' to discredit
traveller's tales, and particularly when the traveller is not of
their own tribe. But there is no longer any need for apology. I
am now in a position to produce Signor Sella's photographs as
evidence to the flowers of the Skenis Skali. And if Dr. Radde is
not enough, I have also at hand the recent testimony of a scientific
botanist, M. Levier, to the existence of what he has called, without
exaggeration, a vegetable Brobdingnag in these Caucasian glens.[1]

Before, however, inviting my readers to plunge with me into the
pathless wilderness, I must first lead them along the Suanetian
highroad—a highroad in the most literal rather than in any ordinary
acceptation of that word—which crosses from the post-station of
Alpana on the Rion to the Skenis Skali, and follows that stream
to the foot of the Latpari Pass.

This pass, 9256 feet in height, is crossed by an easy horse-path,
open during the three summer months. Early in October, however,
it is closed by snow, which does not disappear till July. For some
eight months in the year there is no access to Suanetia, except for
men on snow-shoes, or pedestrians who are prepared to face the
rough paths and torrents and stone-swept gullies of the defile of
the Ingur. Mr. Phillipps-Wolley, the only Englishman who has
taken this track along the river-banks, speaks of it thus:—'It is
not too much to say that, unloaded, any man must be in good
condition and at least a fair mountaineer, with a steady head, to
in any sort compass that walk in three days; loaded, these men
do the distance in about five; but a life spent in such walks would
not be a very long one.'

To travellers accustomed to British methods of administration
it may seem strange that the Government should not be at the
pains to construct at least a tolerably safe mule-road to Suanetia.
The native nobles are ready to provide the labour, but the money
and material have not hitherto been forthcoming.

The Department of Public Works is one of the weakest points

---

[1] See Chapter ii.

in Russian Administration, and its conduct is becoming every
year more and more a subject of criticism among Caucasians
who have travelled outside their own country. Even among the
more intelligent and advanced mountain tribesmen there is a
growing demand for help and encouragement in the development
of the natural resources and the commerce of the country. I have
heard village chiefs refer with high approval to the works now
being carried out in Egypt, and repeat tales they had heard from
fellow-pilgrims at Mecca of the splendours of Bombay. The Russian
Government has been successful in pacifying the Caucasus. It is
very much to be hoped that the enlightened men to be found among
its administrators may now prove equal to the further task that lies
before them, and that they will not allow their plans to be frustrated
by the apathy of underlings or by the traditions of bureaucrats.

From the north good walkers—I do not mean climbers—can
reach Suanetia without any difficulty. The passes from the Baksan
may form material for a subsequent chapter. But the natural access
to the district is from the south, and the road used for all official
and general purposes starts from Kutais. It has been very frequently
and fully described by travellers—best of all, perhaps, by M. Levier.[1]
For some fifty versts the traveller takes advantage of the Mamison
road up the Rion Valley. At the post-station of Alpana he finds
a by-road, which first pierces a picturesque limestone gorge and
then emerges on a broad sunny basin, where vines climb in classical
fashion among the tree-tops and broad maize-fields clothe the hills.
The landscape is still hilly rather than mountainous : of a character
found commonly in the outskirts of the Apennines, more rarely in
those of the Alps. Frequenters of the Italian Alps may be reminded
of the Trentino, of the lower basins of the Sarca about Comano.
Travellers can drive over a low pass to Zageri, the seat of government of the Leshgum. Their luggage will be conveyed in an *arba*
or native cart, a basket mounted on two small front wheels and
trailing behind on the ground, drawn by oxen. Zageri is the residence of the local Nachalnik, who inhabits a small wooden house of

[1] See Von Thielmann, *Journey in the Caucasus*, 1875 ; Telfer, *Crimea and Transcaucasia*,
1876 ; Levier, *A travers le Caucase*, 1895.

a very simple description. Visitors must not, however, trust to his hospitality or present aid in securing horsemen for Suanetia, for in the summer he is apt to be away on an official tour. On one recent occasion, a predecessor of the present district officer was found to be engaged in the more agreeable task of cementing the Russo-French alliance by escorting in her excursions a Parisian lady, who paid an extensive series of visits among the Russian officials

ZAGERI

of the Caucasus, and subsequently, as I was told, went on to the Transcaspian. Her bloomer costume created much surprise in Suanetia, to which she penetrated.

At Zageri we are on the frontier between the great mountains and civilisation. Here wheels and telegraphs and regular posts come to an end. The Priestav of Suanetia lives a hermit's life, dependent for his letters on an irregular Cossack, and for his provisions, such as salt and sugar and tea, to the despatch of special convoys over the Latpari Pass—a three days' journey. The village stands on the right bank of the Skenis Skali in a broad cultivated valley. The landscape is bright and full of local colour, particularly on a feast-day, when the Mingrelian gentry, the peasants and their wives, ride across the hills from the distant villages, and the green in front of the *dukhan* is enlivened with the martial figures of the men and the red skirts and bright handkerchiefs of the women.

For a long day's ride the traveller follows up the stream of the Skenis Skali into the mountains. Half a mile behind Zageri the entrance to the gorge is guarded by a ruined castle. The scenery may remind the Alpine wanderer of a Bergamasque valley. High-arched bridges and chestnut-embowered villages are wanting ; but the variety of the timber, the richness of the undergrowth, the scale and colouring of the slopes, make up for any lack of pictur-esque incident.

The mid-day halt is made at Lentekhi. This hamlet is in an important and very beautiful situation, at the junction of three valleys, all of which lead to passes to Suanetia. The most eastern is the main valley of the Skenis Skali, which is the way to the Latpari Pass. The central glen, that of the Lashkadura torrent, leads to another pass, a more direct way for pedestrians to Latal— when you know it. Dent's party in 1888 did not know it, or find it, and wandered rather vaguely over the heights and hollows. Through the third glen mounts a horse-track which circles round the western flank of the Laila Glaciers, crosses a high pasture where the Dadish Kilian Princes have a house and keep their horses in summer, and descends below Betsho. From the horse-pasture another very rough track leads over the hills to Sugdidi. A short cut across the glaciers, by which a hunter can, it is said, reach Lentekhi in one day from the highest hut on the Suanetian side, also descends—if I mistake not—into this valley.

We have bidden farewell to wheels. The region of *dukhans*, or wine-shops, has also been left behind. In the villages henceforth the only accommodation met with will be an occasional Cancellaria— that is to say, a small building, containing as a rule no furniture whatever, unless a raised platform can be called furniture. But the interior will generally be found clean, and in stormy weather the traveller is glad of shelter and solitude, and may well prefer the 'court-house' to a climber's tent or a native dwelling.

The path through the forest to the highland basin in which the principal villages of Dadian's Suanetia are situated mounts through a forest of astonishing magnificence. It was late on an August afternoon in 1887 that I started to ride up the valley. Night fell while we were still far from Cholur; the moon gleamed

THE CANCELLARIA, CHOLUR

for a time through the branches on the foaming waters of the river; then the shadows grew deeper in the forest, and more than once we missed the path. As the upper valley opened dimly before us strange lights shone in every direction; ghostly figures raised on high platforms were silhouetted against the flames; wild cries and chants and the beating of metal drums rang through the stillness of the woods. The maize was ripe in the fields, and the bears on the neighbouring hills were only to be restrained from their favourite

food by the whole force of the male population. Each watcher was
posted on a wooden perch, whence he waved his birch-bark torch and
shouted to his fellows.

The night was too dark to push on to the courthouse at Cholur—

THE PATH ABOVE LENTEKHI

so we knocked at the gateway of a castellated farm. The buildings
were of the type common throughout Suanetia. A high wall with
one or two towers on it enclosed the living-rooms, farm buildings,
and a small court, to which heavy double-barred gates gave the
only access. The bolts were fast, and in answer to our knockings
a female voice parleyed with us from within, and assured us that

since all the men were watching in the fields we could not be admitted. A barn outside gave some shelter, and our horses were supplied with provender.

The ascent to the Latpari Pass is by steep zigzags through a beech-forest. Imagine the Bisham woods, near Marlow, 2000 in place of 200 feet high. At last the green shade is left behind, and scattered birches fringe the upper pastures, across which many tracks, worn deep in the loose slaty rock, lead to a wide depression in the range, the nearer summits of which do not reach the snow-level. There is nothing sensational in the scenery, and the traveller's attention is engrossed by the lovely flowers and the rare insects and butterflies that wander about among them.

Let him pray for an unclouded sky ; better, let him help himself to secure it by camping high, so as to reach the crest at an early hour. For the view from the Latpari Pass is not a sight to be missed. Here, at a height of 9200 feet, the wanderer finds himself brought face to face with the white mountains that he has seen from Batum or Kutais. Opposite, beyond the trench of the Ingur and a low range of foot-hills—broad green downs, unbroken by crags or wood, clothed in deep flowery grasses that fall only to the sharp scythe of October frosts—rise the granite precipices of Shkara and Janga. The spectator's position with relation to the Central Group is comparable to that of a climber of the Cramont to Mont Blanc. That view was De Saussure's ideal of Alpine magnificence. Shkara is 1300 feet higher than Mont Blanc ; the line of the Caucasian precipices runs west from it without a break for ten miles ; then it does not end, but withdraws to enclose a bay out of which a great glacier sweeps down in a cataract of pure ice, while beyond the gap the keen spire of Tetnuld soars in isolated beauty against the sky.

It is a landscape which no picture or photograph can render adequately. For its effect depends not so much on the curves of the skyline as on the boldness and scale of the mountain structure, and the beauty of its details. The spurs or buttresses that hold up the gigantic cliffs of the central chain are splendid in their abruptness ; they rise immediately above smooth green hills, which

nowhere attain a height of more than 8000 to 9000 feet. The
traveller accustomed to the Alps is amazed at the quantity of
snow and ice that clings even to the steepest parts of the range,
the swelling bosses of glacier, the thick folds of snow that drape
the mountain forms. The frozen cascade of the Adish Glacier
is unique among ice-falls, and, when the sun shines on its towers
and caverns, gleams with the most varied colours. Tetnuld is
almost an ideal mountain : the snowy face the Grivola turns to
Val d'Aosta is a miniature reproduction of it, but Tetnuld is a
Grivola higher than Mont Blanc.

There is more to be seen from the Latpari Pass. Turning
west we overlook the labyrinth of green hills and glens, the forests
and pastures and corn-lands of Free Suanetia. It is ringed by a
high distant range of granite domes and spires, between which
long glaciers, like white ladders, lead the eye skywards. For
the present, to quote M. Levier : ' I will avoid any minute
enumeration of the points, pyramids, needles, crests, combs, ridges,
cols, the line of which develops itself before the astonished gaze.'
This lively botanist goes on to apologise to ' Alpinists ' for his
omission of a ' learned catalogue bristling with exact names for
summits whose nomenclature is still undetermined.' We no more
expected it of him than he would thank us for cataloguing the
flora and inventing barbarous names for newly-recognised species.
Each explorer has his own task. That of surveyors and discoverers is to establish names for mountains, as that of botanists is
to find them for plants. But the proper place for a catalogue
is an Appendix, and for the moment I spare my readers.

One object on the horizon, a golden mass, the colour of which
tells of the greater depth of atmosphere through which it is seen,
must, however, be named. The double crest of Elbruz is unmistak-
able. Farther to the right stand two great rock-towers, linked, like
those of a Gothic cathedral, by a lofty screen. These are Ushba,
the Storm-peak, the tutelary mountain of Suanetia. The broad
snows of Dongusorun and the horn of Shtavler, the summit between
the valleys of the Nakra and the Nenskra, appear farther to
the left. As we descend, following a terrace along a projecting

brow the long spurs of the Laila come into view, fringed with
sunshine and turning their shadowy forests towards us. We see
from time to time the white water of the Ingur flashing far
below in its deep gorge. Zigzagging through azalea copses and
white rhododendron thickets, full of midsummer bloom, the path
passes amongst weathered birch-stems, the branches of which
frame the great pyramid of Tetnuld, spotless white between the
green earth and blue heaven. Opposite us opens the broad
glen that leads to the glaciers of Janga. Its solitary village,
Iprari, is noticeable from the absence of any towers. The Russians
razed its battlements to the ground in 1876 in retribution for the
murder of two officers. At last the track plunges down steeply
to the courthouse of Kalde, which stands on a little meadow beside
the Ingur, hemmed in by green slopes except where the crests of
Ushba fill the gap above the river.

Let us now turn to another of the paths to Suanetia likely to be
used by mountaineers. In treating of Gebi and its inhabitants, I
took occasion to point out that, in olden times, a frequented track
led from the Rion to Suanetia across the comparatively low passes
that separate the southern valleys. In fact, up to the sixteenth
century, the Suanetians held the upper basins of the three great
rivers of Imeretia, the Rion and Skenis Skali, as well as the Ingur.
They lost them through rash indulgence in their primitive practices :
they slew a local noble of some importance, whom Brosset calls
Prince Djaparidze. As a punishment they were closely blockaded
by their neighbours, and after some twenty years of isolation were
reduced in A.D. 1534 to cede to the Georgian sovereign all their
villages and churches, east of Ushkul, with the treasures contained
in them. The document has been preserved, and contains many
village names, e.g. Edena, now extant only in mountain nomenclature. The territory deserted by the Suanetians was only partially
occupied. The Skenis Skali sources became a wilderness across
which it is at present an undertaking of some difficulty to force
a passage with animals. But the novelty of the experience
and the strange sights seen on the way fully make up, at any
rate in recollection, for its toils and inconveniences.

The region we are about to penetrate lies a day's journey west of Gebi and south of Karaul. The frequented track of the old Pasis Mta, which connects the two places, skirts its eastern border. Dr. Radde was the first traveller to visit the Skenis Skali glens; I followed in 1868 from east to west, and in 1887 retraced my steps in the opposite direction. Our first passage was made in very broken weather, with a train of ten Gebi porters. On the second occasion I succeeded, as Dr. Radde had done, in forcing horses through the forest. I saw in perfection the wonderful landscapes, and secured outlines of both sides of the chain, which settled some moot questions of orography in a way since confirmed by the Surveyors.[1]

It is an afternoon's ride from Gebi to the ruined huts at the head of the Rion Valley. The snowy range only appears at intervals in the background, but the valley scenery is enchanting. The path passes among cultivated fields until a bridge—sometimes missing —transports the traveller to the right bank. Henceforth the way lies through a glorious wood, where the smooth stems and fresh foliage of the predominant beeches are mingled with gigantic birches, tall alders and maples, and noble pines. The last disappear towards the head of the valley. The undergrowth of azaleas is of extraordinary density, and the Caucasian rhododendron shows in places its great heads of cream-coloured blossom, delicately stained with clear yellow and pink. Bright streams cross the path; with no other implement than our hands we may capture a dish of trout. When the ice is melting the fish take refuge from the muddy and chilly violence of the Rion in these tributary rivulets. Whatever the traveller's destination—whether Karaul, Ushkul in Suanetia, or Cholur on the upper Skenis Skali, he will mount by steep zigzags to the great pasture which covers the spurs of the ridge forming the western limit of the Rion basin. Here he will meet with the herds, horses and cattle of Tartars from the north side, resting after their passage of the glaciers. They come from far—even from the country of the Karatshai, west of Elbruz.

---

[1] The forest has also been traversed by Mr. Phillipps-Wolley, by Mr. Holder's party, and by Signor V. Sella in 1890.

'How many horses have you?' I asked of one fur-bonneted, keen-eyed native. 'Sto,' a hundred, was the reply.

When the crest is reached, the track, well-marked as yet, turns along it towards the main chain. From this uplifted terrace, 8000 feet above the sea-level, there is a noble view back over the lovely curved hills and hollows of the Rion basin and the snows that encircle it. On the left, the crests of Laboda and Ziteli, the Stir-Digor mountains, send down a glacier to feed the first tributary of the Rion. Burdjula, the peaks of Adai Khokh, Shoda, are all conspicuous. But north and westward the view, if less lovely in composition and in detail, is attractive by what it half reveals and suggests. Above the level wall, over which run the snow-passes to Karaul, rise the icy combs of Koshtantau, Dykhtau, and Shkara, Dykhtau almost concealed by the intervening mass of

NATIVE TRAVELLERS

Fytnargyn. Beyond Shkara the twin towers of Ushba invite us to Suanetia.

At this point it may be well to insist on a lesson the Alpine traveller has to learn, generally at his own cost, in the Caucasus. Where there are no made paths the tracks run along the ridges, and not in the hollows. In our own country the old ridgeways had a like origin; they avoided swamps and hidden enemies. But this is only half the lesson. When there is no ridge handy, or it is needful to traverse a forested valley, the torrent bed is apt to be the only serviceable path. The route from the top of the first pass to the Suanetian settlement in the Zena Valley is a combination of ridges and torrent-beds. If heavy rains have fallen and the torrents are full, it may easily become altogether impracticable. On my first passage we tried a short cut in the descent to the Skenis

Skali. We soon found ourselves scrambling in and out of deep water-channels, creeping under or over prostrate and mouldering trunks. We saw from above what looked like a smooth glade. Our self-congratulations were premature. The smooth and flowery surface was some seven feet above the ground; we waded or cut through a dense growth of broad-leaved plants, until a bear's track gave

us a line to the banks of the river. At this spot, one long day's march from Gebi, there is a birch-bark shelter. It is a pleasant halting-place in fine weather; the eastern glacier of the Skenis Skali shines above the leafy solitude; there are fish in the river, and chamois, if you can find them, on the hills. But in a rainy season mosquitoes and small stinging black flies are apt to murder sleep—at least for those who are not provided with one of Mr. Tuckett's ingenious gauze canopies.

The little pass to the next valley might easily be made practicable for animals. Nothing but a Caucasian horse could cross it in its natural

THE SOURCE OF THE SKENIS SKILA

condition, and even Caucasian horses have to be relieved of their loads. It is approached by two gullies, one of them so steep that I found myself using my hands to climb it. Our Ushkul horsemen performed wonders here on my second passage. One was a dark, tattered, stumpy barbarian: he uttered prayers and exhortations. Another, a splendid, fair-faced, good-tempered giant, heaved the struggling animals up the worst places. The third wore the clothes and had the manners of a Persian gentleman.

He walked in a pink cotton frockcoat, wore a turquoise ring, and had his ears pierced.   He moderated the language or the zeal of his colleagues, and gave wise counsel and help at the critical moment.   Truly the Suanetians are a mixed and variable race!   The fathers of these men had nearly murdered us twenty years before : with my present companions I had nothing but pleasant dealings, and it was with regret we saw their bright faces and dark turbans disappear for the last time as they rode off home.

The descent lies into the glen of the Zeskho, the central source of the Skenis Skali.   At its head the chain in old days used to be frequently crossed by Suanetians, bent on lifting their neighbours' cattle.   It must require some enterprise to ' lift ' an ox over a pass of 11,000 feet.   These old disorders are now only a memory.   But they are a very living memory.   If any mischief or misfortune takes place on the north side it is, as a matter of course, and with or without reason, set down to the Suanetians. At present what cattle there are in the Skenis Skali are sent there by their Tartar owners, who pay the Dadian, or chieftain of the district, a few kopeks for each head of cattle on the pasture.

At the head of the Zeskho, where the disused cattle-pass lies, the crystalline schists of the main chain present a bare tame outline. Farther west, however, bold granite horns, the last outliers of the Central Group, mark the ridge which, on the north side, sweeps round the hollow of the Ailama Glacier.   The only way down into the valley is by a torrent-bed, full of loose boulders.   When the trough of the main stream is reached, the best plan, supposing the water not to be in flood—a frequent occurrence—is to plash along among the pools and half-dry channels.   This part of the journey is not without solace.   The jungle of raspberry and currant bushes that lines the banks gives excuse for frequent halts for refreshment, in which the natives set the example.   They find further sustenance in the succulent stems of a huge umbelliferous plant, which they chew as they walk.   Then one of the train raises his voice in song, the whole body join in chorus, and the woods echo with some old ballad of war or the hunt.   The difficulties of the road, however, generally cut short this entertainment.

' The river, where it falls into a gorge, is crossed to its right bank ; there is no bridge, and one has generally to be extemporised by felling an alder. The ruins of an old castle or tower are here visible among the tree-tops. There are several in these glens—proof that once upon a time, when the Suanetians held Gebi and part of the Racha, they were less deserted.

Beyond this point side-torrents cut deeply into the loose slopes. To get horses across their gullies, where nobody has passed all the summer, ice-axes have to be brought into play ; and it often takes half an hour to dig out a sufficient track. The wood thickens, prostrate trunks block the way ; sometimes the animals tuck up their legs like goats and leap, sometimes our united efforts are needed to lift a log, so that they may squeeze underneath. As it grows dark we gain a glade in the beech-forest level enough to camp on. Water is fetched from the torrent below, the tents are raised, the horses picketed. Cooking is begun, and one of the horsemen comes up with a long, hollow fennel stalk, and carries off in it a live ember to furnish his companions with a separate fire. Are we not in the land of Prometheus ? Suddenly there is a stampede, our men rush about shouting ' the bear,' but Bruin remains invisible—as he generally does in the Caucasus. Peace ensues, and the travellers and their train sit round their fires, toasting flat loaves on knives or daggers, until it is time to seek the shelter of tent or sleeping-bags. I have tried both. The sleeping-bag is extremely serviceable in dry weather and for high bivouacs, but for any protracted tour in so moist and variable a climate as the Caucasus a light tent is undoubtedly essential.

The scenery rises to a wilder grandeur as we draw near the angle of the mountain which divides the Zeskho and Zena torrents. Great pines mingle with the deciduous trees ; their dark companies, draped in grey lichens, climb the steep hillside in order so close that the ground beneath them is hardly visited by sun or rain. A faint track is here and there visible, often little more than a ladder among the roots. It is not until the bottom of the Zena Valley has been reached that any distinct path can be recognised.

A new feature now appears in the landscape. Hitherto, since leaving the Rion, the peaks and glaciers have been subsidiary— a gleam of white or a fantastic rock-tooth framed between the branches of the beeches or the tall pine-stems. Looking up the Zena, the view is closed by a great snow mountain. It is, indeed, a great mountain, the loftiest on the Caucasian watershed, the third in height in the chain.[1]

In the curves of its long crest and continuous precipices Shkara

DWELLERS IN THE WILDERNESS

curiously resembles Monte Rosa, seen from Macugnaga. But here there is none of the barren foreground which defaces the Alpine view. The five peaks tower above downs that are great flower-meadows. Forests bright with the varied foliage that renews itself every spring, beech and birch, alder and plane, climb the hillsides. The nearest glades have been cleared of their gigantic

---

[1] Shkara has been allotted 17,038 feet by the last survey, 16 feet less than Dykhtau. Whether this relation between the summits is permanent, I doubt. The conditions of their snowcaps must affect it; and to Mr. Cockin, the only man who has measured each from the other, Shkara seemed to have a slight advantage. It is safest, however, for the present to accept the official figures.

flowers, and yellowing barley now occupies them. On a little plain in the foreground rise the smoke pillars of half a dozen humble homesteads — birch-bark huts — raised by visitors, or emigrants, from Ushkul. These traces of man's handiwork serve to emphasise the scale of the superb landscape, one of the most perfect in the arrangement of its lines and the combination of sublimity and beauty in its details it is possible to imagine.

As the head of the valley is approached, Shkara sinks for a time behind the nearer hills. The most prominent object is now the rocky comb of Koreldash,[1] the Ailama of the north side, which dominates the forked tongue of the glacier that falls into the head of the glen. A broad and steep sledge-track leads away to the left, and brings the traveller without further difficulty to the Zagar Pass (8680 feet), the lowest gap in the fence of mountains that encircles Suanetia. The view of the snows obtained from its grassy crest is soon lost, while of the region in front nothing is yet seen. A gentle descent over the pastures of a dull green glen leads to the black towers of Ushkul, the first and highest community of Free Suanetia.

---

[1] Dr. Radde called Ailama, Koruldu ; the new map gives the name Koreldash to a much lower ridge. The word doubtless indicates to natives some pasture or hunting-ground they go to at the head of the Zena Valley. This is how, when a need for them arises, summits acquire distinctive names.

CHAPTER X

SUANETIA

Οἱ δὲ Σοάνες δυναστεύουσι γοῦν τῶν κύκλῳ, τὰ ἄκρα τοῦ Καυκάσου κατέχοντες τὰ ὑπὲρ τῆς Διοσκουριάδος . . . ἅπαν γὰρ ἐστὶ τὸ πλῆθος μάχιμον οὐ συντεταγμένον.   STRABO, Lib. xi. c. 2.

THERE are sceptics who venture to deny that the most delightful of old English story-tellers, Sir John Mandeville, ever travelled, or even existed. But this much is certain, that an author writing under the name of Mandeville, in the reign of Edward III., told the following strange tale of the Caucasus:

'In that Kyngdom of Abcaz is a gret marvaylle. For a Provynce of the Contree that hathe well in circuyt 3 jorneyes, that men clepen Hanyson, is alle covered with Derknesse withouten ony brightnesse or light, so that no man may see ne here, ne no man dar entren in to hem. And natheles thei of the Contree seyn that som tyme men heren voys of folk and Hors nyzenge and Cokkes crowynge. And thei seyn that the Derknesse befelle by Myracle of God.

'For a cursed Emperour of Persie that highte Saures, pursuede alle Cristene men to destroye hem and to compelle hem to make Sacrifise to his Ydoles and rood with grete Host in alle that ever he myghte for to confounde the Cristene men.'

The Christians were miraculously preserved by a great cloud, which came down on the heathen host, who have ever since wandered about in the darkness.

An Arabian geographer, El Masudi, describes a Lost Valley in the same region in terms, it is true, trenching less on the marvellous but sufficiently similar to suggest a common basis for the legends. El Masudi's valley is enclosed by a wall raised from below upwards, two miles high and fifty miles in circumference. This barrier renders it impossible to go within the enclosure. By night many lights may be seen in it in different places, and by day are discovered villages, men, and cattle, but everything appears little, on account of the height from which the spectator looks down. Nobody knows what nation the inhabitants belong to, for they are unable to climb up, and no one who ascends to the top can go down to them.[1]

The more old travellers' tales I read the more convinced I become that nine times out of ten there is some truth at the bottom of them, some foundation in fact for the most picturesque superstructures of fancy. Hanyson reads very like an anagram of Soany, Saures might easily be Chosroes, the clouds that gather under the great peaks and overshadow the southern valleys at their feet might very well be represented as covering a land of darkness. The Suanetians keep herds of horses, and much poultry. Both stories, the English and the Arabian, seem to me to be probably based on the vague reports of wanderers who had stood on the ridge of the Latpari and seen the green pastures and white towers of Suanetia far below through the breaks in the storm-clouds. Let us, too, halt here for a moment in our travels in order to collect some details as to the natural characteristics, past history, and present condition of this Lost Valley of the Caucasus.

Suanetia, the country of the Suans—excluding Dadian's Suanetia on the Skenis Skali—is the whole upper basin of the Ingur above the great gorge through which it finds a way out to the lowlands near Sugdidi, a town some fifty miles west of Kutais. It is about forty miles long by fifteen broad, and in size and general features may be compared to the valley of Aosta. The Laila chain will then take the place of the Grand Paradis, the Zagar Pass that of the Col de la Seigne, and the

---

[1] Sprenger's Translation, vol. i.

Latpari Pass that of the Little St. Bernard.   The Dongusorun, the easiest pass over the main chain, will correspond to the St. Théodule.   But the Caucasian valley is in every respect more difficult of access than its Alpine rival.   The unbroken wall of rock and ice which forms its northern boundary is a far more formidable barrier than the Pennine Alps.   It encloses between its complicated spurs and bastions six great snow-basins, those of the Adish, Zanner, Tuiber, Leksur, Chalaat, and Ushba Glaciers.   Other great glaciers fall more steeply and directly from under the peaks of Shkara, Janga, Tetnuld, and Dongusorun.   Two ridges several miles in length run out from the watershed towards the Ingur, enclosing between them the glen of the Nakra.   By a prodigious blunder the five-verst map took the Caucasian watershed along the more eastern of these spurs and entirely ignored the upper Betsho Valley.   All these ridges are composed of crystalline rocks, for the most part granite, which show the tendency observable in the Alps, in the Mont Blanc and Pelvoux groups, to arrange themselves in double parallel ridges.   Unfortunately this structure was not recognised by the authors of the old survey, and in consequence the small map based on it both in the French and English editions of that standard work, Reclus's *Géographie Universelle*, is entirely misleading.

On the south Suanetia is fenced in by the lofty slate range of the Laila, attaining an altitude of 13,400 feet and supporting glaciers which may compare with those of the Grand Paradis group in the Graian Alps.   Near the Latpari Pass its rocks display very markedly the fan structure.   Foreign geologists have described them as 'palæozoic schists,' but the fossils discovered by Signor Sella on the top of the Laila, which have been examined and reported on by Dr. Gregory at the British Museum, do not bear out this designation as far as those peaks are concerned.   The formation, whatever its age, plays a very great part in the Caucasian chain, forming its watershed from the Mamison eastwards.[1]

---

[1] See Geological Note, Appendix A.

Between the granite and the slates, in places usurping the
central position of the granite in the watershed, lies a belt of
crystalline schist ridges narrower than the corresponding belt on
the north side. Their green rounded outlines contrast strikingly
with the precipices of the main chain. It is over these, where
they link the slate and granite, that the gentle slopes of the
Zagar Pass (8680 feet), only 1700 feet above the highest
villages, afforded in olden days, before the forests of the Skenis
Skali became pathless, the main access to the valley from Georgia.
Now the higher Latpari Pass, leading more directly south towards
the seat of government, Kutais, is universally preferred, though
in most years it is not open for horse traffic till the beginning of
July, and is closed by snow early in October. The Ingur, which
with its tributaries carries off the waters of Suanetia, has its
source under Shkara in the glaciers that line the south side of the
central chain. Its first large tributary, the Mulkhura, which drains
the vast snowfields that lie west of Tetnuld and east of Ushba,
exceeds it in volume. The two torrents unite near Latal, the meeting-place also of the streams from the Laila and the snows of Ushba
and Dongusorun. The glens above this point—the Ingur sources—
are covered with the castles of the Independent Suanetians: so
called because they had thrown off all external control for at
least one hundred years before Russian rule was established in the
country. The narrower trench below Latal through which the
united waters of the Ingur flow was 'Dadish Kilian's Suanetia,'
named after a family from the north, probably of Kabardan origin,
which had established a feudal lordship over its communities.

In scenery, this highland basin is in every respect a contrast to
the northern valleys on the other side of the chain. 'Savage Suanetia,' the title chosen by an enthusiastic sportsman for his account
of his travels in the district, may have been appropriate enough if
applied to the inhabitants only. But, as far as nature is concerned,
it has to be reversed. 'Smiling, sylvan, idyllic,' such are the
epithets that rise on a traveller's lips as he suddenly emerges
from the dark treeless glens and chilly recesses of the Northern
Caucasus on to a region of gentle slopes and wide distances, of

forests and flowery meadows, of fields golden with barley. Compared to the warrens, or stone-heaps, that serve the people of the northern valleys for dwellings, the towered villages and castellated farms of Suanetia assume at a distance a false air of mediæval romance. North of the chain, at Bezingi or Balkar, the traveller feels himself at the bottom of a well. He knows hours

A SUANETIAN LANDSCAPE

of climbing are required in order to enlarge or vary the outlook. Here the landscapes are wide and constantly changing: the visible sky is not a narrow strip but a broad arch. The hill-shapes may recall Savoy—the basin of Sallanches; but the forests show richer and more varied foliage than we are accustomed to in the High Alps. The pines no longer predominate, or press on one another until they become mere ragged staffs. They present themselves as dark, shadowy cones amidst the fresh green of the deciduous forest, of beeches and alders, of ash and walnut, of copses that in June and July are bright with purple rhododendron and fragrant with golden azalea blossom. The glades are gay with lupines and lilies and the spires of a ten-thousand-blossomed heracleum.[1] Any comparison from the reality to an imitation must seem more or less inverted and false. But for those who only know the imitation, it may be permissible to repeat a phrase that comes to every Englishman's lips as he wanders through Suanetian woodlands. When the azaleas and rhododendrons thicken, and the tall flowers cluster among them round the mown, open spaces, the epithet 'park-like' is inevitable! One finds one's-self looking unconsciously for the chimneys of the 'family mansion,' and the board with 'Trespassers, beware.' The illusion is abruptly broken when their place is taken by the towers of Ushba.

Mountaineers, as a rule, see Suanetia after midsummer. In June among the blossoms, and again in October when the beeches, the wild fruit-trees and the azaleas turn red, and the birches golden against the fresh autumn snows, the brilliancy of the landscape must be marvellous. Suanetia is a country for travellers and artists as much as for mountain climbers. Space, variety, sunniness —these are the constant and characteristic qualities of Suanetian scenery. The great mountain basin is broken by no heights that approach the snow-line. The glens are divided only by long grassy or forested ridges. Their gentle undulating crests furnish the most effective contrast to the icy clefts and rigid cliffs of Shkara and Ushba. From the beauty of flowers and forests close at hand, the eye is carried through soft gradations of distance to the pure glaciers which hang down like silver stairs from the snowy chain. The atmosphere has none of that sharpness of definition we associate with the Alps in summer. It more resembles

---

[1] M. Levier writes :—'Heracleum mantegazzianum is probably the largest umbelliferous plant in the Caucasus. Its stalks reach 10 centimètres in thickness, its basal leaves exceed a mètre, and on the smallest of the plants which M. Correvin has raised from seed at Geneva I have counted ten thousand blossoms.'

that of the West Coast of Scotland or the English Lakes. The afternoon breezes from the Black Sea bring up showers and vapours to colour the atmosphere, to soften the mountain outlines and magnify their bulk. The north wind from the steppe suffuses the sky with an impalpable haze through which the great peaks glimmer like golden pillars of the dawn. To the natural beauties, the snowy peaks, the flowers and forests of the Suanetian landscape, man has added something. It is a land where every man's house is his castle. The meadows and the cultivated valleys are strewn with high white towers. In one spot a single tower stands isolated, in another they cluster in groups of fifty to eighty. Every hamlet has as many towers as the cities of Tuscany in the Middle Ages. Nothing so fantastic as these family fortresses can be seen elsewhere outside San Gimignano or the frame of an Old Master.

A TOWER AT USHKUL

Mestia alone boasts seventy towers, each 40 to 80 feet high; Ushkul over fifty, and two black castles besides. The houses to which the towers are attached are quadrangular blocks, slate-roofed, without chimneys, and with narrow slits, closed by wooden shutters, for windows. Sometimes they have no windows at all, the light penetrating only through the interstices in the unmortared wall, while the smoke escapes through the roof. Torches made of birch-bark are used at night : a wooden passage, capable of being cut down in case of necessity, leads to the first floor of the tower of refuge.

Let us enter one of these houses or barns. It contains a single large, dark room; two or three boulders form the hearth : the furniture consists of a few wooden stools or benches scattered about the earthen floor ; in the corner is a raised wooden platform with skins and cushions, the family couch. By groping up a narrow passage we may reach the entrance to the tower; ladders or notched logs, easily removable, lead from storey to storey. The

CHURCH WITH FRESCOES AT LENJER

ladders are short, and to gain each storey one has to scramble up the last few feet by projecting stones left in the wall. Skulls and horns of wild goats lie about on the landings ; on the top storey are loop-holes for firing. The towers are built of unsquared blocks of granite or slate, and generally whitewashed. At Ushkul, however, the two castles have been left their natural dark colour.

In the upper and more lawless communities wood was, until quite lately, very sparingly employed. In Lower, or Dadish Kilian's Suanetia, timber balconies, barns, and even houses built of unsmoothed logs are not uncommon, and have increased in number since domestic warfare has ceased, and with it the need of dwellings at least externally fireproof.

The country is rich, strange as it may seem, in churches. The reader must not, however, let his fancy be wrought on by the familiar sound of the word and imagine buildings answering in any

TRIPTYCH AT MESTIA

respect to the church of Western Europe. The Suanetian churches, in dimensions and external aspect, are more on the scale of Italian roadside chapels. They have no towers; where bells exist they are hung on a wooden framework outside the church. This arrangement is common also in Corsica. The average dimensions of the internal nave are about 25 by 20 feet. There is commonly a porch; at Latal a portico, as at St. Mark's of Venice, runs round three sides of the building. The apse is shut off by an iconostasis or screen; it varies in external form and decoration. At Lenjer the apse is hexagonal; in one of the chapels at Latal semicircular and decorated with a colonnade in low relief. The interior, and sometimes the exterior, are frescoed in a style varying from pure Byzantine to what in Italy might be called *Giottesque*. The roof is often decorated with representations of the heavenly bodies, on a blue ground. A large wooden cross, covered with silver *repoussé* plates, is sometimes found in front of the iconostasis. There are few Georgian features in the architecture, and it appears at least probable that the builders were rather under direct Byzantine influence.

In these churches are preserved, under the jealous guard of the village elders, a number of very interesting objects, including manuscripts of great antiquity. Many of them have been described in detail and depicted in the work of M. de Bernoville, already referred to. Among the treasures he was allowed to inspect were the following. At Ushkul, small bronzes, apparently Roman, Persian money, Persian silk embroidered with six figures of the sun, ancient arrows and weapons. At the deserted monastery of St. Quiricus, near Kalde, he found arrows, figures in silver or silver-gilt, a magnificent Greek manuscript, attributed by M. de Bernoville to the sixth or seventh century (its subject is not stated), a silver box in the form of a book, used for the preservation of the sacred elements, having on one side the Crucifixion, with the Virgin and St. John and two angels, represented in *cloisonné* enamel on a silver ground. The workmanship is said to be of the highest order. The border is set with uncut precious stones; on the reverse side is a scene which seems to be the descent of Christ into Hades. M. de Bernoville, who has figured this case in his volume, describes it, however, as the Resurrection of Lazarus. I am inclined to believe that this may be the object, the removal of which by a Russian official became known throughout Suanetia, and led to almost insuperable difficulties being placed in the way of later travellers desirous of investigating any church treasures.

At Mestia we read of two processional crosses, a number of very beautiful old *repoussé* silver pictures with Georgian inscriptions, a great cross enriched with scenes of martyrdom, two silver cups, Italian in character, massive silver jugs. Some of these Signor Sella succeeded in photographing. At Lenjer is a manuscript of the Gospels, copied at Jerusalem in 1046-48—no inscriptions or manuscripts prior to the eleventh century are forthcoming ; at Latal a Gospel in an ornamental binding, manuscripts rolled on

ANCIENT CHURCH ORNAMENTS AT MESTIA

sticks, bells bearing Greek and Latin inscriptions ; at Ezeri, in the Prince's possession, a silver-gilt box, with Kufic inscriptions, and a massive silver bowl of Persian work.

It is obvious that an expert from South Kensington might spend a very interesting holiday in Suanetia, and that the history of the country may be further elucidated, if no greater discoveries are made, by a student competent to look over the ancient rolls and manuscripts.

This seems the best place to give a brief sketch of the history and origin of the Suanetians. Students will find in the second volume of Dubois de Montpereux's work on the Caucasus, or in M. de Bernoville's *Souanétie Libre*, fuller information and ample references.

Strabo describes the *Soani* as a powerful nation, who were governed by a King and a Council of Three Hundred : he adds that they were in the habit of using poisoned weapons in war. The statement in the received text that they could assemble two hundred thousand fighting men must, even if the name is loosely applied to a confederation of the Kolkhian tribes, be taken to be a copyist's error. Pliny speaks of the Svanetæ. It is, perhaps, worthy of notice that Suanetes and Consuanetes appear in the catalogue of the Alpine tribes subdued by Augustus, inscribed on the Trophæum that still shows 'its Roman strength' on the heights above Monaco. Suanetia was included in the Roman Empire, and Christianity, as is shown by the lists of Bishops present at the Œcumenical Councils, took root at a very early date in Kolkhis. When it penetrated to Suanetia is a matter of conjecture, but M. de Bernoville seems to have some reason for his belief that it was derived directly from Byzantium and not through Georgia. The churches found in the district are constructed on a plan not common in Georgia. Their bells, doubtless of much later origin than the buildings, bear in some instances Latin inscriptions, unfortunately without any date.

The country was reserved for Persia in the treaty made between Chosroes and Justinian when they combined to hold the line of the Caucasus against the Northern hordes. Persian objects are still found among the treasures concealed in the ancient churches, together with flint-headed arrows and weapons of a very remote period. When the Georgian kingdom first established a suzerainty over the Suanetians is uncertain. It was before the eleventh century, during which they temporarily asserted their independence. A hundred years later (A.D. 1184-1212), Queen Thamara became the ruler of Suanetia. This heroine plays, in popular imagination and legend, throughout the Caucasian isthmus the part taken by Alexander or Charlemagne in other parts of the world. She was styled by Georgian chroniclers, anticipators of the Hungarian compliment to Maria Theresa, the greatest of their *kings*. If we may believe the ballads still chanted in her honour by the Suanetians, she led the mountaineers to victory over their neighbours, the Abkhasians and Tauli, and, better still, reduced their taxes to the nominal fee of an egg per household.

Two centuries later (A.D. 1400) we find Suanetia taking advantage of the misfortunes of Georgia to again declare itself independent. The mountaineers' audacity grew until they burnt Kutais; they were chastised, and a family of the name of Ghelovani was imposed on them as rulers. Their obscure annals continue to be full of fighting and slaughter. Early in the fifteenth century they had to give up their claims to the villages on the upper Rion, which still, in the case of Gebi and Chiora, bear traces of their influence. In the eighteenth century the people on the Ingur dispensed with the ruling family of the Ghelovani, who, as the Dadians, still exercise feudal rights in the valley of the Skenis Skali on the southern side of the Latpari Pass. The Kabardan family of the Dadish Kilians, coming from the north, had meantime acquired large possessions, and some sort of control over the four lower communities on the Ingur, while the hamlets round the sources of the Rion had become absolutely independent. They realised the new ideal of a society where the free-will of the individual overrides all other considerations, and the only check to crime is the reciprocal extinction of criminals.

From this time forth all certain knowledge of the valley was lost. Its skin-clothed inhabitants paid occasional visits to the lower country in search of salt, but what slight traffic there was passed into the hands of the few Jewish families who had established themselves at some unknown date in Lakhamula, the lowest village above the great defile of the Ingur. Upper Suanetia was left, 'the world forgetting, by the world forgot.' We are, however, able to represent its condition from the reports of its first visitors in the latter half of the present century.

The picture they bring before our eyes should not be without interest to the advanced politicians, or dreamers, of Western Europe and Russia itself. For here we find some of their wildest imaginations carried out in practice.

I regret that I cannot give a more full statement as to the land tenures and the transmission of property, as well as some account of the old habits and beliefs of Suanetia. So far as I know, these matters still await thorough treatment; and no one should be more capable of giving it than the Surveyors, who have spent as many months among the mountain people as we travellers have days. The Government would confer a lasting benefit on students interested in the Caucasus by publishing reports from their officers from time to time of the information they have collected. The paper of a Russian writer, M. Akinfieff, printed at Tiflis in 1890, has come under my eyes, but only in a summary which does not inspire me with complete confidence.[1] What follows here is based on notes from books, and on conversations I have had with M. Nikoradse and other persons in the Caucasus.

Each farm or fortress was inhabited by a single family, the members of which did not separate except at the death of its head. The village, according to Professor Kovalevsky, consisted originally of members of the same family or *gens*; now, however, the village generally includes several distinct families. Members of the same family do not intermarry. A community is made up of several adjacent villages. But a community has proved too large a unit. Thus in 1866, when Dr. Radde was at Ushkul, the men of Murkmeli shot at every one who came down the path from Chubiani, both hamlets belonging to the same commune. There had been some quarrel over rights of common pasturage. Public enmities were supplemented by countless private feuds. When a woman changed hands or husbands, the parties concerned could not always agree on the value in cattle of the lady exchanged. Hence arose assaults of persons and batteries of towers. The punishment for 'breach of promise' was death at the hands of the woman's relatives. As parents had the right of betrothing children in their cradles, such breaches were not rare, but the more prudent bachelor evaded the difficulty by bigamy, by marrying once for duty and a second time from inclination, a practice which does not appear to have been thought objectionable. When too many girls were born in a family, a pinch of hot ashes was placed at birth in the mouth of the unfortunate baby and its body disposed of in the courtyard. This barbarous custom is vouched for on excellent authority by M. de Bernoville. In older times the Suanetians resorted largely to wife-lifting or exogamy; yet at the last census there were four males to three females in the Ingur Valley. Morality, in the ordinary sense of the word, is lax, and

---

[1] See *Scottish Geographical Magazine*, June 1895.

there are reported to be traces in the relations between brothers and sisters-in-law of an old form of what may be called family marriage.

The affairs of each hamlet, in so far as they were not settled by appeals to arms, were regulated by an assembly of all adult males. Before any decision was arrived at by the assembly every man had a right to be consulted, and a late comer could reopen the debate. Dr. Radde narrates his personal experience of such an incident in the discussion that arose with regard to his proposed visit in 1864 to one of the churches at Ushkul.   There being no local authority of any kind able to enforce a decision, arms were constantly resorted to, and the villages lived in perpetual warfare.

Free Suanetia, even before it had attained to Home Rule, had carried out Church Disestablishment and Disendowment with curious thoroughness.   The priests disappeared, the ecclesiastical property was secularised, a village council or 'vestry,' said to have become an hereditary body, assumed its control, and kept the key of the church, which, no longer reserved for pious uses, was employed chiefly as a treasury and banqueting-house.   It appears that these local elders absorbed the tithes in kind formerly paid to the church.   The old Byzantine Christianity was forgotten, and in its place there grew up the wildest jumble of Church rites, Persian sun-worship, and old Pagan beliefs and sacrifices.   The marriage ceremony consisted in sewing together the garments of the bride and bridegroom ; baptism was travestied ; the ancient funeral ceremonies were revived or continued.   Of these Professor Kovalevsky has furnished me with the following description :—One of the nearest relations of the deceased follows the body to the grave, leading by the horns a fat ox.   Immediately after the burial the ox is killed, and the heart and liver are placed on a wooden platter.   This is taken by one of the local elders (who are not consecrated, or in any way recognised as priests by the Georgian Church), who lifts up the plate, using at the same time the following words: 'O God, accept this our sacrifice.'   The portions so dedicated he keeps for himself.   The rest of the animal furnishes the funeral banquet.[1]   A year after the death a commemorative feast is held at the grave.   The relatives bring

---

[1] Signor Sella was present at one of these banquets.   See Illustration, p. 217.

cheesecakes, portions of meat, and the spirit locally made from barley, the provisions the ghost is supposed to need on its journey. A portion is blessed by the elder, and kept by him for his own use.

It is said that Suanetians who have reason to distrust their relations sometimes order their own funeral feasts, and take part in them during their lifetime. Every year after the harvest there is, as in Roman Catholic countries on All Saints' Day, a general commemoration of the dead, and large offerings of food are made to the elders.

FUNERAL FEAST AT MAZERI

Signor Sella has preserved in his photographs a vivid record of such a scene. Mr. Phillipps-Wolley saw seven oxen slaughtered, boiled, and distributed at Gebi, a place long united to Suanetia, and still preserving traces of its historical connection. I have also witnessed there a similar primitive banquet. The animals were killed and cut up in the churchyard.

There are no monuments resembling those of Ossetia or of the Turkish villages. Grave-mounds surround the churches, or are found under particular trees. But the dead are often put out of sight without heed of locality. In the centre of many hamlets there is a venerable tree or trunk—at Latal a walnut, at Mestia a birch, at Lenjer a cherry—under which are placed two or three rude stone seats. Tree-worship survives in many parts of the Caucasus. The sacred groves of the Circassians are described in Bell's and Longworth's *Travels*, those of the Ossetes by Hahn. There is a sacred wood close to the deserted monastery of St. Quiricus, near Kalde in Suanetia. In the Alps a few groves that possibly owe their survival to the same worship still exist. There is a patch of old beechwood near the shrine at Forno, above Lanzo.

Of Christian observances the Lenten Fast is the chief still held in any honour. The men are said to assemble outside the churches on Twelfth Day and the first Sunday in Lent, while the women are never allowed to approach them. Three days in the week are kept as holidays, Friday, Saturday, and Sunday. Carlyle somewhere says that the only virtue of his countrymen consists in keeping the Sabbath. Judged by this test the Suanetians might be held to be even more virtuous than the Scotch!

The Suanetians were, it must be added, arrant thieves, cattle-lifters, and sheep-stealers, who would on occasion carry off a girl as readily as a sheep across their saddle-bows. M. de Berno-ville relates how one such captive was released by the Russian Expedition of 1869. Their foreign relations were in consequence habitually strained. They in fact consisted for the most part in warlike undertakings and predatory forays on their neighbours' pastures. The great glaciers of the main chain, passes of the nature of the St. Théodule and Col d'Hérens, were no obstacle to these sturdy marauders. The Turkish mountaineers had to build watch-towers, and keep guard, in order to protect their flocks and herds. I myself saw in 1868 stolen oxen being driven hastily across the Dongusorun Pass, and so frightened were our porters of their probable reception on the north side, after their country-men's misdemeanours, that we had the greatest difficulty in inducing them to remain with us. Dr. Radde recounts the robbery of five hundred sheep by Suanetians of the Skenis Skali.

Strangers naturally seldom came to Suanetia. I can count

on the fingers of one hand the travellers who had visited the
country before 1868. Among its inhabitants there was no tradition of hospitality, such as is almost universal in the East. They
not only turned the stranger from their doors, but they exacted
a payment for letting him pass them. An attempt was made to
enforce such a demand on my last visit to Adish.

Medicine was practically unknown, and even now the traveller
who cures by his drugs is looked on more or less as a miracle-
monger. Goitres are prevalent, and epilepsy—possibly attributable
in part to the vile spirit extracted from barley—is not uncommon.
The natives are said to be peculiarly liable to fever when they
descend to the lowlands, and an incident I shall have to relate
affords a strong proof of their sense of danger in doing so.

Primitive poetry and local ballads often give a nearer insight
into the condition of life and the manners of a race than religious
rites and beliefs. The former are indigenous ; the latter as a rule
more or less exotic. Dr. Radde has fortunately preserved several
very curious Suanetian ballads, such as are still sung under some
ancient tree, or on the march along the mountain paths. They
celebrate the golden time of Thamara, past forays across the great
chain into the land of the Baksan (the name of Terskol, a glen at
the foot of Elbruz, occurs Tartars), or among the Abkhasians to
the west. The following ballad, which records the fate of a hunter
—an early 'mountaineering accident'—gives so lively a picture
of Suanetian manners that I must venture on a rough translation.

Metki was a hunter of Pari, in Dadish Kilian's Suanetia. He
became the lover of the Mountain Spirit. It appears from Dr.
Radde's version that, besides having an official wife, he was also in
love with his sister-in-law, and that to the latter he revealed the
secret of her mysterious rival. How the Spirit revenged his
indiscretion, Metki, or rather Metki's ghost, tells as follows :

'Metki is unhappy, and to be pitied. The men of Lentekhi were assembled for the dance. Into the circle of the dancers sprang a white hare :
after running round the circle it leapt between Metki's feet. Metki said to
his fellows, "Remain you quiet here ; this has never happened to me before.
I must follow the tracks of the hare !"

'High in the valley are the tracks. He came to a place where the mountain goats live. He came to the steep rocks. The white hare was transformed into a white mountain goat. Metki clung with the right hand and the left foot to the steep rocks. There came a neighbour from the same village, and he lamented when he saw how Metki hung, and heard how Metki spoke: "Once on a time I wounded you; remember that no more, but carry the news of my misfortune. Tell my father I fell from here, from the wild-goats' dwelling. Let him make ready wine with honey, and feast the neighbours; and bid my mother that for the repose of my soul she give to the folk bread and cheese and millet; and bid my wife that she bring up the children well, and my sister that she cut short her hair, and my brothers that they take good care of the house, and live not in enmity. Bid my friends, when they bewail me, that they sing true in the chorus. Bid my Thamara that she meet me at the foot of the mountain, that she go quickly on the level path, and climb weeping to the mountain.

'"Over me flutters the raven. He craves my eyes for his meal. Under me, at the foot of the mountain, waits the bear who shall eat my flesh.

'"The star Venus is my enemy!

'"Venus rises, and the day and the night part asunder. May my sins rest on the Mountain Spirit. O Spirit, save me, or let me fall quickly into the gulf."

'As the red of morning shone, and the day and night were parted, Metki fell; but all his misdeeds shall rest on the Spirit of the Mountains.'

The Suanetians are not (as M. Chantre alleges) mainly a pastoral people. They keep a few flocks of sheep and herds of horses. Bullocks are used to draw sledges, and are eaten in winter. But flocks and herds are seldom found, as among the Tartars beyond the chain, on the high pastures, and consequently there are often no paths to them. To reach the upper glacier basins you must find and follow almost invisible and overgrown hunters' tracks. Pigs, the smallest breed I ever saw, and geese wander round the homesteads, which are guarded by dogs. The villages are surrounded by barley-fields, fenced in with neat wattling. The foot-paths between them are pleasant. As the traveller descends the valley he meets with other crops, millet, flax, wheat, and tobacco, and Indian corn is grown in outlying plots below the most western villages at a height of about 3500 feet. The inhabitants have

learnt recently to cultivate potatoes and other vegetables. They cut
a certain amount of hay on the high pastures. Sometimes they
cross the chain in summer, and hire themselves out as labourers
to the indolent Tartars, just as the Lucchesi do to the Corsicans.
But there is no love lost between them. The Mussulmans look
on the Suanetians with contempt as pig-eaters. I heard the
Suanetians hiss 'Cherkess' at our Kabardan Cossack; and the
Cossack — a mild, amiable creature, the reverse of our popular
idea of a Cossack—despised and distrusted every Suanetian from
the bottom of his soul.

It seems to me difficult to recognise any prevalent type among
the Suanetians. *Variety* is the most marked characteristic. The
village head-man of Mestia, huge and bull-like, was like a figure
on an Assyrian monument. Fair men with blue eyes and tawny
beards are common. The ordinary costume is the long brown frockcoat of the Caucasus, with cartridge-pouches on the breast. On
the head is worn either a flabby Ossetian wide-awake, a *bashlik*,
or else one of the tiny pieces of cloth, like kettle-holders, common
in Mingrelia. The women at Ushkul have, or had in 1868, one
rough sheet of sacking for clothing, and are shy. In other villages
they wear the red robes common in this part of the Caucasus, and
white or coloured cotton kerchiefs on the head. At Latal they
wear flounced petticoats, such as might be seen in a back street
of Genoa. Some one may start a theory that the Latal ladies
are the descendants of refugees from one of the Genoese colonies
on the coast, destroyed by the Mohammedan invasion! One per
cent. of the population is said to be goitred.

The Suanetian language resembles Old Georgian. It has
some affinity also with the dialects spoken by the more
eastern highlanders, the Pshavs, Chevsurs, and Tushins. The
late Mr. D. R. Peacock, H.B.M.'s Consul at Batum, prepared a
limited vocabulary of the Georgian, Mingrelian, Laz, Suanetian,
and Abkhasian dialects for the Royal Asiatic Society.[1]   Even

---

[1] *Journal of the Royal Asiatic Society*, vol. xix. part I. See Dr. Radde's and Captain
Telfer's works already quoted. Hahn states that Greek words occur.

a hasty glance shows that the first four tongues have many words in common, while the Abkhasian seems to stand absolutely apart from all of them.[1]   The problem that has been discussed is : Are the Suanetians—so far as they are not merely a mixture of refugees who have found shelter at different times in this mountain Alsatia—of the Georgian stock, or do they belong to some primitive Kolkhian race ?   The first view is taken by Radde and Kovalevsky, the second by De Bernoville, whom M. Chantre copies in the short notice contained in his encyclopædic and splendidly illustrated work.   The linguistic argument seems to me in favour of the former view.

In this strange and interesting political and social condition, Suanetia appears to have remained for more than a century.   Off the world's highways and out of the world's contests, the mountain communities went on turning, like the earthen pot, round and round in their own rock-girt pool, until they were swept at last into the stream of the nations.   Meantime the Free Suanctians were free and independent to their hearts' content.   They were as lawless as the Cyclopes of the *Odyssey*.   They knew no restraint to their passions.   No man could call either his wife or his house his own except in so far as he could defend them by force.   The right of murder was the foundation of society.   Such a state of things was too ideal to last in this prosaic, order-loving age.   In 1833 Russia assumed suzerainty over the district, and as years went on her suzerainty became more than nominal.

Shortly after the Crimean War a Russian force penetrated,

---

[1] M. Chantre prints a very poetical legend purporting to account for the absence of any written form of the Circassian dialect.   A learned Adighè or Circassian, an Arabic scholar, sat down to endeavour to make an alphabetical representation of his native tongue.   He had not proceeded far when his labours were interrupted by the sudden appearance of a venerable figure.   The stranger addressed him to this effect : 'Give up your hopeless task.   Can you put into human writing the rolling of the thunder among the peaks, the crash of the falling avalanche, the deep roar of the mountain-torrents, the blast of the waterfalls ?   Can you represent the sounds of the stones as they clatter down the gorges, of the branches of the forest as they moan in the tempest, the screams and songs of the birds as they call to one another from height to height ?   How then can you hope to imprison in letters the free speech of the tribes of Circassia ?'

for the first time, the mountain-barriers. The expedition produced no permanent political result.

In 1857 the Russian Government was brought face to face in a very dramatic manner with the difficulties every civilised government in turn meets with when, from reasons of high policy, it tolerates disorder within its frontiers. The first breakdown in the system of non-intervention was brought about by the violence of a certain Constantine Dadish Kilian, one of the feudal princes of the lower valley. This ruffian, who had already in a private vendetta slain one of his uncles and wounded his cousin, was known to be fomenting trouble. Sent for to Kutais by the Governor and ordered to live elsewhere than among his vassals, he did to his ruler as he had done among his own people. He stabbed that official and three others. The Dadish Kilian met with the usual fate of murderers; and as a result of his crime a Russian force was sent into the valley, the culprit's castle was razed to the ground, and a garrison of ten men placed in his village. The Independent Communities were, however, still left alone. This was the state of affairs at the time of my first visit. In the upper hamlets Russian orders did not run, and the Government was openly defied. Private wars still raged, individual against individual, family against family, hamlet against hamlet, community against community.

The first travellers to visit Suanetia were two Russian officials, General Bartholomai and Herr Bakradze. They wrote pamphlets, describing chiefly the ecclesiastical treasures and inscriptions existing in the district. Herr Abich and Dr. Radde, the well-known botanist, and curator of the Tiflis Museum, visited the valley in 1864 and 1866. Two years later Dr. Radde was followed by the first party of English travellers, who owed much to their predecessor's book and friendly advice.

In the following year (1869) Count Levashoff, then Governor of Mingrelia, assembled an armed force and marched with some pomp over the Latpari. M. de Bernoville, a Frenchman, who was allowed to take part in the expedition, has given a detailed account of its progress. The Suanetians met the Russian force in arms

on the heights above Mujal, but in the end they made their submission.   The leader of the insurgents— or patriots—sent a peace-
offering in the shape of a cart laden with boiled beef and vessels
of the horrible native spirit, brewed from barley, called 'raca.'
M. de Bernoville gives a picturesque description of the scene that
followed.   First came a troop of suppliants for redress : an old
man whose son had been assassinated, a pale husband whose wife
had poisoned him and fled to the tower of a neighbour, a youth
whose entire family has been slain in a vendetta.   These were
all put off and ordered to present their complaints to regular
judges—when they were appointed.

This formidable incursion, which was not followed up by any
practical steps for throwing the country open by means of new roads,
seems to have rather irritated than awed the Suanetians.   In 1871
the Russian Government, which up to this time had only maintained a post of a dozen Cossacks at Pari, a hamlet in the lower
and comparatively civilised portion of the district, found it necessary to plant a garrison of a hundred men at Betsho, on the banks
of a branch of the Ingur, from the head of which a glacier-pass,
commonly used by the mountaineers, gives access to, and, therefore, possibility of relief from, the Baksan.   How little respect
the presence of these troops ensured for the representative of the
Russian Government is amusingly shown by Captain Telfer, R.N.,
who has given a full account of his travels in the district in company with a Russian official in 1874 : [1]

'One of the objects of the Chief's official tour in the upper valley of
the Ingur was to superintend the fresh elections of the village officers in
the several communes ; and notice having been given upon our arrival
that the voters for Kala and Ushkul were to assemble in the morning,
the male population of those two communes began to muster in front of
our encampment at nine o'clock, and when all had assembled the proceedings were opened with an address from the Chief.   The instantaneous
and unanimous expression of opinion being that the Chief should himself
select the most fitting men, the Colonel had to explain at some length

---

[1] Telfer's *Crimea and Transcaucasia*, 1876. See also *Edinburgh Review*, No. 237.

that he could only approve the choice of the people, as it was quite impossible for him to make judicious appointments, seeing that every man was a perfect stranger to him. Some dissatisfaction was shown at this reply, but after a time the crowd moved away, and almost immediately hurried back, pushing to the front one of their number who was doing his best to resist. The favourite refused to be the "elder"; in the first place, because his three years' term as "rural judge" had just expired and he desired to be released from further responsibility, and because he thought no greater misfortune could visit him than that of becoming *mamasaklysy*. "I killed a man in the next village to this ten years ago ; I have paid his relations the full amount of blood-money, but they are not satisfied, and I believe that they are seeking an opportunity for revenge ; if I am made *mamasaklysy* I know what I will do—I will kill another of the family, the man who wants to kill me." This was the explanation offered ; but the Chief told him that if he persisted in making such a statement he should arrest him, and have him tried for murder; on the other plea, however, that of having already served as judge, he was entitled to decline the new honour, and a fresh election must take place. The determination of the people was not, however, to be altered, for they clamoured in favour of the late judge, and *vox populi* being *vox Dei*, he was prevailed upon to accept the office.'

The occasional dangers and annoyances incident to a district-officer's post in the Caucasian Alsatia may be estimated from the following further extract from Captain Telfer's narrative :

'The "elder" and the priest made their official report, which was to the effect that an old feud between the villages of Zaldash and Mujal had resulted in the violent death, the previous January, of a son of Kazboulatt Shervashidze, the *mamasaklysy* of Mujal, and as the people of Mujal muster stronger than they of Zaldash, the allies of the deceased man's family had kept the assassin and his friends besieged in their tower since the commission of the crime, for which blood-money had never been paid. The Chief was inclined to the belief, from the evidence at hand, that the murder had not been premeditated, and that one man slew the other in self-defence; he accordingly despatched a messenger to Zaldash, to tell the accused and his two brothers that they were to leave the tower and come to him forthwith. A first and a second summons remaining disregarded, the Chief himself rode off to Zaldash, accompanied by his interpreter, the priest, and a Cossack, and ordered the trio to descend, which they promised to do, provided they were not constituted prisoners. After being repeatedly urged to give themselves up unconditionally for the easier investigation of the charge preferred against them, a ladder slung to a long rope was let over the parapet, and the three brothers descended to the ground, when he who was accused of the murder hurriedly approached the Chief, and insisting upon kissing him on the naked breast, pronounced his submission and readiness to follow.

'This farce being over, the brothers were ordered to the front, and as the party moved off necessarily at a walking pace, a loud voice at a loop-hole called upon it to halt, under a threat to fire. The explanation offered by the brothers was, that a man of Ipari who had fled his village for murder, had sworn to defend with his life the murderer of Zaldash, in return for the protection afforded him from his own enemies. The interpreter shouted to the scoundrel that no harm was intended to the brothers, and that they were not being carried off against their will: the Iparian, however, who kept his rifle levelled, still threatened to fire and kill the Chief or the priest, if his friends were not immediately allowed to reascend the tower. Hereupon the youth pleaded to having sworn to stand by the runaway of Ipari, proscribed like himself, to the last extremity, and to avoid further bloodshed begged that he might be permitted to stay, for the Iparian, he said, would most assuredly fire. The advantage being decidedly in favour of the bandit in his unassailable position, the Chief deemed it prudent to release the assassin from his bond, leaving the settlement of the matter to a future occasion, when he should be better prepared to enforce his authority.'

On another occasion two travellers provided with Russian re-commendations were, despite the Chief's personal remonstrance, refused lodgings and compelled to sleep under a tree. When we find a magistrate unable, even when on the spot, to enforce the simplest order, or to procure provisions for his own party, it is easy to understand that for ordinary visitors travel in Suanetia thirty years ago was not altogether easy.

The danger of this policy of letting ill alone and allowing government representatives to be insulted with impunity, was shown in 1875, when a serious outbreak was only averted by the forbearance of the officials concerned. The survey preliminary to a readjustment of the land-tax roused the discontent of the Suanetians, who surrounded the detachment at Betsho, and prepared to resist in force their relief over the Latpari Pass from Mingrelia. The Russians threw 300 Kabardan Militia into the valley by the Betsho Pass. Captain Telfer has related from Russian sources the story of the disturbance and its suppression, which was effected without any fighting, except in the dislodgment of an obstinate ringleader from his tower, where he had to be formally bombarded with a howitzer.

Even this warning, however, did not suffice to convince the Government of the expediency of impressing its strength on the handful of unruly mountaineers. Temporary tranquillity was purchased by concessions, and no force adequate to overawe the turbulent communities was left in the district. The result was lamentable. During the summer of 1876 a small detachment of soldiers was sent to Kala, a group of villages at the northern foot of the Latpari Pass, to arrest a fugitive criminal. The Suanetians fled to their towers and took up arms in defence of the right of asylum. At nightfall the Russian force retreated from the hamlet, having lost its three officers, and leaving dead Colonel Hrinevsky, 'the Chief' of Captain Telfer's narrative, and his interpreter, who were shot through the roof of a barn. Such an outrage was too much even for the patience of the Caucasian authorities. The Government inflicted an adequate, but by no means excessive retribution, made a great many good resolves as to new roads and other measures, and tightened to some extent, as it might well have done earlier, the reins of administration. Troops and mountain-guns crossed the Latpari. At first the Suanetians from their towers defied the invader, after the manner of Orientals; but they had reckoned without artillery. The mountain-guns soon brought the stones about their ears. Iprari is now a collection of barns without towers; its teeth are drawn. A certain number of its inhabitants have had experiences of Siberia, and, strange to say, returned to tell them. The authorities at Vladikavkaz are less lenient than those of Tiflis. A late commandant of Ciscaucasia justified the capital punishment of brigands by the judicious remark that to send men from the climate of the mountains to Siberia would be to put a premium on crime!

The Government has appointed responsible headmen or *starshinas* in every commune, has sent more Georgian priests, has established several schools, erected sheds or court-houses where travellers can find shelter, and placed its representative at Betsho in a position to command a certain amount of respect and obedience. The framework of local government has thus been laid down. But the machinery is naturally still rude and ineffective. Thus, at Ushkul the Starshina does not understand a word of Russian, and the official documents he receives are carefully preserved, unopened and unread, in one of the church chests! Some thieves from Adish (formerly so notorious a robbers' den that in 1864 Dr. Radde did not dare to pass through it by daylight) stole from our camp in 1887 what they could lay their hands on under cover of night and storm. But this was an exceptional experience ; Russian justice speedily overtook the culprits, and the offence is not likely to be repeated. I walked about in 1887 and 1889 alone and unarmed by day and night over the hills, as freely as I should in Switzerland. A change is slowly coming over the people : schools, perhaps the only effectual civilisers, are doing their work.

There have been no further serious troubles during the last twenty years. The princes mediatised, the natives once taught the effect of field artillery on their stone walls, and the discomforts of a journey to Siberia, the country has been free from public disorders, and private vendettas and robbery have been kept within limits a tolerant administration may wink at. Since in Paris, where a lady is in the case, murder is held no crime, it may be lightly punished under similar circumstances in the Pari of the Dadish Kilians. To waylay a Jew pedlar after he has converted his stock into money may be looked on as a merry jest in Suanetia as well as in Sherwood. But since 1875 a new generation has grown up, which knows the meaning of 'school,' has learnt to cultivate potatoes and keep bees, and to welcome English travellers for the money they leave behind them. By 1920 it seems probable that the Suanetians will have begun to collect crystals and make bouquets of yellow lilies—there is not a scrap of Edelweiss in the Caucasus ; the son of the murdered Jew will have set up a general store at Betsho; the priest at Mujal will keep a 'Gostinitza London,' and the village headman will have a roll of porters and a tariff for the Tuiber and Zanner Passes.

The Suanetians are a mixed race, a tribe of refugees; they have the qualities as well as the vices of their ancestors, and amongst them there are undoubtedly individuals of capacity, who, now that reciprocal slaughter is forbidden, will turn their wits and energies to some better account. The pacification of their country without serious fighting has been one of the successes of the Russian Administration in the Caucasus. It has been effected chiefly by patience in overlooking petty offences and by the gradual introduction of some control and new ideas. It is hardly, however, a complete success. In the same time a more energetic and wealthier government might have spent much more money, and done much more for the district. Roads might have been made, mineral resources examined, and perhaps utilised. The defile of the Ingur might have been opened. A district of ten thousand inhabitants would hardly have been left to be administered by a native civilian with ten men, lodged in a row of shabby wooden sheds. But the Caucasian Administration is compelled to do its work cheaply;[1] it aims at making things easy, under certain conditions, to the mountain tribes. Its subordinate officials have less money and less energy to expend, and are more easily influenced by their surroundings than British Civilians. Not infrequently they are members of subject races. So long as they can keep the peace they are apt to let progress shift for itself. They avoid, no doubt, some of our mistakes and indiscretions; but they are less capable as administrators. So long as Great Britain maintains among Orientals her unrivalled reputation for uprightness, justice, and tolerance, she need not fear any contrasts that may be drawn by her subjects when the great Empires meet in Central Asia.

---

[1] According to Professor Hahn, however, the force at Betsho costs the Government annually 300,000 roubles.

CHAPTER XI

TRAVEL AND MOUNTAINEERING IN SUANETIA

(1868-87-89)

The mountains were all dark with clouds upon their heads. Such an impression I never received from objects of sight before, nor do I suppose I ever can again. Glorious Creatures ; fine old Fellows ! I turn back to these great places, participating in their greatness.

CHARLES LAMB.

HE passage through the forests of the Skenis Skali from Gebi to Ushkul has been described in the preceding pages. I broke off my story at the point where, on a great crocus-studded hay-meadow, gently sloping towards the Ingur, the first English explorers of the Caucasus caught sight of the black towers of 'Queen Thamara's Castle,' the old fortress that watches the easiest entrance to 'Free Suanetia.'

As the green featureless glen we were descending opened out towards a larger valley, a great company of towers met our astonished eyes. We could count at least fifty, clustered in three separate knots, and most of them covered with a rude white plaster. Square in form, they were redeemed from a resemblance to factory chimneys by their roofs and battlements, pierced for musketry. Round their base clustered barn-like dwellings built of dark slate. The scene was weird and strange. My mind wandered far for a

comparison : first to some woodcut familiar in childhood, an illustration to Lane's *Arabian Nights,* then to Tuscan San Gimignano.

We hurried on towards these habitations with all the eagerness
of men who have been rained on for several days, and have had
little to eat or drink beyond high sheeps-brains, wild raspberries,
and water flavoured with the dregs of tea-leaves. In 1868 our tent
was not waterproof, and our commissariat was simple in the
extreme.[1]   We found quarters in a barn slightly above the village,
a gloomy building without windows. Many of the houses at

USHKUL

Ushkul have no windows, and depend for light on what can pass
through the chinks between the unmortared stones of the walls.
In this gloomy lodging we spent two nights and a day, surrounded
by the most savage and dangerous-looking set of people I have ever
come across, outside Arabia. The men went about armed with
flint-lock guns and pistols ; even the small boys carried daggers.
Their arms seemed almost their only possessions ; their clothes

---

[1] I observe that a recent traveller, Mr. Trevor-Battye, says of Whymper tents, ‘to
pretend that they are waterproof is not even reasonable humour.’ The last I had proved
perfectly waterproof under the most severe trials possible in a temperate zone. It was made
by Messrs. Silver, of Willesden canvas.

were sheepskins, or rags and tatters, their coats as often as not
sleeveless, their headgear dirty *bashliks* tied up into turbans, or small
shapeless pieces of cloth, from the size of a crown-piece upwards,

STREET IN USHKUL

fastened on the top of wild, un-
kempt locks. The women were
as a rule hideous, and their
dress was shapeless; the
children wore a single piece of
sacking, or nothing at all. We
could not sit outside our barn
without being mobbed: if we
retreated for peace into the
black interior, we were pursued by individuals who planted
themselves a yard off, took a
steady stare which lasted any
time from five to fifteen
minutes, and then began to
overhaul our persons, with as
little scruple as if we had been
figures in a waxwork show.
Here a line had to be drawn
and the sightseers requested
'not to touch any of the objects
exhibited.' But still, on one
pretext or another, visitors crowded in, and as the day wore on,
grew more and more aggravating. Towards evening a short
revolver practice, and a bold statement by our Mingrelian interpreter, an old servant and travelling companion of Gifford
Palgrave, that our weapons were self-loading, produced a certain
pause in the persecution. But we barricaded ourselves in for the
second night, not without some apprehension as to how it would
pass, or how we should get away from the place next morning.

Our final departure was a singularly dramatic scene, and gave
promise at one time of a tragic ending. After an attempt on the
part of the people to separate us, by shutting our interpreter

and our Chamoniard, François Dévouassoud, up in the barn, had failed, we succeeded in hoisting our slender baggage, partly on the one horse we had secured, partly on our own shoulders. Then forming in close order, and holding our revolvers in our hands, we made ready for a sudden start. Meantime some of the inhabitants, yelling and jabbering, barred the way, others brandished swords, daggers, and pistols on either wall of the sunk lane which led through the village : a few ran off making signs they would fetch their guns. The women, screaming and apparently endeavouring to restrain the passions of their relations, added to the picturesque confusion.

Things seemed getting worse and worse, and the issue more and more doubtful, when a demand of some sort, shouted out by a man on the right-hand wall, suggested a simple stratagem. I flung a handful of kopeks into the crowd, and at the same moment we all made a sudden push down the lane. The crowd scrambled and fought for the coppers, the men in the roadway yielded as the cold muzzle of the revolver touched their faces, and in less time than it has taken to describe the incident, we were outside the hamlet and among open fields. With our fifteen barrels we now felt comparatively safe. When roused to passion, the Suanetian will occasionally use his dagger in open fight—I have more than once seen daggers drawn—but he much prefers the safety of a neighbouring thicket, whence he can take a deliberate aim with the help of his forked gun-rest, and shoot his enemy unobserved. The owner of our horse, a native of another village, who had disappeared during the disturbance, now came up to tender his services and his congratulations, while our Mingrelian interpreter explained to us the voices on the wall : ' Let us tie them up, let us rob, let us kill.'

Such was my first introduction to Suanetians. It will be allowed that, if I have written some hard things of them, it has not been without provocation. There is no doubt, however, that in the last twenty-five years the Suanetians have changed very much for the better. But readers who may be disposed to consider my early descriptions overcharged, because more recent experiences do not correspond with them, may do well to look into narratives contemporary with mine.   Dr. Radde, the Curator of the Tiflis Museum, was even in 1866 no raw traveller, and this is the account he gave of the inhabitants of Jibiani after his first visit :—

'The impression left by my stay at Jibiani cannot exactly be called peaceful. Constantly surrounded by from sixty to eighty natives, amongst whom were many children and even women, it was only by the greatest patience and forbearance that we could protect ourselves from their obtrusiveness. Presents, friendliness, and a scrupulous and often affected indifference to insolence succeed best with such a people; but there comes a point when it is necessary to draw a line, and to take decided measures to put an end to their excessive rudeness.

'During my stay two wounded men presented themselves, and I frequently heard gunshots from an old castle called Lenqueri, which stands on the left bank of the Zurischi (?). In this castle lived eight robbers, natives of the neighbouring hamlet of Murkmur, which, with Jibiani, forms part of the same community, Ushkul. A quarrel about the pasture-grounds had involved the two hamlets in open war, and the bitterness of the quarrel was such that the whole population took part in it with powder and shot, two-edged daggers and swords, while the robbers issuing from their castle carried off at every opportunity the herds of the opposing party, and spread murder and rapine through the district.'

The Doctor added :

'Among this population men are frequently met with who have taken two or more lives. Murder is not only sanctioned, but in many cases commanded by their code of morality.'

Certain Georgian writers have argued, on the strength of the name Edenis Mta, that the Garden of Eden was situated among the sources of the Rion. They might fairly have gone on to suggest that Cain took refuge in Suanetia, and founded that 'régime of reciprocal assassination' which, according to M. Renan, is the earliest stage in human society.

Nineteen years later I returned to Ushkul. After descending from the Latpari Pass to the guest-house at Kal, we turned up the path that leads to the sources of the Ingur. Except one striking glimpse of the Kalde glaciers and Janga, there is little to see in the trough beside the stream until the fifty towers of Ushkul rise among the yellowing barley fields, and the shining crest of Shkara crowns the green hillsides of the middle distance. I must confess that it was not without a certain involuntary tremor that I walked between the well-remembered walls, straight into the den of thieves from which we had once been so thankful to escape. On my companion François Dévouassoud's face I noticed a more than usually pensive air, as if his recollections were too much for him, and he took the occasion to remind me that our camp had been plundered at the neighbouring Adish a fortnight before. His relief and my pleasure were consequently great when a man dressed as a well-to-do Georgian stepped forward and introduced himself to us. He proved to be one Bussarion Nikoradse, a Suanetian orphan, who, I know not why, was educated at government expense for the priesthood, but has preferred the post of a schoolmaster at Kutais. Nikoradse was spending his summer holidays among his native people, and he cordially invited me to share his lodgings—a room which he had provided with a floor, a table, and a bedstead, thermometers and a field-glass—luxuries of civilisation unique at Ushkul. Our host obviously exercised much influence over the villagers. The people were in every way strangely changed for the better. Twenty years before every man had seemed to have the terror of sudden death in his eyes—that strange, hunted look, as recognisable as the gambler's frown, that marks a land of vendetta. This wild expression was now far less universal. When Mr. Phillipps-Wolley passed in 1882, the priest dared not eject the turbulent crowd from his room lest he should be shot for his pains. Now I was left in undisturbed quiet in our lodging, and was seldom mobbed in my frequent rambles. Provisions were supplied without difficulty, and the three horsemen whom we subsequently secured to go with us to Gebi served us with something less than the usual Caucasian intractability. Even papermoney had a purchasing power, and payments no longer had to be made in piles of metal kopeks. After all, the change has been gradual compared to that effected in Hunza, where the greatest brigands of Central Asia served contentedly as Sir Martin Conway's porters a year after the British occupation of their fastnesses.

During my stay of nearly two days I was able to do full justice to the sights of Ushkul. There are two castles : one close to Chubiani, the other high on the hillside, which—according to local tradition—were Queen Thamara's winter and summer residences. Thamara, as I have noted elsewhere, plays in the Caucasus the part as an architect taken by Alexander in Syria, the Saracens in the Alps, and the Devil generally. Everything remarkable in the way of buildings is placed to her credit.

During my stay I never tired of sitting on the rocky knoll crowned by the black towers of the lower castle, and watching  the lights and shadows shift on the grey cliffs and white glaciers of Shkara. When the eyes needed rest there was the village beneath me ; I could watch all that was going on in these primitive homesteads. It was not very much. There was hay to be brought in on wheelless wains, drawn by oxen, there was corn to be beaten out on the paved threshing-floors, which form a sort of terrace outside the houses, or to be ground in the little watermills beside the stream, cakes to be baked, a sheep, perhaps, to be killed and cut up.

WATERMILLS AT USHKUL

Little boys, perched on the rude boards set with stones which are used as threshing implements, exhorted their beasts with odd cries, while their parents, clad in sad grey rags, superintended the business. Other children played a rough game in which an old cap was scrimmaged for.

My host acted as cicerone. We visited the remains of the chapel in the Castle ; we wandered up to the church which stands isolated above the hamlets. I was taken to a certain historical barn, where I was told a party of Franks had many years before been entertained. I remembered that 'entertainment' very well. Two or three young trees planted in front of the church represent an ancient sacred grove which has been destroyed by weather or war. Throughout Suanetia there are traces of tree-worship in early times. In several of the villages a single tree of great age and size is found near the church on a sort of village green with, beneath its shade, ancient tombstones, and a stone seat apparently used in village assemblies.[1] We saw the outside of the hunter's home where Mr. Phillipps-Wolley was lodged, decorated with

'fifty off-forepaws of bears in varying stages of decomposition.' I went carefully over the house and tower in which our host had constructed his apartments; it varied little, if at all, from that I have described in the last chapter.

I naturally did not limit my exploration to the three villages that form Ushkul. A pleasant walk of two or three hours up the grassy dale of the Ingur leads to the junction of the Shkara and Nuamkuam Glaciers at the very base of the enormous cliffs of the great chain. The ice is in retreat, and has left behind it a tract which is full of

THE HUNTER'S HOME, USHKUL

interest for the student of glacier action. As far as I can learn from their works, some English glacialists are not much given to studying the Reports of the United States Survey. It seems to me a pity, for they convey useful cautions to the inconsiderate advocates of glacial erosion. Here, in front of the Ingur Glacier, were to be seen on a small scale, as in a model, most of the features found on the outer edge of the region once covered by the great North American ice-flood. Within the limits marked

---

[1] For the Caucasus, see Bell's and Longworth's *Travels in Circassia*; generally Frazer's *Golden Bough*, vol. i., and Fergusson's *Tree and Serpent Worship*. Similar stone 'Chairs of Justice' are found in some of the villages of Val de Lys, south of Monte Rosa. See Brosset's *Rapports sur un voyage archéologique dans la Georgie et dans l'Arménie*, 1847-48.

by the half-dozen great erratic blocks, ranged in a curve, which mark the terminal moraine of the last advance, there is a series of mounds and pools, formed by the damming of streams. Of lowering in the trough of the valley there is no sign whatever.

Above the meeting of the ice-streams and on their true left lies the Belvedere Alp of the Caucasus. After a steep climb I found myself in a lovely meadow, the nearest to the snows of an army of green hills, unbroken by copse or wood, except here and there by a slender birch or a tangle of the cream rhododendron. The surface was one sea of flowers, pink and white daisies, gentians, forget-me-nots, and waving grasses. The spot was not, however, altogether unknown to man, for, wading ankle-deep in the thick bright carpet, I found on the brow which commanded the best view of the mountains two stone-men—no common stone-men, but carefully built pyramids tapered up with scrupulous neatness to a point. Could they be the work of Russian Surveyors ? Hardly, for at that time the new map was only in contemplation in this district, and it would be an insult to the maker of this portion of the five-verst map to suppose that if he had really visited the ground he would have misrepresented it as he has. I would rather believe that some bold hunter raised these piles as altars to that Spirit of the Summits who—as the ballad tells—led astray the adventurous Metki.

Whoever the builder may have been, he showed his taste. The view from this point is unsurpassable of its kind. The source of the Ingur lies below ; the spectator stands on a level with the snow-basin out of which rise the great rock-walls and buttresses that support the five peaks of Shkara. They carry snow and ice to an extent hardly ever seen in the Alps. This richness of frozen hangings is a joy to the traveller, but a terror to the climber. To the right stretches the long and formidable crest, reached from this side by an Alpine party in 1893, and in 1895 from the Dykhsu basin, which extends to Nuamkuam.

I despair of creating in the minds of those who have not travelled in Suanetia any true picture of the extraordinary sublimity of the face of the Caucasian chain that overlooks the Ingur sources.

There is nothing in the Alps to compare to the view from the ridge above Adish; on one side Shkara and Janga, on the other the ideal glacier, that wonderful ice-fall which pours down in one unbroken cataract from under the white pyramid of Tetnuld, a mountain as high as Mont Blanc and as graceful as the Weisshorn. And as a background to this magnificence there is a wide western view over leagues of rolling hills and delicately curved spurs, where, ringed in by peaks too numerous to be named, Ushba and the Laila first catch the eye, the leaders of a host once strange and indistinguishable, now shapes and names familiar to many of our countrymen.

The Italian side of Monte Rosa is cut up into sections by the high lateral ridges that divide the valleys and abut against it. The southern faces of Shkara, Janga, and Tetnuld are only separated by such low banks as the Col de la Seigne, and from any eminence they come into view together.

No doubt the aspects of nature viewed by the prisoner between high mountain walls are often extremely impressive. But most of us, I think, in the long-run prefer the broader landscapes, which admit all the infinite variety of light and shadow, of atmosphere and distance. Space, light and shadow are the characteristics of Suanetia. Its scenery has no parallel in the Alps, or elsewhere in the Caucasus. The traveller feels his senses inadequate; he longs for a memory to carry away more of the beauty that is set before him in such profusion.

I have been tempted for convenience of contrast to throw together my two visits to Ushkul. The rest of my Suanetian experiences I shall deal with in chronological order. In 1868, after escaping from our barn, we were led by a native, who must have had an exceptional number of vendettas on hand, by a curiously circuitous path as far as Latal. In place of following the direct track down the main stream of the Ingur, or crossing into the basin of the Mujalaliz, we were taken up the glen of Kalde, not, however, by the proper path, for the villagers of Iprari were among our horseman's numerous enemies. Perhaps we did well to avoid them, for they were the men who treacherously slew two Russian officers

in 1876. The last time I passed in sight of their homes their
towers had been razed to the ground, and a few selected ruffians
were enjoying free quarters in Siberia. But we innocent strangers
did not suspect the object of our deviations, and were well content to be brought back to the glaciers.

We hurried through ill-famed Adish, and, leaving behind us
the comparatively bare glens of the Ingur sources, followed for
miles the low spur which, projecting from the base of Tetnuld,
separates the narrow trench of the Ingur from the broader valley
of the Mulkhura, known as the Mujalaliz.

This brow is a more or less level natural terrace some ten
miles in length. The walk along it is the most beautiful I know
in any mountain country. Nowhere else do the sublimity of
snows and the beauty of woodlands so completely join hands. No
descriptions can convey, except to a very sympathetic reader, who
supplies a great deal from his own experience and imagination, the
faintest idea of the natural charms here united.

A map, if he can read one—few Englishmen, and hardly any
Englishwomen, know how much instruction, what romantic pictures
may be derived from maps—a map to those who can profit by it may
give some suggestions of the views that meet the traveller in every
direction. Overhead soars the splendid pyramid of Tetnuld. On
one side the eye ranges down the deep pine-clad defile of the Ingur
to where the triple crest of the Laila sends down long glaciers into
the forests. It follows the great sweep of the main chain, from the
towers of Ushba round to the massive crags of Tiktengen, tracks
the glaciers as they wind between granite precipices, until, at the
edge of the forests, they release their streams to dance down among
the meadows and corn-fields of the Mujalaliz, the valley of towers.

All these visions the map may suggest to such Alpine travellers
as can read its shorthand. But the beauty of the foreground is
beyond all possible anticipation. Level lawns of smooth, lately
mown turf are surrounded or broken by thickets of laurels, rhododendrons, and azaleas. Yellow lilies, lupines, and mallows flower
amongst them; bluebells and campanulas carpet the ground.
Woods of ash, hazel and fir, beech, birch and pine offer a pleasant

shade. A painter might camp here for a month, and, if he could imbue himself with the spirit of the scenery, bring home sketches which would astonish those who think mountain landscapes are wanting in variety, natural composition, atmosphere, and colour.

In 1868 we followed, more or less, this glorious terrace almost to Latal. Very much bewildered at the hill-paths we were led along, we did not appreciate the reason of our meanders. In fact, our track was still regulated by the blood-feuds of our horsemen, and the consequent need they felt to keep clear of the hamlets of their enemies.

Our second great sensation on my first visit was the view we enjoyed on a clear morning from the brow between Latal and Betsho. I have crossed that little pass five times, besides spending one long solitary day in strolling about its by-paths. I can see as I shut my eyes how the birches group themselves, how the path winds, the exact corner where Moore stood still and shouted as Ushba first broke on our astonished eyes. Its peaks had up to that moment been concealed by clouds, so that it came upon us with all the force of a complete surprise. The view of the mountain is not perfect; the rock-screen on the west, which for the present may be called the Mazeri Peak, hides part of its base; the crests are neither wholly detached, nor does one stand in solitary grandeur; the spectator is a little too much under the great mass. But the dimensions tell: fancy yourself at Cormayeur, and in the place of the Aiguille du Géant a Matterhorn of the height of Mont Blanc. You would have the counterpart of the relations of Ushba with Betsho, and the Caucasus provides as a foreground the loveliest woodland landscape imaginable.

That brief vision of the summits, one of the few we had in Suanetia in 1868, was soon over; the mists again wrapped round them. We went on our way past the broad meadow, then tenantless but for haymakers, where Betsho was to be created in after years. It was not until we reached Pari, the old seat of the Dadish Kilian who slew his Governor, that we found Russians, the first we had seen since leaving Kasbek. These were ten Cossacks, on whose good offices we relied for our transport in crossing the chain. Our passage of the Dongusorun Pass will find its place on a later page.

I must now ask the reader to leap nineteen years, and join M. de Déchy and myself on our descent from the great glaciers that separate the head-waters of the Baksan from the Asian slope. The valley of the Mulkhura is divided by nature into two basins; the highest, known as the Mujalaliz, is a broad smiling oasis of corn-lands and meadows. Below a ravine lies the second basin, that of Mestia, partly devastated by the torrent from the Leksur Glacier.

I and my companion had with us three Chamonix guides, and some eight Urusbieh men as porters. We were consequently no small addition to the society of Mestia, and on our arrival had, as usual, to be 'at home' to the entire population.

The first mark of progress was that we had a roof to be at home under, a modest wooden shed or Cancellaria; the next was the presence of a representative of order, responsible to the Government, in the shape of a burly Suanetian, whose chain and medal—like a waterman's badge—proclaimed him to be the Mayor or Starshina. He was a very big man, of wild aspect, with a broad face like a Nineveh Bull. A very small sharp boy acted as his interpreter. The acquirements of this precocious youth were explained when, on my afternoon stroll, I came across a school-house, a wooden cottage, the walls of which were pasted with newspaper pictures of single Cossacks pursuing Turkish armies, and of common objects of civilisation, some of which must have sorely puzzled the brains of the young Suanetians. It was holiday time; the master was absent. The environs of the village, or rather villages—for Mestia consists of several hamlets and no less than seventy towers—are charming. Close to the guest-house is a very ancient birch-tree, with stone seats under it. The open ground is fringed with azaleas and rhododendrons, the glacier streams meet in a birch-hung cleft resembling the gorge at Pontresina, and at an amazing height in air the spire of Tetnuld flushes red in the face of the sunsets. The peak farther off, seen over its northern slope, is Gestola.

It is a pleasant ride of about two hours, or a much pleasanter walk—for in Suanetia the bridle-lanes are stony ditches, while the field footpaths resemble those of our own country—down the open valley to Latal. For most of the way the traveller passes between barley-fields divided by neat wattled fences. The foregrounds are shifting combinations of golden grain, white towers, and graceful birches. On the slopes of the middle distance the sombre tints of the evergreen forests lie like shadows across the

SUANETIAN HOMESTEADS

brighter hues of the beech, poplar, and alder groves. In either direction the view is closed by noble snow-peaks, the Laila in front, Tetnuld behind.

At Lenjer, a group of hamlets about half-way to Latal, there is a church with a hexagonal apse. The masonry is very superior to that of the houses or towers, the blocks being of limestone and carefully squared. The external walls are frescoed after the manner of an Italian chapel. There are some graves near the church, and others near an old fir-tree, which has stone seats under it, as at Mestia. The rarity of graves in Suanetia is striking. This strange people will bury their dead anywhere.[1] M. Levier was in 1890 present, at Pari, at the exhumation by the Russian officials of the corpse of a victim killed in some private feud. It had been laid a foot or two under the common path. The Suanetians, it appears, have this much reverence; they object strongly to the face-cloth being raised, and it would be as much as an official's life is worth to do so.

Latal is a very large group of villages, the lowest in Independent Suanetia. Its hamlets stand on knolls, many of them obviously ancient moraines, above the junction of the Ingur and the Mulkhura. The vegetation shows traces of a warmer climate, and walnuts abound. The homesteads are less crowded, and stand apart in the fields. There are two or three churches or chapels, and the apse of one is decorated externally with an arcade. They are all kept locked up, and on none of my visits have I succeeded in getting access to them. The women are more prominent here than in the upper villages, and occupy their full share of the ring that surrounds the traveller who halts for lunch under the shade of the great village sycamore. On one of my visits the common fountain, a long wooden trough, was in use as a bath by a lady of the locality, who seemed but little embarrassed at the appearance of strangers.

Beyond the familiar little pass that leads to Betsho we found the new capital of Suanetia. Betsho is as much an official and artificial creation as St. Petersburg itself. But very little money and not too much energy has gone to its erection. An unfriendly critic might describe it as two wooden sheds and a bungalow. In the modest bungalow lives the Priestav, or Commissioner, as he may be called, who rules Suanetia. The shed opposite his house, once a barrack, is now a ruin, and untenanted save by a casual Mingrelian, who has established himself, with his poultry and a few barrels of wine, in a floorless, half-roofed corner of it. The upper shed, a long, low building built across the valley, contains the quarters of the police staff, and a Cancellaria

[1] Levier, *A travers le Caucase.* 1894.

or courthouse, sometimes placed at the disposal of travellers. The slopes of the valley of the Dola torrent are well wooded, its bottom is open and cultivated, and the towers of two considerable villages rise among its meadows. The view up it is closed by the great peaks of Ushba. Their vertical height above the court-house is 10,700 feet, and their distance under ten miles.

The attraction of Ushba, which acts as a candle to the

THE GOVERNMENT BUILDINGS, BETSHO

Alpine moths who gyrate round it, careless of all else that lies close at hand, generally keeps English visitors at Betsho. It affords, however, from many points of view, the worst quarters in Suanetia. Provisions are scarce, and horses or porters often unprocurable. The natives being accustomed, perhaps, to be requisitioned for public services, are not eager to meet the requirements of the Priestav's guests, and in that official's absence his subordinates are not always cordial in their reception of strangers. It is possible, however, to get large Russian loaves baked here, and these are almost indispensable to travellers who do not bake for themselves.

On the first day of our stay in 1887 the weather was unsettled, and M. de Déchy was occupied with his photographic apparatus and other details. Accordingly, I started without him for an exploration of Ushba, taking with me two of my Chamoniards. We were off at 5 A.M. An hour's walk across meadows and corn-land up the open valley brought us to Mazeri, a picturesque village overshadowed by a castle of the Dadish Kilians. Here the Gul glen, which leads straight up to the small glacier that lies under the eastern cliffs of Ushba, falls into the Betsho valley. At the angle we attempted a short cut, with the result usual in Suanetia : we imbedded ourselves in an impenetrable tangle of hazels and azaleas. After this experience we humbly asked our way at the next farmhouse to the *lednik*, which is Russian for glacier. To our surprise we were understood, and directed to a beaten horse-track, improved for the benefit of the Russian officers, who send up occasionally in summer for a load of ice.

The path mounted steadily through a fir forest, and then traversed flowery pastures. The white clouds played in and out between the two great peaks ; towards noon they lifted. By that time we were level with the middle region of the glacier, and it became necessary to consider how far our reconnaissance should be pushed. Since the sky seemed to promise a few fine hours I set my heart on gaining the top of the crag opposite Ushba, which forms the south-east extremity of the semicircle of rocks that encircle the head of the Gul Glacier. In such neighbourhood it showed only as the footstool of Ushba ; yet a summit of over 12,000 feet,[1] the height of the Wetterhorn, may be called a mountain even in the Caucasus.

The glacier pours down in a short ice-fall—easily turned by the rocks on its left bank—from a recess between the base of the two great towers and our summit—Gulba, I propose to call it.

---

[1] Mr. Donkin, from observations while climbing on Ushba, estimated the height of Gulba as 12,500 feet. The Gulba of the one-verst map is a much lower summit.

The moraines of the Gul Glacier are gigantic and out of all proportion to its size. Their dimensions become instructive when their true origin has been recognised. They represent not the excavating capacity of this small, and not very steep, ice-stream, but the extent and looseness of the cliffs that surround its *névé*. They are formed of the missiles the demon of Ushba is constantly hurling across the path of his assailants. These vast piles of spent projectiles may well give cause for reflection to those who do not feel confident that climbing a frozen chimney under fire is altogether a reasonable form of recreation. The caution is the more called for, as from this point of view the proportions of the great mountain are not fully displayed, and its cliffs conceal some of their terrors.

Now we were at its very base, Ushba looked less formidable than might have been expected; less formidable than it is in reality. The Meije and the Cimon della Pala have certainly both a greater air of inaccessibility. The mountain is, of course, much foreshortened. It must be remembered, also, that the great snow-trough between the peaks is rather dangerous and laborious than difficult. Were it not for the missiles—stones and icicles—that sweep it from time to time, the ascent to the saddle would not be beyond the powers of any strong party when the slopes are in fair condition. Mr. Cockin came down them in the dark, and with 'one shoe off'! The rocks of the southern peak are very formidable, and it seems doubtful whether the ridge leading to the top from the saddle can be climbed directly. There may be other ways, either on the western or eastern face of the final peak. Possibly its conquerors will, as in the case of the Matterhorn, reach it by disregarding altogether the tracks of their predecessors. Very favourable conditions, however, will be required for the ascent.

The local conditions in July 1887 were the reverse of favourable. Never in the Alps have I heard a mountain keep up for hours a continuous discharge of miniature avalanches. On the whole of the upper slopes the surface snow, under the influence of the mid-day sun, was peeling off. It was not falling in masses, but sliding gently downwards. When, by climbing some banks of broken rocks, we had overcome the ice-fall, we found it almost more than we could do to plough up the first slope of *névé*. The surface gave way at every step under our feet. The stillness of

GULBA

the upper air was broken by a singularly soft and ominous hissing sound, like that made by a disturbed snake.

The rocks on our right were steep, but our best chance was clearly to grapple with them at once. We took advantage of a sort of shelf, by which, with more labour of arms than legs, we raised ourselves on to the western buttress of our peak. It projects into the *névé*, part of which flows from a recess behind it. Beyond this snow, at a distance of a few hundred yards, a pair of rocky pinnacles divided us from the basin of the Chalaat Glacier. The rocks were probably not more difficult than those leading up to the Schreckhorn Sattel. The impression they made on me was probably due to the quantity of ice and loose snow spread about them, and also not a little to the superabundance of loose boulders. Latter-day Swiss climbers can hardly realise the extraordinary service that has been rendered them by their predecessors in clearing the ordinary tracks up rock-peaks of treacherous handholds.

At the point where we first looked directly down a grim precipice on to the Chalaat Glacier, the crest of the mountain narrowed to a thin comb. We made the cliffs smoke with the boulders we dislodged for safety's sake. But the climbing was not difficult, and we speedily gained the nearest summit. There was a second beyond, perhaps a foot or two higher. An ice-gully separated them, but with a little delay we crossed it, and at 3 P.M. —in three hours from the lower glacier—were installed on our belvedere.

From Betsho, I must confess, Gulba is 'a poor thing,' blunt and stumpy; but when on the top one discovers that the mountain is in fact a wedge, and a very thin one. The cliff on the east is, from the picturesque point of view, perpendicular, and stones sent down it towards the Chalaat Glacier disappeared at once from sight, leaving behind them a sulphureous reek.

'Animi causâ devolvere rupem
Avulsam scopulo placet, ac audire sonantem
Haud secus ac tonitru scopulis dum immurmurat altis,'

writes, in his clumsy hexameters, an old Swiss Latinist. This pleasure we enjoyed for a minute or two, but as soon as we had cleared a solid space to sit down upon we found something better to do than to imitate such mediæval frivolity.

Gulba may be a little mountain, but it is a great view-point. The sky overhead was ominous, but the lower clouds had lifted, as they often do before a storm, and nothing was hidden from us except the actual tops of the Central Group, Tetnuld and its farther neighbours. Beyond the highest reservoirs of the western branch of the Chalaat Glacier rose two spires of snow, part of Chatuintau. Almost at our feet lay the meeting-place of the Chalaat and the Leksur glaciers. The great basin of the Leksur Glacier and the ridges round it were spread out as on a map. All 'Free Suanetia' was laid as a carpet before us—a maze of low smooth ridges and deep glens, heights clothed in shadowy forests, hollows where the shafts of sunshine played on yellowing barley-fields and towered villages and white torrent-beds. The long chain of the Laila lifted its glaciers on high; they showed as pale streaks under the storm-clouds advancing from the Black Sea. Beyond the Ingur, far off in Abkhasia, we noticed another glacier-bearing crest, part of the southern limestones. From these distant objects the eyes returned to rest on the vast bulk of Ushba, the eastern face of which was fully displayed. From this height its cliffs and ice-raked slopes looked far more formidable than from the lower glacier.

The first part of the descent demanded care, for the loose boulders were particularly troublesome. As soon as it seemed to me safe, I gave the order to try the snow in the bay on our right. The slopes were not crevassed, nor was their angle steep enough to make the tendency of the surface to slide any danger in the descent. We rode down in fifteen minutes, on little avalanches of our own starting, a distance we had taken two hours to climb by the rocks.

As soon as the rope could be taken off, I left the guides to follow at their leisure, and set off at my best pace for the valley. The great peaks were already black with thunder-clouds, and it seemed only a question of minutes when the storm would break.

At the foot of the descent I found a camp had been set up since the morning by Prince Wittgenstein and Prince Shervashidzi. The former, who has since died, was a Russian officer who had held high posts in Central Asia. He talked English perfectly. The latter is a Caucasian noble. Their camp was interesting as an example of the old native habits in travel. Four solid stems had been first fixed in the ground, and cross-beams nailed to them to support walls and a roof. On this simple framework boughs were being dexterously woven by a crowd of camp-followers. Bright Persian rugs and saddlebags were spread on the ground and gave colour to the scene. In settled weather life in such an arbour must be agreeable, and even on a rainy day the owner of many *bourkas* can defend himself from a perpetual dripping. What success the Princes met with in the object of their travels, the search for gold, I never learnt.

Four hours after leaving the top of Gulba I pushed open the door of the courthouse at Betsho, and discovered my companion sedulously immersed in those tiresome occupations which are the price the mountain photographer pays for his successes.

Two years later, in 1889, I again found myself in Suanetia, this time with my friend Captain Powell, as the guests of Prince Atar Dadish Kilian, the representative of the old princely family who were once the rulers of Lower Suanetia and still hold the document by which the Tsar Nicholas confirmed them in their rights as feudal lords of the country. Ezeri, the Prince's residence, consists of a number of detached towered hamlets, spread over a broad shelf of sloping meadow-land some 6000 feet above the sea, and only a few miles west of Betsho. The situation is pleasant and picturesque. Beyond the Ingur the snows and forests of the Laila are all in sight; Ushba shows its enormous tusks over the low hill behind the villages; down the valley there is a fine view towards the gorge of the Ingur.

The Prince, now a man in the prime of life, was educated at Odessa, and then sent to travel on government business in Japan and Manchuria. He speaks French, and is an educated gentleman. None the less he plays the part of a native noble in the mountain home to which he has been allowed to return. He lives like a feudal chief in the Middle Ages, surrounded by retainers, and receives his rents in services and in kind. He keeps more or less open house to guests. From the old home of his family he sends out his messengers to Ossetia to buy horses, to Sugdidi for provisions, to Kutais for household necessaries. He has extensive possessions, many castles and farm-houses in the valley and pastures on the hills. His horses are kept in summer at an establishment in the forest west of the Laila, on a track that leads to Lentekhi.

He has abandoned his old castle, and built for himself a wooden house in the form of a large Swiss cottage. An outside staircase leads through a balcony to a large hall, furnished with heavy wooden benches and vast chairs, such as might serve as stage furniture for *Macbeth*. The inner apartments are provided with Persian divans. Meals are served in the hall, and the waiters are native retainers, who join from time to time in the conversation. The fare is abundant, and every meal ends with an Oriental dish as old as Isaiah—curds and honey. The chief ornament of the table is a noble silver bowl of Persian workmanship. We had as fellow-guests a Mohammedan chief from the Karatshai, and another member of the Dadish Kilian family, with a very pretty bride from Kutais. The day after our arrival was Sunday. To our astonishment we were awakened by a church bell. We could hardly believe that we were in Suanetia. The Georgian priest lately established at Ezeri held a service in the half-ruinous church, which stands in a beautiful situation on a brow beyond the village, approached by an agreeable footpath between the barley-fields. The congregation muster outside the church. We were too late for the service, but were allowed to inspect the *repoussé* silver images studded with rough turquoises still preserved in the interior.

The rest of the day was given over to sports on the green before the Prince's house. Native spirit, brewed from barley, was handed round to the men in loving cups, various games were played, the women danced, and the boys tumbled about with some young bears which had been caught in the forests.

Our supper, which was seldom served before 10 P.M., was followed on this occasion by the entrance of a chorus of women, who sang long ballads, dancing in a circle to the refrain. In these ballads, and nowhere else, is buried the lost history of Suanetia. I implored our host to collect and publish them. He summarised the purport of some of them for us. One told how a company of

Suanetians had been overtaken by the Turkish mountaineers on the Tuiber Glacier, and how in the midst of the battle an avalanche had fallen and, overwhelming the combatants, stilled in a moment the clamour of the strife. Prince Atar assured me that arms of very ancient date and human bones had been recently found in the moraine at the foot of the glacier and were believed by the people to be relics of the legendary catastrophe. Other ballads

SUANETIAN WOMEN

were tales of private love and revenge, Æschylean horrors, chanted with much force and emotion by the chorus. We did not end without the praises of Thamara, as indispensable in Suanetia as 'God save the Queen' in the British dominions.

On the following day we set out to make the first ascent of the Laila, long an object of my ambition. Two days before we had from Betsho made an excursion up the valley that leads directly to the base of the highest summits. It had no mountaineering result, but the ride through a forest of flowers was of the most enchanting beauty.

The path crosses the Ingur and winds amongst copses, and meadows full of hay-cutters, round the spur east of our valley. Then, traversing the water of the Laila, it follows the tumbling stream into the heart of the mountains. How can I suggest the tranquil loveliness of that wood, or the beauty and variety of the flowery meadows it enclosed? Near the head of the glen its main branch turns westward, and ascending through glades laid out by that great gardener, Nature, as if to frame vistas of Ushba and the snows of the main chain, we entered a basin into which the ice of one of the Laila glaciers, now directly overhead, fell in avalanches, fragments of which had rolled as far as the yellow lilies and wild-roses that grew all about us.

We laid our sleeping-bags beside a clear spring-fed pool, shadowed by maples and beeches. Ushba was first a double flame in the sunset, then a black cathedral front against the starry heaven. Beyond it loomed the immense pale cone of Elbruz. As I write the words, the ghost of Dr. Johnson seems to repeat, 'No, sir, it may be called immense, and a cone, in a book, but it is no more than a considerable protuberance.' We cannot all of us look on mountains with the Doctor's comprehensive and almost cosmic eye, and, perhaps, if he had seen Elbruz he might have pardoned me for measuring it by the scale of six-foot humanity. To ants even a molehill must seem something more than a protuberance.

Before dawn rain splashed through the beech-leaves, and we had to retreat from before our mountain, which on this side looked formidable enough. We amused ourselves on the way down by trying who could find the most blossoms on a single stalk of the yellow lilies. Fourteen won the competition. Pursued by rain-storms we fled through Latal, and away from the scanty resources of the Priestav's deputy at Betsho and the native *dukhan* to the hospitality of Prince Atar on the heights of Ezeri.

Prince Atar announced his intention to join us in our second attempt on the Laila. Caucasians dine too late to start early, and it was 1 P.M. before our cavalcade was ready and we set off to ride across the meadows and down the steep zigzags to the Ingur. At a village on its left bank lived an uncle of the Prince: at

his house we halted for tea. He was a hearty person, but our
conversation was necessarily limited. He set my mind, however,
at rest as to the native origin of the names I have used since
1868 for the two most conspicuous mountains of Suanetia. ' *Ushba,
Tetnuld*,' he exclaimed, as he sat on his balcony and waved his
hand to the two peaks, which were both in sight. Samovars
always take a long time preparing, and male Caucasians are as

A MOUNTAINEERS' 'AT HOME'

prone as the women of other nations to linger over afternoon tea.
To arrive before dark we had to push our animals at a trot up a
staircase-path where boughs threatened to sweep the rider from
his saddle. After two hours' ride we found the shepherds' quarters,
a good log hut.

Of course the first idea of our Caucasian companions was not
bed—or rather sleep, but supper. They set to work to boil a
sheep in the hut. Next to boiled mutton, the smell of it is a chief

object of my detestation, and I and Powell spread our sleeping-bags on the turf outside, where we were haunted by cows and nipped towards morning by frost.

At daybreak we were led by our native companions to a pass in the ridge that separates the wooded glen holding the great western glacier of the Laila from the Ingur Valley. It commands a superb prospect. I have seldom seen such beautiful effects of morning light and shadow as those thrown across the vales of Suanetia, such richness of colour and variety of mountain form combined in a single view. In front of us was the western face of the Laila; a broad glacier flowed from a well-marked saddle, on either side of which rose steep icy ranges. The three highest peaks were at the head of the glacier, and from a hollow north-west of them a smaller glacier afforded easy access to the crest overlooking Suanetia, a mile or more from where we stood. We determined to make for this point. But we had to descend 1000 feet in order to reach it.

The hunters, whom the Prince had taken as his escort, led us, or rather misled us, according to their lights. In their minds the word Laila had a distinct meaning; it was the point at which they occasionally crossed the chain when seeking a short cut to Lentekhi. Towards that pass they were conducting us. Politeness to our host kept us with them to the point where, to reach our peak, it was essential to turn to the left up the smaller glacier. There they insisted there was no way, no *doroga*—or path—except up the main glacier, and the Prince unfortunately believed them. We each took our different tracks. Without adventure of any sort, without even using the rope, Powell, Maurer and I mounted the ice and snow-slopes to the broad saddle, conspicuous throughout Suanetia on the west of the Laila peaks. This point has been reached from the Ingur Valley by subsequent travellers without the long circuit we were led into. The remainder of the way to the top was as easy as the ascent of the Titlis. First we hastened over some broad rocks, next across a long snow-plain, then up a bank of ice with just enough snow on it to save step-cutting; finally, up a steep slope of slate, broken by weather into small fragments that slipped away, like a sea-beach, from under our feet. Its top was the first of the Laila summits, the crest seen from Ezeri. The second was a few feet higher, but we had lost so much time that we could hardly afford to go on to it. Signor Sella climbed it a week or two later, and subsequently Herr Merzbacher of Munich visited all three summits.

The Laila is admirably placed for a panorama. It rakes the central chain of the Caucasus and overlooks the great forests westwards. But, apart from its topographical interest, the view gains a peculiar charm from the carpet of green and gold that is thrown down at the feet of the stupendous cliffs of the great chain, to the contrast between the vales of Suanetia and the snows of the Caucasus. The position of the climber relative to the great chain may be compared to that of a traveller on Mont Emilius behind Aosta to the Pennine Alps. To suggest the comparison is to enforce, on those who have seen both, the superiority of the Caucasian view. And it can hardly be said too often, the transparency of the Caucasian atmosphere softens the outline, deepens the shade, magnifies the bulk of the peaks. The mountaineer who has spent several hours on a fine day on the crest of the Laila will ever after carry in his mind a recollection of a sight, or rather of a series of visions, of exquisite aerial effects, of transfigurations, in which what the author of the Book of Proverbs calls 'the highest parts of the dust of the world' appear as the silver spires of a temple raised by no mortal architect.

The ascent is so very easy and, when taken the right way, comparatively so short, that there is little excuse for any traveller, who has higher ambitions than to be a chimney-jack, leaving it out. It fills me with surprise when I remember that I did not myself seek this Pisgah until my third visit to Suanetia.

The Prince and his hunters were visible on a patch of rocks some distance below the snow-pass. We rejoined them at the base of the peak, and regained Ezeri very late the same evening. The next morning broke unclouded, and was succeeded by one of the finest and hottest days I have ever known in the Caucasus. I strolled alone up the shadeless dale behind Ezeri, to a gap from which a path descends directly to Mazeri, above Betsho. Thence I followed a zigzag path to the brow on the right, for which Signor Sella got the name of Mesik.   He visited it in October, the day after the first snowfall.   I found the turf enamelled with gentians, forget-me-nots, and pyrethrums.   This crest commands an unique view of the south-west peak of Ushba, and an almost complete panorama of Suanetia and its ring of mountains.   It will be one of the lady's walks of the twentieth century, when Caucasian travel is organised, as Syrian has been for the last fifty years, by the establishment at Kutais of dragomans with the needful camp-equipment.

I close this record of my rambles in Suanetia with a keen sense of regret at their incompleteness.   As I look once more at the well-worn sheet of the old five-verst map, I recognise how many lovely green downs and ridges, doubtless as beautiful as those I have tried to describe, remain still unknown to me.   I long for more idle days spent in lounging on a haycock on the verge of some fresh mown glade, until the sunset fades off the crest of Tetnuld, and the stars and the fire-flies come out together. I am haunted by the faint perfume which the last azalea blossoms are pouring forth from thickets, under which the lilies and lupines that have escaped the scythe brighten the borders of the wood.   I even begin to indulge in audacious doubts as to the orographic insight of my juniors, and to fancy that I might perhaps have found the way up the maiden peak of Ushba better than great climbers have done, had I concentrated myself more on the attempt. When I get to this point I know that I am dreaming, and hasten to put away my papers and my idle thoughts.

CHAPTER XII

THE ASCENT OF TETNULD

THE literary success of Mr. Grove's *Frosty Caucasus*, great as it was, did not produce in this country any immediate revival of Caucasian Exploration. Its failure in this respect was, I think, due mainly to two causes—the war of 1877, and the impression created by the fever which fell on Mr. Grove and his companions during their descent to the Black Sea.

It was to M. de Déchy, the Hungarian traveller, as I have already said, that the credit of recalling our thoughts to the Caucasus was to a great extent due. His three journeys, in 1884, 1885, and 1886, had resulted in several interesting climbs and some valuable topographical explorations, and also—what was more generally effective—in a large series of excellent photographs, which brought for the first time the scenery and people of the Caucasus vividly before men's eyes. In 1885 I became the channel through which his work was made known to the Alpine Club, and it was partly perhaps through this communication that my friends Mr. Clinton Dent and Mr. W. F. Donkin were, in 1886, induced to try their luck in the Caucasus. They set out with the intention of following Mr. Grove's suggestion, and attacking the peak at the

head of the lower reach of the Bezingi Glacier, which he and
A. W. Moore had identified with the Tetnuld of Suanetia.   They
were successful, but when they gained the summit we now know
as Gestola they found that there was another Tetnuld—the true
Tetnuld—in the field.   It is a peculiarity of Caucasian peaks,
Elbruz, Ushba, Dongusorun, Janga, the Laila—I might name
others—that they have a way of proving double-headed.[1]   Since it
provides double employment for climbers, it may surely be reckoned
to them as a merit.

In all probability Gestola will, with Tetnuld, be ranked in the
future among the easy peaks of the Caucasus.   But the first
ascent was by no means tame.   By a failure to allow sufficiently
for the rapid changes in the condition of Caucasian slopes, or
perhaps from inadequate reconnoitring, the party found themselves
—very much as we had done on Kasbek—in the position of Mr.
and Mrs. Diskobolus in Edward Lear's ballad.   They were on the
top of a wall from which there was reason to doubt if they 'could
ever get down at all.'   Mr. Dent tells me that he is about to
repeat the story of his adventure, with which he long ago thrilled
the Alpine Club.   I shall not, therefore, anticipate here such
confidences as he may think it expedient to lay before the public.

This ascent was the main result of the journey.   An attack
on Dykhtau—the climbers called it Guluku—was not pushed
very far.   Mr. Donkin fixed a number of points about the great
Bezingi Glacier, and then the mountaineers rode back by the
way they had come to Naltshik and the nearest railway station.
This very brief and limited experience of Caucasian travel
sufficed, however, to furnish Mr. Donkin with the material for
a chapter which stands out, I think, from the monotony of Alpine
publications by the vivid impression it leaves behind it, not only
of the incidents of daily life in the mountains, but of the sensitive
and happy nature of the writer, who saw and enjoyed so much
in so short a time.

The discussions raised by my friends' journey made me feel

---

[1] Tetnuld and Gestola, however, are entirely distinct peaks, as much so as the Dent Blanche
and Dent d'Hérens.

that I could no longer resist the temptation to go myself and see once more the great mountains, of many of which I had in 1868, owing to broken weather, had but fleeting glimpses. I felt confident—and as the event proved, rightly—that one unclouded view would clear up most of the confusion that still encompassed the nomenclature of the Central Group, and enable me to determine between the various identifications of the two summits first measured and named by the makers of the five-verst map as Dykhtau and Koshtantau.

In August 1887 M. de Déchy and I, with my old friend and guide, François Dévouassoud, and two of his relations, found ourselves at Betsho, the centre of Russian administration in Suanetia. The condition of the snow had forced me to give up any designs on Ushba, the Suanetian Matterhorn. The experience of subsequent and more competent peak-hunters has since fully proved the wisdom of that decision. My thoughts naturally turned to the other great mountain which dominates the upper basin of the Ingur, Tetnuld. The views we had already gained had sufficed to remove all the doubts raised in the previous year, and to establish the entirely separate existence of Dent and Donkin's peak. We had seen the two mountains from the west, rising at least a mile apart and separated by an immense glacier basin.

Shkara, Ushba, and Tetnuld, owing to their being so conspicuous from the valleys at their base, and even from the distant lowlands, are at this moment among the best-known peaks of the Caucasus. Twenty-five years ago they were unrecognised, and hardly even named. Shkara, when seen from the distant lowlands, was described as Pasis Mta, because it is not very far from the passes at the Rion (Phasis) sources, just as Monte Leone was called the Simplon—or St. Plomb—by the contemporaries of De Saussure.

Tetnuld and Ushba preside over Suanetia, as the Jungfrau and Wetterhorn do over the Bernese Oberland. Owing to its peculiarly graceful form, Tetnuld was one of the first peaks to attract attention from Caucasian travellers. M. E. Favre speaks

of it as 'the gigantic pyramid of Tetnuld.'   Herr von Thielmann
writes :—

> 'Tetnuld, the most beautiful of all the mountains of the Caucasus, stands
> out from the chain in the form of a gigantic pyramid of the height of 16,000
> feet. The dazzling whiteness of its snowy mantle, combined with the grace
> of its form, produce an effect similar to that created by the Jungfrau, while
> to complete the comparison a conical peak, smaller but equally beautiful,
> like the Swiss Silberhorn, rises up by its side.'

IPARI

Before leaving England I had studied photographs of the
mountain, and found, as I thought, the right way up it. The most
convenient starting-point was obviously Adish.   From the pastures
above that village the snowfields at the western base of the
final peak could, by crossing a spur, probably be reached with less
trouble than by ascending the glacier they feed, which drains into
the Mujalaliz or valley of the Mulkhura.

Our first stage was to Ipari.   As usual at Betsho—I might

say in the Caucasus—the horses did not come till past noon,
and it had long been dark when we all reassembled in the court-
house at Ipari. Half the party came by the Ingur, the others by
Mestia and the Uguir Pass. The former route is considerably
the shorter. The path from Ipari to Adish, a three hours' ride, is
most romantic. Fancy the Valley of the Lyn with two mountains
of over fifteen thousand feet closing every vista, the white pyramid of Tetnuld in front, the rock-towers of Ushba behind. One
of the views of Ushba was the most perfect imaginable. But there
are so many perfect views of Ushba! The particular charm of
this was in the water, and the foliage of the foreground, and the
way in which the lower hills formed a framework for the great
peaks. The path continues by—and often in—the stream until
the barley-fields and towers of Adish come suddenly in sight.
Adish, as I have before pointed out, is the most isolated,
and one of the wildest of the communes of Free Suanetia. It
has no priest or headman : but in 1865 the villagers are said to
have been formally baptized ; they are certainly still unre-
generate, and utter barbarians in their manner of dealing with
strangers. But, strong in our escort of two Cossacks,[1] we had no
fear of the inhabitants, and made our mid-day halt in an enclosure
at the top of the village. High prices were asked for provisions,
and the villagers quarrelled noisily among themselves as to the
distribution of the money, or invented grounds for petty demands,
which they pressed on us with noisy persistence. Compared,
however, to our encounters in 1868, this appeared to me but
a poor performance. Violence of tone and gesture are conventional
in Suanetia : there was no real passion. We scattered smiles
and kopeks in return for a sheep and other provisions. One man
demanded payment on the ground that we had lunched on his
land, and on being laughed at had recourse to the traditional
pantomime of fetching his gun ; another laid hold of my ice-axe,

---

[1] The reader must be reminded that, in records of Caucasian travel, a Cossack is not an
ethnographical but a military term. The two men we had with us on this occasion were one
a Suanetian, the other a Kabardan from Naltshik. The surveyor's ' Cossack ' at Karaul was a
Tauli. Many of the Cossacks, both men and officers, are Ossetes.

which I had stuck in the ground while mounting, and required a ransom for it. A few kopeks, however, settled all questions. The whole affair was nothing more than an attempt at petty extortion, enforced with habitual violence of tone and gesture.

We had intended to sleep out high above the village. But 'the basest clouds' had succeeded a glorious morning, and we were content to establish our camp in a birch grove an hour above Adish, and close to the foot of the great glacier. The glory of

THE ADISH GLACIER

its ice-fall exceeded my remembrance. It is unequalled in the Alps, and only rivalled in the Caucasus by that of the Karagom Glacier. M. de Déchy rode on to examine the marks he had set up two years previously. The ice had advanced nearly forty feet. The steeper glaciers of the Caucasus were mostly showing signs of slight advance in 1887 and 1889. Many of them had shot fresh streaks of brown and grey rubbish over their green moraines. The advance of glaciers depends mainly on the amount of snow-supply in their upper basins, and it is therefore those which travel fastest—that is, those which have the greatest volume and the steepest beds—which take the lead in oscillations. For example, the Glacier des Bossons begins to encroach on the Valley of Chamonix long before the Mer de Glace shows any sign, and the Upper Grindelwald Glacier advances before the Lower. With night, heavy rain began to fall. Our Willesden canvas resisted the downpour, but the guides, who had pitched their tent badly and in a hollow, were inundated. The Cossacks made an arrangement in birch-boughs and *bourkas*, which, as the event proved, was not only water- but sound-proof.

In the grey dawn Dévouassoud withdrew the tent curtains, and in the gloomiest tones made the solemn announcement—'Our mutton has been stolen.' Further research showed that the thieves had been singularly audacious, and that our loss was far more than a few joints of meat. The luggage had been piled under a waterproof sheet between our tent and the Cossacks' shelter. The cover had been lifted, the lock of M. de Déchy's hand-portmanteau removed, and the contents ransacked. A revolver, some *steigeisen* presented to me by Viennese friends, and my companion's store of clothes, had been abstracted. His medicine-chest had been opened, but the contents were left untouched. The waterproof cover had been skilfully and carefully replaced, so that the more serious theft was not suspected until long after we had missed the mutton.

This vexatious, but by no means disastrous, theft had its most serious result in a telegram which by some means found its way through Germany to the English newspapers to the effect that, owing to the robbery of all my goods, I had been compelled to give up my Caucasian journey. Some of my friends were in consequence needlessly alarmed, and I received much undeserved sympathy.

We had little doubt as to where the thieves came from. After such an experience, we could hardly leave our camp to the mercy of the men of Adish, while we attempted Tetnuld. In the drenching rain we decamped as best we could. It was a noisome struggle with wet ropes and canvas and photographic cases that had to be carefully tended to keep them from suffering from damp. Adish

seemed almost deserted as we passed through it.   At noon the
heavens cleared; and we had an exquisite view from the brow
above the Mujalaliz, where we found troops of haymakers at work,
quite regardless of weather, as indeed haymakers have to be in
Suanetia.

We ran down the steep hillside and installed ourselves in the
priest's house at Mujal.   It is a good wooden cottage, and on

SUANETIANS

the first floor are two large clean rooms, with a broad balcony
running round them.   The village is one of a group lying in an
open basin of barley-fields, enclosed by wooded slopes, on the left
bank of the stream, about a mile below the junction of the torrents
from the Tuiber and the Zanner Glaciers.   Beyond the river the
white towers of Mulakh break the hillside, and high in the air
the mightier towers of Ushba show between the rainstorms their
vigorous outline.   Tetnuld is hidden by its spurs, and at the head

of the valley only the white snout of the Zanner Glacier is seen
beyond the dark cliffs and forests of a deep gorge.

Next day we despatched the priest's son with 15 roubles (28
shillings) to Adish to try to recover our goods. In case of his
failure we sent the Suanetian Cossack to Betsho to inform the
Priestav of our loss.

About noon I, with two of the guides, made a futile start for
Tetnuld. We got on the wrong side of the gorge leading to the
Zanner Glacier, and after spending some hours of storm under an
impenetrable pine, came back again. The weather all day was like
that of the English Lakes, storm and gleams, and we had some
wild visions of Ushba hung with cloud-banners.

The following day was all storm and no gleam. We had, however, our fill of entertainment indoors. It was a day of arrivals.
First there was the advance of the Russian forces to avenge
the Rape of the Shirts. They consisted of a splendid old Cossack
sergeant—quite the popular ideal of a Cossack—and his two men,
a mild, broad-faced Russian youth and a weak Suanetian. This
trio marched on Adish, and, very much to our surprise and their
credit, successfully arrested the ten leading villagers.

Another arrival was promised us—no less a person than the
Bishop of Poti, the first Bishop who, in historical times, had
penetrated Free Suanetia. From so fever-stricken a see one might
naturally look for a pale ascetic. Our prelate, however, was much
the reverse—a man of sturdy frame and sense. But I am antici-
pating. It was towards evening before the path that descends
the beautiful slopes above the village became alive with horses.
The cavalcade was divided into many detachments, camp-servants
with huge saddle-bags, long-haired priests, singing-men with dark
locks and melancholy stag-like eyes. Last came the Bishop himself,
a large, thick-set man in imposing ecclesiastical vestments, attended
by his secretary and a Mingrelian gentleman who talked French
and had spent some time at Geneva. Through the latter I had
some talk with the Bishop, who told me that the first sermon
he preached to the Suanetians would be on the necessity of
giving up their eclectic practice of keeping the holy days of three

religions and doing no work between Thursday night and Monday morning.

The supper that evening showed the resources of Suanetia. We all, except the Bishop, sat down to it—a company of at least thirty. Roast mutton and boiled fowls were followed by roast pork. Knives fell short, and plates shorter. But the baser sort at the lower end of the table used their *kinjals* (daggers) for

A BOY AT MUJAL

knives, and the flat loaves—excellently baked for once in the Bishop's honour—served as plates first and were eaten afterwards, after the fashion of Æneas. And there was wine at discretion — capital, sound Mingrelian wine, which no one but the guides despised for its goatskin flavour. It was long past midnight when I retired between the folds of my insect-proof curtains, watched by a solemn group of long-robed priests and peasants, resembling nothing so much as the by-standers depicted in the Raphael Cartoons.

The sky next morning was less charged with vapour, and there was a touch of north in the wind. I was determined to start again for Tetnuld. M. de Déchy was anxious not to lose the advantage of the expected visit of the Priestav from Betsho, and his assistance both in recovering his lost apparel and in making final arrangements with the villagers to serve as porters.

It will be most convenient if I give here the result of our application. Early in the afternoon of the second day, after I had started for Tetnuld, a party of villagers came in from Adish.

Soon after the Priestav arrived, and the villagers were summoned before him. The two men who had demanded money of us were first questioned : 'What do you mean by asking money from my guests—honourable persons who are escorted by Cossacks ?' Their side - arms were taken away, and their hands tied behind their backs. Then came the turn of the fifteen heads of families. They protested that the village was innocent; that the robber must have been a chance traveller. 'That cannot be,' said the Priestav;

'you know perfectly well that there is no road, and there are no travellers in your valley.' They were given two hours to produce the property. Nothing being forthcoming, their side-arms were, after some pretence of resistance on the part of one or two, taken from them, and they were ordered to remain in custody at Betsho until the goods were returned. 'I am anxious,' said the Priestav, 'to show Mr. Freshfield, as an Englishman, that we can act with vigour in case of need.' And certainly no English officer could have come to the help of his countrymen with more

A SUANETIAN HUNTER

vigour, good judgment, and (as the event proved) success, than M. Aetovsky, the excellent Priestav, came to ours. In the end M. de Déchy's effects were recovered—with the exception of the revolver—and sent back to him months afterwards at Odessa.

Had we been content to take the Tuiber Pass (11,815 feet), the ordinary route from Suanetia to the Tartar valleys east of the Baksan, crossed two years before by my companion, there would have been comparatively little difficulty in procuring porters. We were calling on the villagers to reopen a pass

of which nothing but a tradition survived, and which only one
man in the valley pretended ever to have crossed. Had any
traveller a hundred years ago tried to make the men of Grindelwald cross their glaciers to the Valais, he would certainly
have met with considerable difficulty. M. de Déchy deserved
the highest credit for his patience and pertinacity in overcoming
the very natural unwillingness of the men of Mujal for the
adventure we forced upon them. Our plan was as follows :—
I should set off at once with the three Chamoniards, bivouac
high, and attempt Tetnuld by the glacier which flows down
from its peak to meet the Zanner. Twenty-four hours later
M. de Déchy should start with our Cossack, the native porters,
and all the baggage, and pitch our tents beside the Zanner
Glacier, where I should endeavour to join him at night. Should
I fail to do so, we would each do our best, by lighting fires,
to give intelligence of our safety and our whereabouts, and I
and the guides would press on next morning until we caught
up the Heavy Brigade on the ascent to the pass. As we had
neither of us ever seen the great glaciers leading to the peak and
pass, the scheme was, I flatter myself, bold as well as ingenious.
As far as topography is concerned, it may fairly be compared to a
proposal to climb the Schreckhorn and meet again at the Zäsen-
berg, or on the way to the Mönch Joch—no one having previously
been as far as the Eismeer for a quarter of a century.

Warned by experience, I took the precaution to hire a native
to show us the way through the gorge. Crossing the torrent
just above the junction of the Tuiber water, we found an old
track of the faintest kind, which after a time failed us altogether. It was warm and moist among the dripping flowers
and foliage; the guides were the reverse of exhilarated, and our
chances of success did not seem very brilliant.

The ice twenty-seven years ago—as may be seen by the photographs taken by Count Levashoff's expedition in 1869—poured
over a steep cliff. On the top of this it now lies, ending at
6640 feet, which is practically the same height at which Abich
found it in 1856. A rough scramble brought us to the edge of

a hillside it had scraped bare. Pushing aside the hazel branches, I got the first view up the southern glacier—the Nageb Glacier of the new map—to the peak. Our route was plain; it was the one I had marked out on an old photograph before leaving England. Given fine weather and no ice on the final ridge, Tetnuld could hardly escape me.

In the foreground, at the foot of a rocky spur of the mountain, two great glaciers met. On the left the Zanner tumbled over from its unseen reservoirs in an impassable ice-fall. On our right the Nageb Glacier fell first in a great broken slope of *névé*, then in a long ice-fall, at last in a gentle slope, until it joined its stream to that of the Zanner. We descended on to the ice, and then mounted the Nageb Glacier for a certain distance, until the crevasses made it convenient to cross the moraine and enter the hollow between the ice and the rocks on its right bank. This was partly occupied by beds of avalanche-snow alternating with flowery slopes. On the last of these, at a height of less than 9000 feet, we determined to spend the night. An overhanging rock offered good shelter, and there were all the requisites for a luxurious bivouac: water, rhododendron stalks and roots for a fire, and flowery grass for beds. It was not high enough, but the ground above was easy, and it seemed better to start early than to freeze higher up. We had two sleeping-bags, sufficient wraps, and provisions for two days, so that the guides were heavily loaded. The space under the rock was soon levelled, stones thrown out, and a flooring of elastic twigs and grass laid down. Then we piled up a blazing fire, toasted Suanetian loaves, and watched with satisfaction the last clouds melt into the sky and the peaks of Ushba stand out against a golden sunset.

I felt very comfortable and was soon fast asleep. I was awakened soon after midnight by a sudden sense of light. The moon had scaled the high wall of crags on the east and was looking down on us. The sight of four climbers in sleeping-bags can hardly have been attractive to a goddess who had once discovered Endymion: she showed, however, no disposition to withdraw her excellent brightness. It was a moment, I felt, not for poetical reflection, but for practical action. I rolled myself out from under the boulder, set a light to the spirits of one of those admirable inventions known as 'self-cooking soup-tins,' and roused the slumbering guides. In fifteen minutes—a 'record' time in my experience for a start—we had laced our boots, shared our soup, and shouldered the light packs containing the day's necessaries.

For a short time the rough ground in the hollow between the ice and the mountain afforded us easy walking. The shadows of the crags diminished as the moon's beams flowed down the snowy avalanche-tracks between them. Where the cliffs and moraine met we were driven out on to the glacier. In the white uncertain moonshine it was not easy to discover a way among the narrow ridges between the ice-trenches. Our first attempt to pass the marginal crevasses failed, but at the second we gained without difficulty the centre of the glacier above the lower ice-fall.

It was still some way to the foot of the first great *séracs.* The ice was turning to *névé,* snow covered the surface, and the rope had to be brought into use. During our halt we faced the vast frozen cascade, a mile broad and 500 feet at least high, stretched out in front of us, high over which, crowned by stars of astounding brilliancy, for the moon was passing westwards, the virgin peak of Tetnuld glimmered against the dark blue heaven. On the previous day I had observed that the southern arm of the fall beyond some rocks which divide it was comparatively unbroken. But François Dévouassoud, who in the old Chamonix spirit is ever ready for an attack on crevasses, saw no reason for us to go out of our way, and we kept a straight course. It was magnificent, but a mistake on his part.

The struggle that followed, although it lasted a great many hours, did not seem to me long; for the actual path-finding among the broken masses of *névé* soon grew sufficiently difficult to be amusing. The whole situation was stirring. The scenery was more fantastically lovely than a child's dream after the Panto-mime. The snows around us seemed to emit an unearthly light. Huge towers of milk-white substance shone against the dark background of sky, green icicle-hung vaults yawned between them.

Presently the clefts and caverns grew more frequent and troublesome, the bridges over them more frail and ill-adjusted. We
seemed often to lose our way among the deep undulations. At
moments all progress appeared to be barred.

In such cases the boldest course is sometimes the best—at any
rate before dawn, while the frost holds. We struck at the slope
where it was steepest, and the crevasses were filled by pieces
fallen from the impending cliffs. By the help of small, half-choked
crevasses, François dashed through and up the sides of a huge
tumble-down snow-quarry, and we found ourselves at last on the
platform which stretches under the western base of Tetnuld. The
final peak, previously hidden for a time, was again full in view;
the stars still formed a coronet round the highest crest. Slowly
they faded, and a glimmer of coming dawn played behind the
southern shoulder of the peak and rested on something vast and
white, far and high in the west—Elbruz. As the sky grew paler,
arrows of daylight flashed round the edge of the world across
the upper vault; other arrows seemed to rise to meet them from
the depths of the distant sea. It was very long before any light
touched the Earth, but at last the great dome of Elbruz was of a
sudden illuminated, and the twin towers of Ushba caught the flames,
first red, then golden. In a few minutes the lesser crests of the
'Frosty Caucasus' were kissed by the sun, the shadows fled away
for shelter under the loftiest ridges. The upper world of the
mountains was awake. The inhabited world — the grey hills and
dales of Mingrelia and the sea-spaces beyond — still waited in
sombre twilight.

The next stage in the ascent was to gain the snow-terrace,
which slopes across the cliffs of Tetnuld up to the base of the
long southern ridge that falls in the direction of Adish. A steep
bank seamed by crevasses brought us to the terrace, the snow on
which proved to be very soft and powdery. The distance to be
traversed was great, and progress became slow, exceedingly laborious,
and, owing to the cold in the shadow of the mountain, somewhat
painful. Dévouassoud suggested that we might force a path up to
the western ridge, which was immediately above us. I declined.

The way, if there were one, lay up steep slopes of rocks, snow, and ice. If the ice entailed step-cutting, the task would have been endless; if soft snow lay on ice, extremely dangerous. I did not think the chance of finding the slopes in good condition justified the attempt, and we abided by the comparatively certain route I had laid down from old photographs.

We turned to our right and ploughed up the terrace. The only variety was afforded by a short, but steep, bank of ice. The loose snow on it had to be scraped off, and good steps made for the descent. It was bitterly cold in the shadow, but I had no suspicion at the time that the cold was of a kind to make frost-bites probable. After crossing a tiny plain we pushed our leader over the *Bergschrund*, and he tugged us up a last bank, on the top of which we broke through a cornice and came out into glorious sunshine. It was 9 A.M.; we had been over eight hours climbing from our bivouac. We sat down to lunch on a little terrace, which lies at the base of the long southern ridge of Tetnuld, and is very noticeable from the Latpari Pass.

The prospect was glorious. The upper glens and sources of the Ingur lay at our very feet. We could have cast our shoes on the towers of Adish; we looked across the face of the great cliffs and ice-falls which are opposite the traveller on the Latpari Pass. We commanded the great *névé* of the Adish Glacier, which spreads out between Tetnuld and the rock-peak called Lakutsa on the new map, and is backed by Katuintau and the western top of Janga—a shining tableland, never before looked down on save by the stars.

This was the decisive moment of the day. I examined anxiously the long lovely ridge which curved down to us from the still distant summit. It promised well; it was fairly broad, nowhere very steep, and but little ice glittered on its crest. Still, it was long, and the softness of the snow made it seem longer. At every step the leader sank over his ankles. Consequently leading was exhausting, and we had to change frequently. From time to time there was a little variety, a few yards of ice or a sudden steep rise, which forced us to zigzag and use our axes. Once we were driven on to the flat top of a snow-cornice, a cornice so prodigious that it could be seen even from Mujal, and strong enough to have borne an elephant.

All the way the views were sublime, and we were free to use our eyes. Those who are familiar with the down-look from the top of the Wetterhorn will understand our situation if I say that on the edge of Tetnuld one enjoys for hours a similar sensation. The snow falls away in a short white curve, and then you see, literally between your legs, the meadows of Suanetia, 7000 feet below. Close at hand were our gigantic neighbours, Janga and Shkara. In the west, Elbruz loomed larger and loftier at every step. As the dome of Brunelleschi dominates the campaniles of Florence, or St. Paul's our City spires, so it raised its vast curves above all the lesser heights. Even Ushba sank to a footstool before the great white throne, inhabited, as the Caucasians believe, by the Prince of the Power of the Air.

So three hours or more passed; my aneroid was marking 16,500 feet (equivalent to about 15,700 to 15,800), but ever in front rose a fresh frozen bank. I looked across to the north-west ridge, and an eminence I had noted on it was below us. 'Nous approchons,' I said to François. 'Nous allons arriver,' he replied cheerily. The snow grew thin; some steps had to be cut into ice. There seemed less bulk in our peak; the converging ridges were below; there was little but air above us. Twenty minutes later a white bank cut the sky; it sank, our eyes overlooked it, our feet trampled it. I ran on for a few level yards; there was nothing more; two ridges fell steeply beneath me. Tetnuld was ours; another great peak of the Caucasus was climbed.

It was 1.15 P.M. We had been nearly four hours over the last 1700 feet of crest, twelve and a half hours, including halts, from our bivouac. I am afraid I enjoyed the next hour more than the secretary of a scientific—or quasi-scientific—society ought to have done.[1]

---

[1] The Royal Geographical Society, of which I was for thirteen years (1881-1894) one of the Honorary Secretaries, is scientific in its aims but popular in its constitution. Owing to the absence of any qualification for its membership—save sex and an annual subscription—the four initials F.R.G.S. do not necessarily indicate that their possessor is either a traveller or a geographer. It is high time some conspicuous and easily recognisable line was drawn between the qualified members of the Society and those who are simply subscribers.

I might have been boiling thermometers, or feeling my own pulse, or securing accurate bearings. But I would put in a plea for the makers of 'first ascents.'[1] They open the way, and make it easy for others to follow them. We mountaineers are not the camp-followers, as some critic has impertinently suggested, but the pioneers of science. *Fiat experimentum in corpore vili* : I have no objection to the application of the proverb. Where our bodies have opened a new observatory, let the Scientific Bodies follow at their ease and their leisure. Had I tried to measure precisely I should not have succeeded. As it was, I estimated Tetnuld as 'slightly over 16,000 feet.' The new survey makes it 82 feet under 16,000 feet. The survey makes Gestola 14 feet higher than its sister peak. But I should like to be certain both peaks were measured from the same side of the chain. There have been very considerable discrepancies in some of the heights from time to time communicated to me by the Surveyors, as results of the new measurements. Undoubtedly they are, as a whole and approximately, accurate, but I feel confident that—as has been the case in the Austrian Alps—further corrections will in several cases have to be made in the official figures.

We had time to study in detail the vast panorama commanded by our space-searching summit. The broad snow-fields of the Zanner, over which next day we hoped to force a pass, called for particular attention. What a superb ice-gorge led up to the gap between us and Gestola ! The green valley over its shoulder should be Chegem. Dykhtau was a surprise ; the southern face was this year all white, while Donkin's photograph had prepared us for a bare cliff ; Koshtantau, all but the pyramidal top, was masked by the cliffs of Mishirgitau ; Shkara dominated everything on the watershed ; Janga was a little higher than ourselves : between them they cut off the view of the eastern snows. The part of the horizon occupied by snowy peaks was narrower than in most Swiss and

---

[1] I am fortified in my plea by the fact that I have my old friend, Professor Tyndall, with me. His famous description of the first ascent of the Weisshorn concludes as follows : ' I opened my notebook to make a few observations, but I soon relinquished the attempt. There was something incongruous, if not profane, in allowing the scientific faculty to interfere where silent worship was the " reasonable service." '

many Caucasian views, but the heights were on a scale more imposing than that of the Alps.

Beyond the sunny hills of Mingrelia and the sea-haze I made out plainly the distant snow-flecked ranges towards Kars and Trebizond : Ararat I failed to recognise, though there were some distant pink cumuli which probably marked its whereabouts. General Chodzko, the first Director of the Caucasian Staff, who camped on the top of Ararat, asserts that he identified Elbruz from it. The distance between these peaks is 280 miles; Tetnuld is 30 miles less. On the Alps I have, from a height of 12,000 feet in the Ortler Group, seen Monte Viso at a distance of over 200 miles.

As we were on the point of starting a guide kicked an ice-axe and set it sliding. It happily hitched on the very verge of the Adish slope. In cutting the few steps needful for its recovery, we had another opportunity to realise what that slope is. The descent of the ridge proved perfectly safe and easy, and in about an hour we were back at the saddle. Here I felt some headache, our only suffering from the rarity of the air : it passed off after a light meal, and was probably more due to hunger than anything else. Light clouds had begun to form in the seaward hollows; they collected in the dales of Suanetia, and now suddenly, as if at a given signal, streamed up to us. I was reminded of the procession of the Ocean Nymphs in the *Prometheus Vinctus*. They passed lightly overhead, lingered a while round the peaks, and before sunset had again melted away.

The descent was without further incident. The snow was very heavy, but our hearts were light. We had a momentary difference when the leading guide, justly dreading our track through the *séracs* so late in the day, began to make for the northern corner of the great basin. François and I had to insist on a sharp turn to the left, which brought us to the top of the long straight slope by which I had proposed to ascend, south of the rocky boss. We wallowed up to our waists, but the slope was steep enough to make progress, even by wallowing, comparatively rapid. We were soon on hard and bare ice, and the rope could at last be taken off. Jogging steadily on, we regained our boulder and the white rhododendron bank at 7 P.M. There was no longer a mist in the sky. Ushba rose a dark shadow against the sunset.

Generally in such a situation the thoughts go backwards to fight over again the day's battle; but ours, and our eyes, were strained onwards. Could anything be seen of our companion and his baggage-train on the opposite hill? We searched in vain the sides of the Zanner ice-fall. I quickly came to the decision to stop where we were, since our bivouac was already prepared, in the trust that if our party were on the road, which we should doubtless learn as soon as it was dark by their beacon-fire, we might catch them up next day. Presently our own beacon flamed up, and after the guides had turned in I rested long beside it in a comfortable hollow, watching the slow muster of the heavenly host and waiting for the responsive glow—which never came. Soon after ten I too crept into my bag, thankful that I had not to seek the narrow shelves of some crowded Club-hut.

END OF VOLUME I

PRINTED BY T. AND A. CONSTABLE, PRINTERS TO HER MAJESTY
AT THE EDINBURGH UNIVERSITY PRESS

A SKETCH MAP OF THE CAUCASUS.

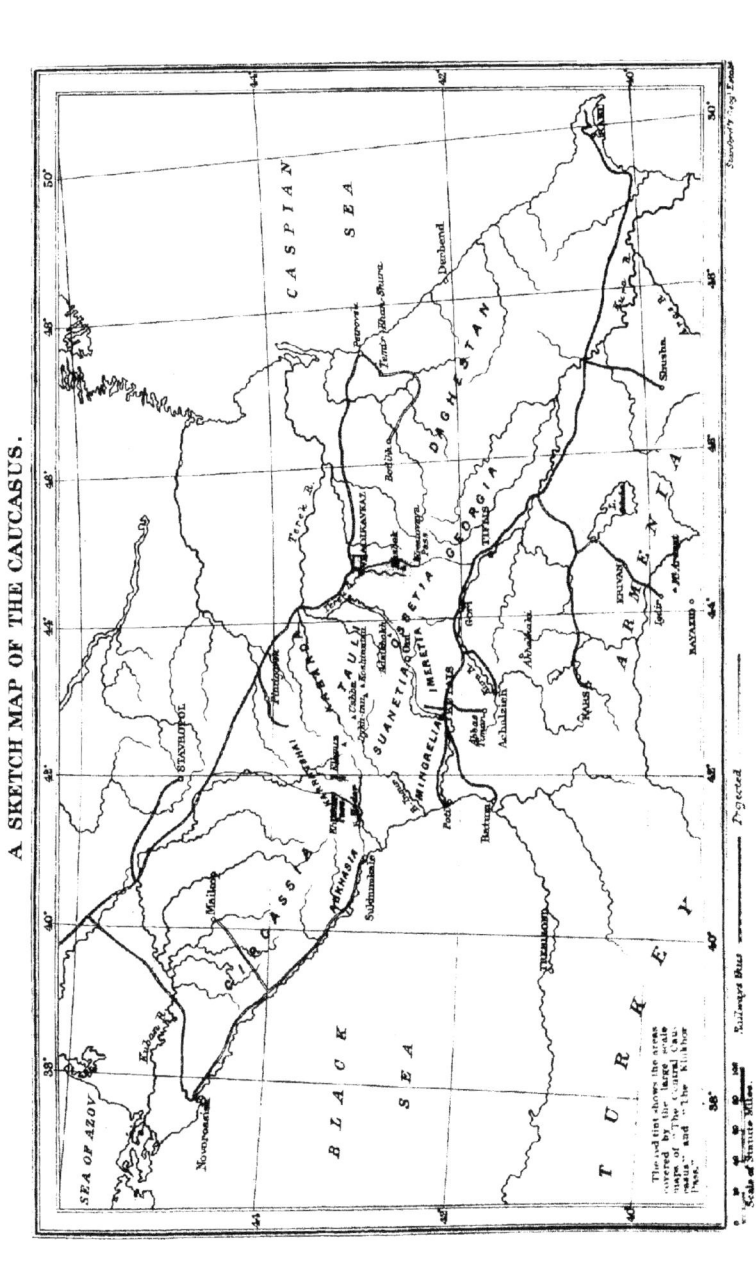

843213

Printed in Great Britain by
Amazon.co.uk, Ltd.,
Marston Gate.